SUPERTRENDS
OF FUTURE
CHINA★

**BILLION DOLLAR BUSINESS OPPORTUNITIES
FOR CHINA'S OLYMPIC DECADE**

SUPERTRENDS
OF FUTURE
CHINA

**BILLION DOLLAR BUSINESS OPPORTUNITIES
FOR CHINA'S OLYMPIC DECADE**

JAMES K. YUANN
JASON INCH

W World Scientific

NEW JERSEY · LONDON · SINGAPORE · BEIJING · SHANGHAI · HONG KONG · TAIPEI · CHENNAI

Published by

World Scientific Publishing Co. Pte. Ltd.

5 Toh Tuck Link, Singapore 596224

USA office: 27 Warren Street, Suite 401-402, Hackensack, NJ 07601

UK office: 57 Shelton Street, Covent Garden, London WC2H 9HE

British Library Cataloguing-in-Publication Data
A catalogue record for this book is available from the British Library.

SUPERTRENDS OF FUTURE CHINA: BILLION DOLLAR BUSINESS OPPORTUNITIES FOR CHINA'S OLYMPIC DECADE

ISBN-13 978-981-281-439-5
ISBN-10 981-281-439-6

Typeset by Stallion Press
Email: enquiries@stallionpress.com

Printed in Singapore by B & JO Enterprise

To Our Families

Foreword

*by Howard Balloch**

My grandfather, who lived in Fuzhou for more than 20 years as a tea trader during the dying days of the Qing dynasty, left the family a book called *Sketches of a Vanishing China*. It is a beautiful collection of watercolor paintings of a bucolic rural China that vanished in a devastating cycle of civil war, foreign invasion and civil war again during the first half of the 20th century. The next quarter-century saw the emergence of revolutionary *Xin Hua*, or New China, which began its own vanishing act in 1976, the year I first came to China. That year had seen geological upheaval in the Tangshan earthquake and political upheaval with the death of the three revolutionary leaders, Zhou Enlai, Zhu De and Mao Zedong, and the arrest of the Gang of Four. Two years later, the story behind this book begins.

Late in 1978, Deng Xiaoping repeated in a speech an old Szechuan proverb: "It does not matter whether a cat is white or black, as long as it catches mice." Setting aside ideology in favor of pragmatism, this old wily revolutionary began the process of giving the future of China back to its children. Gradually beginning the parallel processes of decollectivization, marketization and opening up to the

*Howard Balloch was Canadian Ambassador to China between 1996 and 2001, and is now President of The Balloch Group, one of China's leading boutique investment banks with its headquarters in Beijing and offices in Shanghai, Wuhan, Hangzhou, Hong Kong and New York.

outside world, Deng Xiaoping unleashed two fundamental forces — the people's latent demand and Chinese entrepreneurial energy.

From this inauspicious and almost unnoticed beginning in 1978, Chinese reform has transformed not only the Middle Kingdom but our global economic balances as well. Pushing down prices of what it produces, pushing up prices of what it consumes, and now playing a major role in global capital flows, China is an economic force that must be carefully understood and integrated into the plans of both foreign governments and companies alike, irrespective of whether you are a resource supplier, a manufacturer or a financial service provider. Investors who do not understand China will be as incompetent in selecting winners and losers in their own countries as they would be in the extraordinarily dynamic economy that is China today. And understanding China means understanding the trends at work here and the drivers behind those trends.

At average growth rates around 10 percent over the last 30 years, the macro performance of the Chinese economy has been nothing short of phenomenal. What is equally outstanding is that this growth has been remarkably steady. The only real slowdowns have been event-driven — for example, the 2003 SARS outbreak — and these have been followed by very quick V-shaped recoveries during which the economy has moved into overdrive periods of substantially higher than 10 percent growth until the missing slack has been taken up.

What is at work here? I have long said that the two forces that Deng unleashed — latent demand and entrepreneurial energy — are underlying drivers which will only run out of steam when China as a whole reaches levels of personal wealth that parallel other, more developed Asian countries.

And if this is right, it is interesting to compare the Japan of 1964, Tokyo's Olympic year, with Olympic China of 2008. Per capita incomes, adjusted for inflation, are about the same. Now project forward 25 years to the end of the 1980s in Japan and to the early 2030s in China and imagine similar per capita incomes and levels of spending — on cars and clothes and on leisure and luxury goods — in those two economies. What you will have in absolute, as opposed to per capita, consumption will exceed that of North America and be truly globe-tilting.

The trends and drivers that James Yuann and Jason Inch talk about in this book are key to understanding the way China is being internally transformed and the way that transformation is changing global consumption and demand. They get it. Urbanization, a move up the value chain in both production and consumption, the expansion of the consuming class and radical productivity improvements both in modern industry and agriculture (driven by price growth, value growth and a reduction of people on the land) form a virtuous cycle of growth that does not eliminate business cycles or periods of overinvestment and price declines. Booms and busts will always exist and the authors of this book identify some that are at various stages of waxing and waning. But the drivers that this book explains make the "downs" less deep and shorter in time than they otherwise would be, and the opportunities just that much more exciting. The market corrects quickly here in China as the big underlying forces of domestic demand and entrepreneurial energy keep pushing the economy forward.

The only part of this book with which I disagree is the authors' answer to the question: "When is the best time to invest in China?" Their answer is "Now." Mine would be "Yesterday." I did, as soon as I was free from the proper limitations that apply to envoys of a foreign state, and have now built what started as a two-person consultancy into a dynamic financial advisory and merchant banking firm. For the rest of you, if you haven't yet started, "now" is certainly a better response than "tomorrow," and we can let our authors' answer stand. But read this book first.

Preface

A year ago, when we first started writing this book, China seemed ascendant: Hong Kong, Shenzhen and Shanghai stock markets were pushing to new historical highs, the economy was somewhat overheated but running smoothly under cooling measures, and the run-up to the Olympics was proceeding well with the completion of the Olympic Stadium, colloquially called the Bird's Nest, and other facilities.

Now as we prepare to go to press, the world's economy is in a state of uncertainty over a possible recession in the US, climbing inflation in many countries, food shortages and rising commodity prices, and a record-low US dollar. In China, there is a rollercoaster stock market that lost nearly half its value from historical highs set just eight months before. In early 2008, the country experienced rare blizzards that closed railways, stranding millions of passengers and causing power shortages; the Sichuan region suffered the worst earthquake in China in more than 30 years; and inflation is averaging about eight percent since the start of the year. Despite all this, China's economy still grew 10.6 percent in the first quarter of 2008. China has been growing rapidly for the last 30 years, and it is still growing.

In some ways, China's confidence as a nation has reached its pinnacle with events such as hosting of the APEC meeting in 2001, the Boao Forum for Asia (China's answer to the Davos World Economic Forum) now held annually, and sports events such as the FIFA Women's World Cup hosted in China in 2007. The optimism of the Chinese people, both domestic and overseas, is so strong that it sometimes erupts into nationalistic fervor as it did for the Olympic Torch Relay after controversy in the UK, France and the US. But China as a nation is showing new resiliency in the face of setbacks.

The decade-long preparations for China to appear on the world stage will be capped by hosting the Olympic Games. China's Olympic Decade starts in 2008: August 8, 2008 at 8.08 p.m., to be exact, with the opening of the Beijing-hosted Summer Olympiad. If you are observant and aware of auspicious Chinese numerology, you will undoubtedly notice that's a lot of 8's — 8/8/2008, 8.08 p.m. Chinese consider the number 8 to be lucky because it shares a similar sound to "getting rich" and this date represents a new starting point for China; it is a springboard for billion dollar industries that are just beginning.

For China, the Olympic Decade is important on many levels. Through its athletic events, the Olympics brings a lot of attention to the host country, which usually takes this opportunity to improve the business and social environment. In some ways, it is a face-lift, to improve the country's image to the outside world. China has been longing for this opportunity, for "a thousand years" as many Chinese say, to show how far formerly poor and backwards China has come to join the ranks of modern prosperous countries through its 30 years of reforms and hard work.

Starting three years ago, China began a daily countdown in newspapers and public billboards showing how many days were left until August 8, 2008. Day after day, new regulations (for example, environmental improvement, better labor regulations, even reforming its massive state-wide healthcare program) have been quickly promulgated, increasing the people's optimism. It is this momentum that is carrying China forward, setting the stage for new trends which will create the biggest business opportunities in the next decade for those doing business with China.

This is a book about trends and especially about how to catch them. Some academics can see the trends, perhaps even predict them, but may lack the motivation or resources to act on them. Many businesspeople may have the resources and intent to act, but are often in the unfortunate position of simply following the trends rather than surfing them like a wave. Both, in the end, miss the trends in one way or another.

势, the Chinese character on page xi — pronounced like the *shi* sound in *shirt* — is used in a number of Chinese words for trends. It is useful to understand this pictographic representation for "trend" by the two characters from which it is made:

执

力

On the top half is the symbol for *catch, grasp,* or *execute* (执), and the bottom half is the symbol to represent *strength* (力): The person who catches the trend is strong, or perhaps their strength will master a trend; executing with force is a must to catch a trend.

An ancient Chinese saying cleverly classifies how people react to, and the benefit they derive from, opportunities:

不知不觉	*bu zhi bu jue*
后知后觉	*hou zhi hou jue*
先知先觉	*xian zhi xian jue*

Read here from left to right, top to bottom, it may be roughly translated to mean, if you are not aware, you will have no reaction; late awareness, delayed reaction; early awareness, advance reaction: If you know first you act first.

The time to know the trends, catch them, and act with strength is now. The trends that shape China's immediate future, its Olympic

Decade from 2008 to 2018, are so large that we can call them *supertrends*, and they will result in many *billion dollar opportunities*. China is a country to which the word "billion" is often attached, usually in its relation to population. To put that idea in terms of opportunity, we paraphrase a comment from one of China's current leaders, Premier Wen Jiabao: Any trend multiplied by 1.3 billion people is bound to have a deep and profound impact on business and society, not only in China but also around the world.[1] To us, "billion" is the magnitude of dollars the winners stand to gain by being among the first to recognize and operate in the industries that those supertrends promote.

Deng Xiaoping was the leader responsible for China's opening the door to market economy reforms in 1978 after decades under the Communist doctrines of Mao. He once said, "…To get rich is glorious." This book aims to make you aware of on-the-ground knowledge from China's burgeoning economy that will help you to become rich and glorious. Whether you are in China already and looking for a new path, or outside of China considering your first foray, by following some of the ideas we believe are among the best, or by being inspired by them to find your own, you will open your own door to future success and wealth.

The Chinese character on the book's title page (元) is written and pronounced *yuan*. It is the symbol of money, and the Chinese currency, the *renminbi* (RMB), is colloquially called the *yuan*. To us, it represents the wealth and success that you can hope to achieve by understanding the supertrends and taking action on them to improve your life and business.

This book is not about fearing China's growth in the tone of Japan Inc. in the 1980s, it is not unfairly critical of the Chinese economic development path (as is the current *du jour* approach in many China-related books), nor is it about the question of the various developed Western countries versus China as competitors. Certainly, all such perspectives have a place in the debate, but it is not the purpose of this book to add fuel to the fire. Rather, this book is about China's top business trends and how people from all levels of business and every nationality can profit from them. From multinational corporations to sellers on e-Bay, China's supertrends affect all businesses big and small. They affect you.

The controversy over China's growth may be focused on several key issues: the detrimental local and global environmental impact of China's carbon-emitting, pollution-discharging factories; the exploitation of workers, many of whom are working in the same polluting factories and suffering poor safety conditions and low wages; China's social problems including wealth distribution, aging and slow pace of democratic reform; and in the business sector, intellectual property rights protection. These issues are often presented as either an unfair competitive advantage for China or a reason its rise should be suspect. Many of the worst-case Malthusian scenarios such as a fight over oil supplies are often painted as inevitable outcomes which only concerted international and Chinese political effort will prevent, if at all.

These outcomes discount the power of the market forces that have been unleashed in China: If the saying is true, that no two countries with a McDonald's have ever gone to war, then war with China over oil or some other issue is highly improbable, because China has more than 750 McDonald's and is adding dozens every year.[2]

Like the Malthusian arguments of the past which predicted massive shortages and suffering due to lack of key supplies such as food, many of these anti-China arguments often fail to acknowledge business and markets as potential solutions. Malthus was wrong: We did not run out of food; instead, productivity increases supported a much larger population than he ever envisioned. Therefore, as businesspeople, we prefer to take a more balanced approach to the environmental, social, and political problems of China. To continue a thought from earlier in this Preface, any large problem *divided by* 1.3 billion people may become a very small issue.

We would like this book to refocus the debate and look at China in a more balanced way in order to appreciate the intricacies of its development and the importance of these key future industries as *solutions* to the problems our esteemed academicians, journalists and politicians have identified. Business and markets, productivity improvements and consumer preference, have solved social problems before and we believe they will do so again in China, especially when accompanied by the determination of its government and of a population of poor people striving to improve their quality of life.

The willingness of the Chinese government and the people to improve their living standard through capitalism is powerful, their approach practical and thus far successful.

In terms of the format, this book is written by businesspeople for businesspeople, with practical down-to-earth analysis and advice. We have lived in China for years, and what we see on the ground we put in this book. The supertrends in fact are well-known in China: High-tech manufacturing, environment and energy-saving, urbanization and social development are even a part of the Chinese government's own 11th Five-Year Plan (from 2006 to 2010). We provide a brief introduction to these initiatives in our first section, but it is the impact of the drivers and the trends that we most want to share with you.

This book is definitely not a series of academic-style case studies, a collection of reminiscences and war stories, nor is it an unconnected collection of papers in different styles and presenting different views from an assembly of academics or corporate officers who are usually comfortable in dealing with PowerPoint presentations and paper strategies. Instead, this is an experienced and insightful guide to understanding how to profit from China's rising economy.

The book is divided into several sections. First, there are the *drivers* and the *supertrends*. These are what move the Chinese economy forward, and within them can be found the opportunities that will lead you to success. The big three primary drivers are China's export-driven manufacturing, development of the domestic Chinese market, and foreign direct investment (FDI) which brought capital and technology to China. More importantly, we identify the *drivers of the drivers*, the real forces that push the *primary drivers*. The *drivers of the drivers* are the engines that will continue to power the big three drivers in the Olympic Decade from 2008 to 2018.

The *drivers of the drivers* — government policy, globalization, and people's determination — will propel the Chinese economy of tomorrow and furthermore induce the *supertrends*, which will greatly change the business environment and people's lives. These supertrends — Value-adding and Innovating, Urbanizing and Servicing, Consuming and Aspiring, Inter-networking and E-Commercializing, Affluencing and Greening — will create billion dollar opportunities in products, services, and ideas. These supertrends will lead China's Olympic Decade.

James K. Yuann
Jason Inch

Acknowledgments

We are grateful for the support of our friends and family in the process of writing this book. As well, we would like to thank our numerous reviewers, academic advisors, and colleagues who contributed ideas and feedback to make this a more useful work. Finally, we would like to thank the team at World Scientific Publishing for its participation throughout the entire process.

Contents

PART FOUR: THE WEALTH SUPERTRENDS

PART FIVE: CONCLUSIONS

China, the Land of Mystery: The Good, the Bad, and the Ugly

China has always been thought of as part of the mysterious Orient. When Richard Nixon arrived in China in 1972 and disembarked from Air Force One, Premier Zhou Enlai was there to greet him. Nixon was said to remark, "So we've arrived in the land of mystery, Premier Zhou." Zhou responded, "It may be mysterious to you, Mr. President, but it is not to us." Perhaps apocryphal, this story still gets to the heart of the matter: People in the West are often unsure what is behind the curtain of China.

There are many ideas, beliefs, and stories about China which, to those outside the country, may seem mysterious and difficult to understand, but not to people, including the Chinese themselves, who live and do business in China every day. To them, China is ultimately just China. There is no ancient Chinese secret, though there are many things one can learn from China's trends, and opportunities still to be had for the forward-thinking.

Historically, foreigners have been coming to China from elsewhere for centuries seeking knowledge, fortunes, and adventure.

One of the first documented accounts was a young Italian boy, traveling with his family eastward in search of trade, who arrived at the capital, Beijing, in 1275 A.D. There he stayed for nearly two decades, extending his skills as a linguist and was made a courtier by the then reigning *khan* of the Yuan Dynasty.

Twenty years later, the boy returned to Europe a man, bringing exotic knowledge and inventions from the mighty Mongol Empire. *Cathay*, as it was called then, was unknown to most. So, when his thoughts were recorded into a book recounting tales of strange customs, magnificent treasures, geographic descriptions unparalleled at the time, even cannibalism, heroism, and adventure, it became a best-seller which remained popular for decades after his death.[1]

The man whose name is synonymous with exploration is well-known to all as Marco Polo. His influence on people at that time was great and served to build interest in the wonders of China. His meticulously detailed geographic information guided the likes of Columbus on his journeys, and the Marco Polo name today lives on to great effect as the moniker for a famous bridge near Beijing, even a popular bakery chain from Taiwan.

In the centuries following Marco Polo's first magical, terrifying and awe-inspiring impressions of China in his book, other travelers would continue to seek Cathay, writing about a country of *kowtows* and *sing-song* girls, the place where a certain kind of porcelain (which Westerners eponymously named china) was invented, the source of much of the world's tea, up until its somewhat dramatic closing in 1949. Before that China had already undergone several cycles of isolationism and exploration, and it is now once again open (for business) and the journey eastward to find its riches has started once again. This is the *meng ya*, 萌芽, the seed that is to grow in the Chinese Century only now just beginning.

Thomas Friedman's *The World is Flat* credited Columbus with starting "Globalization 1.0". For this book, which is not so much about globalization as it is about being prepared for China-related change and making the most out of China opportunities, we shall honor the first great traveler who came from the west to the east, Marco Polo, as the one who inspired and ignited the passion to take a chance and go to China for the possibilities it offered.

Journey to the East

In October 2007, six new direct flights from the US to China were announced, and under a May 2007 agreement, the total number of direct flights via US carriers alone will increase to 23 a week by 2012.[2] This figure does not include the Chinese carriers that fly to the US, and it is of course only a fraction of the total flights to and from China to non-US destinations. Boeing estimates that China will need more than 3,400 new large-bodied aircraft for a total fleet of 4,460 by 2026.[3] New infrastructure had to be built, and China will create about 97 new airports throughout the country at a cost of approximately US$62 billion, giving it a total of 244 airports by 2020, with 13 of those airports capable of handling more than 30 million passengers per year each, according to an announcement from China's Civil Aviation authority in January 2008.

Large volumes of air traffic into and within China are one major indicator of several trends: Increasing globalization in politics and the economy, non-stop business opportunities, leisure travel, and urbanization.

China's new airports are among the largest in the world, many built in the last decade and several, including Shanghai's Pudong International Airport, already constructing additional runways to handle increased volumes of air traffic. Compare this to the early 1980s, when China had few international flights, near-deserted international airports like Shanghai's *Hong Qiao* International Airport which had no tow-carts or luggage belts so bags were tossed to passengers from the back of a truck, and if you saw any foreigners on a plane bound for China, they would likely be Hong Kongese, Taiwanese, or guests of the same going to see their mainland Chinese factory.

The increasing flights to and from China and the expansion of China's domestic air carriers mean that there will be far more people coming into China from abroad to the point where today, foreign carriers are courting the Chinese firms for partnerships even after attempts at M&A or joint ventures failed, as with a failed investment by Singapore Airlines into China Eastern Airlines in 2007. Simply put, every air carrier wants to make inroads into China because of the huge growth in air travel both inwards and outwards.

Arriving on a jet plane, don't know if they'll go back again

Where do all these passengers come from? According to 2004 statistics, the majority of travelers to Shanghai were from Japan, Hong Kong, the United States, France, Germany, Singapore, and Korea. All of this is perhaps reflected best by the fact that in 2006, more than 44 million foreigners entered and exited from China, a nearly 100 percent increase from just five years earlier when China entered the WTO in 2001 and, with exception to the year of the SARS disease, inbound travel is on average increasing at 10 percent a year.

China's entry and exit statistics for foreigners are again projected to double by 2012 to more than 80 million.[4]

Why are all these foreigners going to China? Some come to study Mandarin or attend one of China's universities. The Ministry of Education said that 195,000 foreign students attended Chinese universities in 2007, an increase of 20 percent.[5] A large number of visitors are on short-term business or travel, but an increasing number of people are choosing to work and even live permanently in mainland China, much as expatriates have been doing in Hong Kong for quite some time. Now, the place that young and older businesspeople alike want to go is probably Beijing or Shanghai, not only because of the more colorful lives those cities offer, but also the exciting opportunities and growth those cities promise.

According to the latest figures, in 2006 in Beijing, more than 70,000 foreigners were employed on long-term residence permits as well as another 7,000 working in diplomatic functions, while in Shanghai 35,000 work permits had been issued. Another statistic reported for Shanghai, stated that the number of foreigners doubled from 2002 to 2006, growing to about 77,000 expats working at foreign-invested enterprises out of a total 120,000 living in Shanghai.[6] All these numbers belie the total number of foreigners living in both cities, which would include students, family members, business visa holders, and tourists who continually extend their stay. For example, according to the Japanese consulate in Shanghai, officially registered Japanese residents total more than 60,000, with unofficial figures at least 20 percent higher. Americans are listed by their embassy at 50,000, Germans at 30,000, French at 25,000, and so on. When populations of Koreans, Taiwanese, and Hong Kongese are added in, the total population of residents of foreign origin tops 500,000.[7]

China is currently home to more than two million foreigners from outside the mainland.[8]

What keeps them here?

For one thing, job opportunities that are superior to those available in their home country. Postings to cities like Shanghai and Beijing were not long ago considered hardships but today are plum assignments, an important line item on any executive's CV.

For younger businesspeople, China often offers positions in management and social status that would not be available to people of their experience level or income in their home countries. With or without Mandarin language skills, talented people are able to find jobs in China's cities and most enjoy a respectable salary that, although generally lower and paid in Chinese currency, the RMB, the money goes a lot further thanks to a low cost of living.

Live Like a King

My experience building and leading businesses for multinational companies in China has been rich and rewarding. The business dynamics in China are different from those in the US or EU: You need to make fast decisions; you need to be flexible and active; and you need to be independent while at the same time accountable to the corporate HQ.

While life back home was often filled with daily routines of going to the HQ offices and attending endless boring meetings, coming home, doing the housework and honey-dos, along with a very predictable income, mortgage, car payments, and tuition payments for children, China is another story altogether.

China is a high-pressure work environment for foreign executives but with the perks of chauffeured cars, gardeners, private cooks and full-time housekeepers. School tuition here is expensive (about US$25,000 per child at many international schools), but the company often takes care of that. Other benefits may include an overseas differential allowance covering all or part of groceries, utilities, housing, car and even domestic help. All in, the total cash package more than twice your US pay means life in China is far more than being comfortable.

With the leisure time that accumulates with so much domestic help, one can enjoy events like the F1 race in Shanghai, golf at a dozen newly designed world-class courses with full caddy service, enjoy various cuisines at top restaurants for half the price of those in New York or LA, or travel to a variety of scenic or historical destinations in China as well as the nearby resorts of South-East Asia. And, the sweetest thing of all, you can get away from the HQ and its corporate B.S. without sacrificing your career, as China has become a key posting to have on the CV for future moves up the corporate ladder.

— *Richard O. Smith, a typical director*
at the China sourcing office of a multinational company

Life in the Fast Lane

Although I've been in Shanghai for several years already, every day still seems new, because something interesting or exciting is going on. The city is constantly changing and business is fast. As a foreign consultant to MNCs in China, I get to work with high-level executives from both domestic and international companies that I'd not be likely even to meet in the elevator back home. Here I contribute to the strategic decisions of billion dollar companies.

While our salaries are usually not as high as the fabled expat salary-and-benefits packages that GMs get, and we often make less than our counterparts in the US or EU, for many of my classmates from graduate school, the city is full of chances to be a manager of a growing company, or be entrepreneurs.

Work-life balance is a mixed concept in China as business happens around the clock, but for every business dinner you need to attend, there's a leisurely business lunch at a sidewalk café to enjoy. For every business trip to a remote city, there's architecture, art, culture and natural scenery to view.

For the young businessperson in Shanghai, taxis are the preferred method of transportation, brand-new health clubs with the latest equipment keep the ravages of pollution and city stress somewhat at bay (weekly massages for US$10 help as well), and meals out are like being on the *Food Channel*: Jean Georges tonight, Michelle Garnaut tomorrow, every cuisine from Brazilian BBQ to Thai. For fun, you can check out the world's largest indoor ski hill, see the Rolling Stones, Linkin Park or Avril Lavigne in concert, or go to the latest Phillipe Starck-designed nightclub where you can party all night to the music of the world's top DJs while dancing on a hundred-year-old building's outdoor patio with Shanghai's futuristic skyline as your backdrop.

— *David Kim, a typical early-30s entrepreneur*
with his own consulting company in Shanghai

All this demand for Western-style living and dining is driving the prices of such products and services higher and higher. Rents for high-quality service-apartments (short-term stays of six months to two years) have been steadily increasing as the pace of new arrivals to the city is outpacing the speed of development of these premium executive residences. In fact, another indicator of China's increasing convergence towards international level standards, the annual Mercer Consulting cost of living survey, puts Shanghai and Beijing at a reasonable 20th and 26th most expensive cities to live in respectively.[9] Another survey lists them as the 100th and 95th most expensive in the world.[10] The trend across all surveys and almost all cities in China is increasing cost of living as more foreigners (the targets for these kind of surveys) move to China and require the international basket of goods those surveys use.

Regrettably for China, neither Beijing nor Shanghai placed within the top 50 for either quality of life or health and sanitation-style surveys,[11] but nevertheless executives hoping to rise in their companies often make the China experience a defining factor, and the quality of life in major Chinese cities is no longer a strong deterrent requiring hardship pay.

High cost of living rankings do not mean the cities are prohibitively expensive, only that to maintain a Western standard of living is expensive. If you can do without trips to the opera and subscriptions to the *Wall Street Journal*, French cheeses and a bottle of Cabernet Sauvignon with dinner, China's cities are very affordable even for new graduates.

The prices for many products and services, from 500 ml Nestlé water (US$0.30), an hour-long foot massage (US$5), an hour of housekeeper or private chef's time (US$1.5–$4) or a two-kilometer ride in a taxi (US$1.6), may work out to be just 10–20 percent of those in higher cost-of-living countries.*

As soon as people get to China, many find they don't want to leave. A typical foreign resident of Shanghai remarked, "Every time my flight from Shanghai approaches San Francisco, I always hope that something awry would force the flight back to China right away." Whether it is the job opportunities, the low cost of living or the increasingly international variety of entertainment and leisure activities, many foreigners are here to stay, despite some of the problems which the Chinese economy is suffering from.

Bamboo is Always Greener on the Other Side of the River

China is dealing with a number of problems that, by many standards, would actually be considered as advantageous or good for a developing country's economy:

- High growth rates, which mean opportunities for more business, more money, more expansion, or simply a good time to start your own company, but are not always a good thing when it comes to the environment and conservation of resources.
- Increasing wealth of urban residents, a trend that is generally positive except for the increasing wealth divide between city and countryside, and quickly-rising labor and operational costs.
- Large numbers of students going abroad to study at top foreign universities. This may also seem overwhelmingly positive, except that China often has trouble getting its best and brightest scientists and engineers to come back as *hai'gui* — sea turtles. According to one Chinese study, of approximately one million students that

---

*A note on the exchange rate: During the writing of this book, the RMB has been appreciating at an unprecedented rate against the US dollar. Before 2005, the rate was fixed at 8.27 RMB per dollar. As this book goes to press, the rate is approximately 7 RMB per dollar, so we use this rate for conversions throughout the rest of the book unless otherwise noted.

went abroad, only 275,000 returned.[12] Or if they do return, providing adequate jobs at international compensation levels for new
undergraduates educated abroad to be satisfied with, lest they
become *hai'dai* — seaweed — drifting in the tides of international
labor differentials.

How China deals with these economic and social issues is of
concern to those with a macroeconomic perspective on China's
development, but in some cases, as with the high growth rate,
solving the problem would create new problems such as how to
employ China's rural migrant workers as they enter the cities. Balancing the urban and rural incomes is a task that tests China's com-
mitment to market reforms as in fact some people are getting rich
first, as originally envisioned by Deng Xiaoping.[13]

China is the New Gray

Stepping out of an aircraft at Shanghai's Pudong International
Airport any time between April and October, the heat will hit you
like a wave yet, incongruously, you may notice the skies are gray and
overcast. It looks like rain, but it's more likely the haze of pollution
that settles over one of China's busiest cities during much of the
year. China's economy is a mix of good and bad and consequently,
has often been criticized on a number of fronts:

- Laws and regulations are like one big gray area, which leaves
  interpretation in the hands of many, which is how power comes
  into play among different organizations, among different regions,
  and in different situations.
- Transparency of most institutions and businesses is at best gray,
  if not opaque, due to a long-standing practice of working in a
  kind of black-box environment where the procedures and decision
  criteria are hidden behind networks of relationships. The Chinese
  bureaucracy is still this way: Despite a large amount of effort to put
  up ministry websites, solicit public opinion and so on, the reality

is that the workings of the legal system including the courts, the decision making processes in the government, are all still difficult to understand, much less influence.

- The high-speed growth and lack of enforcement of environmental regulations quite literally make the dust-filled air and everything it touches a slightly duller shade, resulting in pollution both inside and outside China, affecting quality of life.

- Some workers, such as the floating migrant population, often exist in a legal gray area, neither allowed to fully integrate with the local communities nor be adequately compensated for the sacrifices they make in health and income. Human rights is still a new concept in China, but much has been done to improve the situation of migrant and rural workers in recent years, part of the government's plan to bridge the wealth divide.

- The graying of the working population is also a major concern. Like many other countries, China has experienced a baby boom. But unlike other countries, it also reduced the size of the subsequent generation with the now-infamous One Child Policy, which has resulted in nearly 100 million one-child families and prevented the birth of about 400 million additional people,[†] causing a number of unexpected or negative demographic effects, not the least of which is too many seniors who are living much longer thanks to improved diet and better healthcare, not enough working population to support the pension system, or not enough children to sweep the tomb (a Chinese traditional practice carried out every year to show respect to ancestors).

[†]In the 1970s, Chinese couples averaged six children before the One Child Policy, which has been reduced to an average of 1.8 children per couple now. There are a number of circumstances in China where multiple children are allowed: Rural families whose first child is not a boy, is disabled, or who pay a fine can have a second child. Urban dwellers as well can have multiple children if a fine is paid or, more recently, if both parents came from single-child families themselves. These multiple effects have probably created a mini-baby boom starting in 2007 as the eligible children reach marriageable age right about now and people aim for Olympic Babies (having a child born in 2008) all at the same time.

- Growing materialism and sense of wealth entitlement is starting to exhibit itself in negative ways. China's infrastructure may be world-class, but sometimes the behavior of the people isn't up to the same standard. For example, Chinese in cars treat the roads as their personal space, treating other drivers, cyclists, and pedestrians with indifference. Campaigns to eradicate spitting on the street after the SARS crisis have largely failed, and Chinese tourists traveling abroad are cautioned by their own government to tone down their behavior which may include shouting, jostling, and smoking in public places.
- Its economic data is often underreported due to the sheer size and effort involved in data collection in everything from unemployment figures to the migrant population. At times, data is exaggerated, for example when provincial governors report their progress on key performance indicators. At other times it is underreported, as in the case of undocumented children born after the One Child Policy was implemented. Data about China is better thought of as gray rather than black and white.

The Chinese government has realized all these problems and has undertaken several measures to deal with the largest of them. Fortunately for China, and for you, these problems are not only solvable, they are where the greatest opportunities exist: Multibillion dollar industries that are just waiting for the right companies and entrepreneurs to step in to provide solutions.

China's Dark Side

Finally, there are the problems that are truly devastating to a developing economy's output, social conditions, and reputation:

- China's black market is really more of a gray market since the stores and even malls can be full of counterfeit merchandise and operate in the open, complete with advertising and business cards. The city governments of Shanghai and Beijing, for example, have closed the most notorious fake goods markets, and foreign firms are increasingly winning cases against retailers that sell fakes.

- Occupational deaths from industries such as coal-mining that are the highest in the world. China's media is covering these accidents and acts of negligence more openly.
- Tainted drugs, food products, personal care products, pet food that contain dangerous chemicals sometimes added as a substitute for active ingredients, causing injury and death when ingested. In 2008, the government completed an overhaul of all toy exporters' quality-control processes and acted quickly to recall food products suspended of problems.
- Exploitation of workers in remote kilns, or at piecework factories with abysmal conditions and low wages — two situations that are fortunately starting to change as company executives are thrown in jail and the government has begun to enforce a new set of labor laws from January 2008.
- Business and government corruption, including land grabs by government officials, price collusion by instant noodle manufacturers, nepotism, bribes, and kickbacks, are all still present, but are the target of central government campaigns to reduce the distorting effects they have on the economy.
- Social unrest arising from the extreme wealth divide between the cities and countryside and the inevitable problems as tens of millions of people relocate into cities, leaving rural lives behind. To provide them with affordable housing, the borders of large cities such as Shanghai are expanding quickly with low-income housing projects.
- Territorial disputes between China and neighboring regions create an environment of geopolitical instability. In our view, many of these potential hotspots will be resolved with business interests in mind: China and the US may fight over prices, Taiwan and mainland China may argue over direct flights from Taipei to Shanghai, but the chances of military conflict seem more and more remote.

- The high potential for inflation resulting from China's trade surplus, its currency exchange rate controls, lack of adequate convertibility of the Chinese RMB into other foreign currencies, and booming stock market and land price bubbles.

These issues have been headline news in the Western media whenever a story on the downsides of China's growth appears, whenever a new trade dispute arises or, in the sadder cases, whenever the circumstances are so truly shocking or sad that we can't help but pay attention. While examining these deep, mostly structural problems is beyond the scope of this book, it is important to acknowledge that China is still a developing country and, as such, is bound to face growing pains. One must also be aware of China's full situation because several of these problems have the potential to derail the Chinese economic miracle, for example, worker exploitation, social unrest and inflation.

Working in the coal mines

China's coal-mining industry is essential to energy production in China. About 80 percent of China's power comes from coal, and the government maintains control of the official price, which creates an environment rife for corruption and cutting corners to make more money. Inside China, it seems a week doesn't go by when another illegal coal mine, perhaps reopened after it had been closed for safety reasons, collapses and traps dozens, even hundreds, of miners below ground. The fate of these workers is not good as, being illegal in the first place, the mines have little safety equipment and the owners often do not inform authorities in a timely matter in the case of disaster, preferring to flee the area with cash in hand. So, the combination of poor facilities and poor management leads to an unreasonably high number of deaths. In 2006 and 2007, the government stepped up efforts to crack down on the unauthorized mines and increase penalties for operators. The State Administration of Work Safety announced a 20 percent decrease in coal-mining fatalities for 2007, but that meant that 3,786 still perished.[14] With China's use of coal only increasing and nearing shortage levels, this situation is not expected to end anytime soon.

On the other hand, cases of worker exploitation that were supposed to have been eradicated long ago seem to be back. 2007's case of worker exploitation in the north-western Shanxi Province brick kilns is one such example. It was found that certain factory owners, with connections to local government officials, had been essentially treating workers as slaves, without pay or freedom to leave. A death caused by management-hired thugs brought the issue to light in the media, all the more shocking for the fact that many workers had suffered physically and mentally, even to the point of being kidnapped from elsewhere to work in the kilns. In the ensuing investigation, more than 500 workers in similar conditions were rescued from a number of locations. China is no stranger to labor exploitation charges, perhaps the first widely reported story being the Nike shoe controversy of the early 1990s.

In fact these may be isolated cases, bad apples, to paraphrase the terminology used in the US case of Enron and other companies to describe poor corporate practices. There is evidence that labor conditions are improving steadily. Factory conditions have improved remarkably, especially in those connected with foreign investment. China has both a monthly minimum wage for full-time workers and hourly minimum wage for part-time work, set at the provincial level based on local conditions. The central government can influence the local governments to increase their wages in response to trade imbalance pressure and the growing urban/rural wealth divide.‡ For example, in 2004, the monthly wage in Shenzhen was RMB600 (US$85) per month while in Shanghai it was RMB570 a month

---

‡The minimum wage, as it does in the West, generally only applies to new workers, the untrained, or unskilled labor, many of whom may be newly graduated students or migrant workers, thus it is not indicative of typical wages Chinese workers are receiving. In fact, in the cities, there is a new class of white-collar workers who are earning thousands of RMB a month, buying cars and even their own apartments.

(about US$81). By 2007, this had increased to RMB850 (US$121) per month in the Shenzhen special economic zone area, and RMB840 (US$120) per month in Shanghai. In July 2008, Shenzhen again increased the minimum wage to RMB1,000 in the city. In order to combat inflation, Guangdong Province announced it would raise the minimum wage from RMB780 to RMB860 (US$122) per month.[15] This is still somewhat less than a "dollar per hour" sound-bite that is often applied to China and other developing countries' labor rates, but with living costs in those cities being quite low it is still a livable, if not comfortable, wage.

In regard to part-time workers, the minimum is RMB6.5 (just under a dollar) per hour in Shanghai at present, but local market labor supply and demand are constantly testing these low numbers. For example, in 2007 a newspaper investigation showed that McDonald's, KFC and Pizza Hut were allegedly underpaying their workers in Guangdong, prompting a full investigation by the provincial labor authority. In 2007, McDonald's took the proactive step of raising its wages for 95 percent of staff, with those in Guangzhou and Beijing getting at least a full 15 percent above the minimum wage.[16]

Skilled-worker exploitation?

It is increasingly harder to argue about skilled-worker exploitation in the Chinese cities, where wages have risen quickly (10–15 percent a year in many places) and dramatically upset multinationals' hiring plans. Suddenly, now that skilled Chinese workers are not so cheap anymore, prime office rents are through the roof, and people with international skills hard to find, companies are finding China's labor environment to be very competitive indeed. While it is certainly still valid to talk about China as a low-cost labor country, the government wants to avoid that impression by focusing on more value-added industries, while low-cost labor-intensive products are being produced further west outside of the cities or even in other competing countries such as Vietnam. A recent survey by Mercer Management

Consulting, the world's leading human resource consulting firm, said that China was one of the most competitive labor markets in the developing world for finding and retaining talent.[17]

China Bubbles

Whenever you hear about over-building, skyrocketing land and stock market prices, and giant infrastructure projects, there is always the danger of an economic bubble. Indeed, China's construction projects alone would appear to qualify, but unlike other recent global bubbles such as the dot-com bubble in the US, the Thai land and stock bubble preceding the Asian financial crisis, or Japan's bubble economy of the 1980s, China's situation is fundamentally different: It has a managed exchange rate and capital inflow and outflow controls, allowing it to resist speculation and avoid (for the most part) hot money flowing into the economy. There are only a few things that could upset China's ascendancy to become the biggest economy on earth by 2050 or sooner. Various economists inside and outside China diverge on the details, but there is general agreement that the most likely scenario to derail China's upward trajectory is inflation.[18]

With its consistently high GDP growth and China's foreign currency controls, it may be said that China is pursuing a kind of neo-Mercantilist trade policy (though the fact it has joined the WTO and opened most markets speaks otherwise). It has already accumulated money to the tune of US$1.76 trillion in currency reserves as of April 2008. An in-depth discussion of inflation and currency management systems is beyond the scope of this book, but simply speaking, with so much money accumulating inside a closed system such as China, the prosperity of the people is bound to put upward pressure on prices as they seek to spend their increasing wealth.

Two things have prevented this from happening in China in recent years. First, the RMB rate was kept undervalued from 1998 to 2005, and foreign currency transactions were controlled by the government and held as reserves rather than being circulated into the system. Rather, China would prefer to buy Treasury Bonds from the US, financing the US debt, to allow the US to buy more products from China. Second, the Chinese population in general didn't have a lot of investment opportunities and thus tended to keep or reinvest a lot of their money without consumption, resulting in a national savings rate that has been around 50 percent for most of the last decade, compared with an essentially zero percent savings rate in the US.[19]

This fragile balance started to tilt beginning in 2006. With few places to invest their money (Chinese *outward* investment and the amount of foreign currency citizens can buy is also limited), the Chinese real estate and stock markets have been booming. Shanghai's stock market nearly doubled in 2007; the nationwide property price index has been on a steady increase for the last two years, with the national average in 70 cities increasing 11 percent in the first quarter of 2008, essentially growing more RMB wealth. Now, with China's state coffers overflowing with foreign currency and the RMB money supply starting to bubble up, this potential for inflation is compounded.

When Pork Flies

It all started rather quietly — pork prices in the local wet markets increasing, people buying more chicken instead. It had happened before: Farmers not slaughtering enough pigs causing a minor shortage, prices go up, farmers raised more pigs on this signal, the price fell back to normal or sold at a discount. The pig cycle was as constant a feature of life in pork-crazy China as the yearly rice harvest. Except, in 2007, it wasn't entirely about misjudging the market.

Farmers now had to pay more for grain, food prices were going up even for slop, a wave of blue-ear disease hit some stocks, medicines were expensive. For a while people did without, buying other meats instead, but it is hard to describe how important pork is to the Chinese diet. It is said that Mao Zedong's favorite dish was fatty fried pork in red sauce. With the exception of northern or western areas that tend to prefer lamb,

(Continued)

most of China eats pork in the way Americans eat beef or Japanese eat fish. So, gradually, people started paying the higher prices.

Then the hoarding began. Regular consumers were seen fighting over rare discounts on pork, then some universities announced they would buy enough pork to serve their entire student body for the semester to keep prices stable for students. When all was said and done, pork prices increased more than 48 percent in 2007. Switching over to chicken or beef didn't help much either — they were up 39 percent on the year.[20]

In 2007, warning signs of food price inflation were seen in China's consumer price index (CPI), the representative basket of goods that measures price levels (made up of about one-third food items, among other daily necessities). The CPI started off the year well enough at 2.2 percent in January (under the 3 percent target the central government had set, yet above the 1.5 percent average set in 2006), and throughout the year it continued to rise steadily and topped 6 percent regularly in the last half of the year, ending at 6.4 percent in December or 4.8 percent overall for the year. While hardly hyper-inflation, this was still alarming because the inflation resisted all attempts to tame it: Interest rate increases to discourage lending, deposit rate increases to encourage savings, forcing banks to hold more money in reserves, increasing the amount of foreign currency Chinese residents could buy and hold, stiffer penalties for price collusion, new taxes on stock market transactions, and real estate policies to discourage speculation. Finally, price controls and monitoring of key daily use commodities such as grain, cooking oil, tobacco, salt, meat, milk and the liquefied petroleum gas (LPG) that people run their motor-scooters on, automative gas, diesel and even that most Chinese of foodstuffs, instant noodles. The government has even hinted at wider-ranging price controls on everything from medical care to tuition, even basic water and electricity. All actions and threats have failed. It's not just individuals who were suffering from inflation; the Producer Price Index reached a three-year high in the first quarter of 2008, going up 6.9 percent. Power, materials, labor, everything is going up in price.

The final market force which would usually correct the upward inflationary pressure is the currency volume: If there is too much of a certain currency in the global system, its relative value begins to depreciate, thus reducing the ability of that country to buy more things in the global market. The only trouble with China is, it prevents its currency from decreasing (or increasing) based on global market supply and demand — it controls the value through what is called a managed float exchange rate policy. This control is similar to a cork on a bottle of champagne and, right now, the Chinese economy is a big *Nebuchadnezzar* which could pop at any moment.

Keeping this from happening is the guiding hand of China's central bank, the People's Bank of China, and ultimately it is China's leadership at the top that is trying to manage the ever more complex system to a soft landing rather than a bursting of the bubble. To the government's credit, the inflation hasn't yet reached unmanageable proportions, with a total yearly increase for 2007 of just 4.8 percent, triple the 1.5 percent CPI increase in China in 2006 (India, another fast-growing developing economy, was at 5.2 percent and Russia at 9.4 percent in 2007 in comparison) and interest rates are at a nine-year high but not unreasonable 7.47 percent, allowing further increases if needed.[§] Furthermore, the RMB has appreciated, albeit slowly, so while overheating of an economy is a worry, if you knew that the economy was going to continue to grow at least 5 percent per year for the next 10 years, isn't that a place you would like to be doing business in?

A growing number of economists feel China is likely to continue its strong growth path[21] and China's own government in fact requires a growth rate of at least 7.5 percent during the 11th Five-Year Plan to achieve the goal of doubling per capita GDP by

---

[§]The government raised the benchmark one year lending rate six times in 2007, usually about a quarter percent at a time.

2010,[22] and to keep generating enough jobs for the newly employable entering the market. Then there are the effects of international events on stimulating development:

China's economic growth will not slow down in the next five years with the hosting of the Summer Olympics in 2008 and Shanghai's hosting of the World Expo in 2010 and the subsequent halo effect, and most of all because the Chinese government would never allow a loss of face when the international spotlight is on China. China may even bid for the 2018 World Cup.

A high domestic growth rate also indicates healthy gains in corporate earnings, real estate and retail consumption — all key sectors to be looked at in the later chapters focused on various industries.

Crisis is Opportunity

All of these problems exist, are well-known and often-reported in more articles and books each year than most of us have time to read, yet the public and policymakers outside China never seem to tire of hearing about them with a sense of curiosity, *schadenfreude*, or dread.

It is not the purpose of this book to either ignore the problems or to go over ground that has already been covered in a number of excellent publications about China.

The purpose of the book is to reframe these issues for what they are to enterprising companies and entrepreneurs: Opportunities.

The Chinese word for crisis is 危机, spelled *wei'ji*, with the first character meaning *danger* and the second being part of another word commonly translated as *opportunity* or *chance*. It is almost a cliché now, but in the same way that Al Gore tells us global warming is one of the greatest threats to our environment and way of life, while at the same time saying it's an opportunity to enterprising energy-saving companies and individuals to shine, each of the above-mentioned issues in Chinese development becomes a chance for somebody to solve a problem and, incidentally, make a lot of money in the process.

Indeed, a graphic from *The Inconvenient Truth* movie shows Shanghai and Tianjin, two of China's most populace cities, being mostly underwater by 2050 if the worst-case climate change predictions are correct. The weight of some of the massive buildings in Shanghai is already causing parts of the city to sink into the ground.[23] This is a problem waiting for a solution.

Similarly, relocating hundreds of millions of people into cities is a very tough job, but you will also find opportunities relating to urban living, from construction to the service industries such as management consulting, accounting and human resources, and other services that are urgently needed in the industrializing and growing urban economies.

When it comes to cleaning up the environment, saving electricity, or generating new energy, China needs all three as soon as possible. The resulting opportunities in green businesses of alternative energy, pollution control, waste reduction and ecotourism are some of the biggest in the world. Red China is becoming green.

Finally, China's social issues such as aging, population imbalance, affluence and the wealth divide affect every industry from education and healthcare, to travel and investment. These are the basis for the supertrends and the biggest business opportunities in China's Olympic Decade.

The 21st Century's Biggest Economy

In the coming years, as part of what is increasingly being called the China Century, the largest creation and accumulation of private wealth ever to occur in the history of the planet will happen, in China. This is much bigger than Microsoft. In fact, by some projections, it's bigger than the biggest economy in the world today, the United States, which by 2050 or even sooner China is predicted to surpass in terms of GDP.[24]

China's own National Bureau of Statistics announced China's 2007 GDP growth was 11.9 percent, revised from the initial figure of 11.4 percent. Either way, it was above forecasts and possibly straying into overheated growth. The World Bank in 2006 projected the Chinese economy would grow at 11.3 percent in 2007, and slow to 10.8 percent in 2008. Where most developed countries strive for 3 percent as a respectable figure (the growth for the United Kingdom was 2.8 percent in 2006 and the United States grew at 3.3 percent in the same year), 10 percent and higher growth stands out.

The Chinese government has made it a priority to manage the growth. Among developing countries, those rates are not unheard of, but China has maintained the growth for more than *20 years*.[25] The first priority then is to keep the economy, awash in money from export trade and domestic demand, from overheating as inflation threatens to wipe out the savings of the already poor rural populace and reduce quality of life in the cities. China's Premier Wen Jiabao said at the 2007 National People's Congress that GDP growth needs to be kept under 8 percent in 2007,[26] yet Shanghai's GDP grew by 11.9 percent in 2007, the fastest pace since 1994, according to the National Bureau of Statistics. The Chinese National Academy of Sciences predicts that growth will slow to 10.8 percent as higher interest rates and monetary tightening policies implemented in 2007 begin to take effect, but the potential for overheating of the economy is still there as exports and the trade surplus continue to increase.

As with the national economy's tradition of five-year plans (China is currently in the midst of its 11th Plan), Chinese cities also have five-year plans, and with the biggest cities growing at above the national target, both Shanghai and Beijing have set more conservative growth targets in order to act as the brakes on the economy. Beijing, for example, is aiming to grow at a reasonable-sounding 9 percent a year for the next five years and wants to increase its per capita GDP from US\$7,000 to US\$10,000 by 2012. Shanghai, on the other hand, always the faster-growing of the two, will nearly double its GDP from about US\$165 billion in 2007 to US\$276 billion by 2012, a yearly growth of about 10 percent. Shanghai, which has recorded double-digit growth for the past 15 years, usually greater than 11 percent, perhaps did not want to suffer the loss of face from breaking its streak by merely matching Beijing's target. Next to Shanghai, nearby Jiangsu Province continues to grow at 14 percent plus growth rates as well, showing that the regional economy which Shanghai is a part of is hard to slow down. Shanghai's per capita GDP is projected by the government to reach US\$13,800 by 2012.

Superlatives, Chinese Style

While biggest, tallest, fastest doesn't always mean best, some of China's megaprojects and feats of business daring make for interesting experiences.

Fastest passenger train in operation: The Shanghai Maglev train connecting the airport to halfway to downtown — 432 kilometers per hour.

Tallest bungee jump: Macau.

Biggest ferris wheel: First there was the Tianjin Eye, at 110 meters, then the planned Shanghai Ferris Wheel (which has been derailed, for now, pending additional studies) at 170 meters, but they all pale in comparison to the US\$100 million Great Wheel of Beijing, a 208 meter

(Continued)

monster that dwarfs the 135 meter London Eye. The Beijing Great Wheel will have 48 cars that will carry 40 people each and it will be finished in 2009.

Highest cellular tower: Mt. Everest, 6,500 meters, giving mobile phone service to the handful of mountain climbers, sherpas and yaks.

Biggest shopping mall in the world: South China Mall in Dongguan, Guangzhou, 7.1 million feet of leasable retail area (and may also be one of the emptiest, as leasing has yet to reach capacity). The second biggest mall in the world is in Beijing, at 6 million square feet. The Dubai Mall is projected at 9 million square feet but, not to be outdone, the American developer of the Mall of America is trying to build a 10 million square foot facility (that's three times the size of America's biggest mall, the King of Prussia Mall in Philadelphia) in Wenzhou, the boomtown south of Shanghai that made it big in shoes and cigarette lighters.

World's tallest hotel: Depending on when you set the bar, at the time of writing the world's tallest hotel is the Grand Hyatt Shanghai on the 88th floor of the Jin Mao Tower, but it will be surpassed by the 93rd floor of the Park Hyatt in Shanghai's new World Financial Center building in July 2008, and then possibly by the Hong Kong Ritz-Carlton Hotel in 2009.

Longest ocean-crossing bridge: The Hangzhou Bay Bridge, joining Shanghai and Ningbo, 36 kilometers long at a cost of US$1.7 billion, and opening in 2008.

Biggest airport/building in the world: Terminal 3 and the Beijing Capital International Airport, 2.95 kilometers long, 1.3 million square meters of floor space, at a cost of US$3.8 billion.

When is the best time to invest in China?

Now. As this book is being written, China is finishing preparations for the 2008 Olympics to be held in Beijing. As a preview for the Olympics, China held the Special Olympics in October 2007 in Shanghai and it was said to be the best ever. The city was mobilized with more than 40,000 volunteers to host 7,500 athletes and families, and the event's opening and closing ceremonies were so elaborate and expensive that they rivaled the ceremonies of the actual Olympics in prior years. Opening ceremony tickets were not sold to the general public, only to groups, but there was no difficulty filling Shanghai's 80,000-person stadium. It is a sign of things to come from China and a strong indicator of the power the Olympic effect will have on China, not only in 2008, but in the entire Olympic Decade.

As of May 2008, the Olympic Torch Relay had suffered major protests in the UK, France, and the US, but continued onwards in a more subdued manner throughout South America, Africa, and South-East Asia. At the same time, protests against Western media such as CNN and companies such as France's Carrefour supermarket chain continued. Yet the Olympics will undoubtedly go on and be successful as China's window to the world, but the country will have to find some real solutions to the problems the extra attention on China is likely to bring.

The Olympic effect is a well-known, if not scientifically proven, correlation between development and the cities and countries that host the Olympics. The difference is in the size of the effect, China's GDP and population being much larger than many of the countries that have hosted the Olympics in recent years. China has been aspiring to host the Olympics for decades and, now that time has finally arrived, all levels of the government are fully behind it: Beijing, city governments in regions around the country where other sports venues have been constructed, and the national government wanting to ensure the entire event puts China in a good light, as well as helping to stoke the economy in a more sustainable direction.

The Olympic effect is not just about land prices, it is about the economic activity that results from the construction of the venues (approximately US$1.8 billion in direct spending on venues, billions more on city beautification, neighboring developments both residential and commercial), the media promotions, the everyday citizens participating in sports and leisure in greater numbers, and the business opportunities resulting from increased tourism.[27]

With the upcoming Shanghai World Expo[28] in 2010, hosting the Asian Games in Guangzhou (also in 2010), and other events, China's economy will continue to be stimulated to grow through both internal and external challenges, meaning that now is as good a time as ever, in fact probably the *best time ever*, to begin or increase your business here.

What You Will See in China

Each chapter ends with a summary of the drivers, trends or opportunities mentioned within. When it comes to China from an introductory perspective, we may now better understand China's positive and negative sides, and some bear repeating before moving on:

1. You need strength to catch a trend, and trends are caught by those who know in advance what is going to happen. This book is your guide to become rich and glorious by riding China's *Supertrends*.
2. Increasing air travel over the last five years and predictions of global companies like Boeing for the next 20 years indicate a clear trend: More and more business is being done in China. Are you one of those people on the next plane?
3. China comes with good, bad, and downright ugly problems. Each problem, however, is a potential opportunity for businesspeople to solve. The best trends and how you can make money from them are covered in the following chapters.
4. China's growth will not slow down in the immediate future, thanks to the positive growth effects related to the 2008 Olympics and 2010 World Expo in Shanghai, so what better time to get into the economy?
5. China's markets are now open to foreign competition across most industries. Markets may still be highly regulated or suffer from structural issues (such as IPR enforcement) in some cases, but it is better to jump in than miss the boat.

Overall the message seems clear: China now!

PART ONE

CHINA'S SEEDS OF GROWTH

～ 萌芽 ～

CHAPTER ONE

China's Three Primary Growth Drivers

待文王而兴者， *Dai wen wang er xing zhe,*
凡民也。 *fan min ye.*
若夫豪杰之士， *Nuo fu hao jie zhi shi,*
虽无文王犹兴。 *sui wu wen wang you xing.*

"The common people wait for Emperor Wen to come and uplift them. But the truly outstanding will uplift themselves, even if Emperor Wen doesn't appear." — Mencius

What are the forces behind China's growth, now and in the future? There are three, what many call the primary drivers of economic growth: Exporting, foreign direct investment, and domestic market consumption. Of these, trade and investment are the most important at present.

China has built its economy on exports, much as other Asian tigers or dragons did before it, relying on its mammoth quantities of labor to make it the low-cost leader. Next in importance comes foreign direct investment (FDI). A well-known relationship in international trade is that foreign direct investment usually follows exports and, by this logic, based on the huge amount of FDI coming from the US, a lot of products should have been imported into China from there, too. The theory goes that a company in the United States starts exporting its products to China and eventually decides it would be easier to just make a factory in China and sell directly in the local market, thereby avoiding all the hassle of shipping, customs duties, and so on. In China, though, it may be said that few companies ever succeeded in exporting to China that didn't set up a major investment of some kind in the country first, rather than later. There are three main reasons why this relationship is the opposite of what we might expect according to standard trade theory.

First, products built abroad and sold in China as is would probably not be entirely suitable for the Chinese market, and too expensive for much of the population, whose per capita income is far below that of the US even though China's economy is the fourth largest in the world after the US, Japan and Germany (if PPP (purchasing power parity) is taken into account, China has the second strongest economy in the world today).

Second, it is a rare product that could not be found in China already, or readily copied and sold at a much lower price than the authentic item.

Third, prior to China's becoming part of the WTO in 2001, many of China's markets had high tariff and non-tariff barriers to overcome. So, as a result, a foreign company wanting to sell its products to China would usually be better off setting up a company, factory or assembly facility there and importing things for its own use, finishing them in China and then selling them domestically or, often, just re-exporting them.

China turned the whole model on its head, as did globalization when it was no longer necessary to worry about where one's factory was so long as it was in the lowest-cost location possible, and so it is that most things sold in China are made in China, and if foreign companies want to sell there they have to invest. Foreign direct investment in China has grown to be the biggest in the world in several years of the last half-decade.

While exports and FDI are China's two most important drivers, they also point to a strategic weakness which is that China is depending on outside markets and investors to help it develop. That is where the third driver comes in — the domestic market.

It is true that any economy is driven by investment, exports and consumption, but in this context investment means not only FDI but domestic investment by businesses as well, and if China's FDI has been high, domestic investment has been higher, so much so that the Chinese government is afraid of overheating in the economy due to too much investment and has made efforts to slow investments down by instructing the big five banks (Industrial & Commercial Bank of China, Bank of China, Bank of Communications, China Construction Bank, and Agricultural Bank of China) to tighten lending criteria, raising interest rates and so on. Nevertheless, China's GDP still grew at the fastest rate of growth in more than 10 years — 11.9 percent in 2007. What's different this time is that the contribution of investment, 4.3 percent, was slightly lower than the contribution from domestic consumption, 4.4 percent.* It is too soon to say this is a trend, but it does lend support to the idea that domestic consumption will be the most important driver of future economic growth as incomes grow and retail spending increases as people find themselves with more wealth.

The mythical one billion customers dream aside, China's domestic market is quite simply going to be the biggest in the world — it is just a matter of time. In 2007, consumption was just under 40 percent of China's total GDP growth, and in terms of the total GDP expenditure, personal consumption was approximately 36 percent for 2006 (the latest year data is available). Although half of the US's consumption expenditure (about 70 percent), these two statistics refute the common idea that China's economy is driven by exports alone. Though still low compared to many developed countries, the growing influence of consumption on the Chinese economy is an important driver.

Many say China will be the world's largest market by 2050, but if China continues to grow at the 11 percent plus pace of the last several years, it could be much sooner. Year by year China steadily marches

---

*These figures are based on the NBS's first announcement of GDP growth of 11.4 percent, which it later revised to 11.9 percent after more data became available.

up in the economic rankings and will eventually challenge the US for the title of world's biggest market. The importance of this for China's development is that, with a strong domestic market, China can effectively reach critical mass and continue developing on its own — a popular theory at the moment that is called decoupling.

To decouple means to be able to develop independently, despite potential problems in other countries or even in a global recession. The decoupling idea flies in the face of globalization's idea that our world is now interconnected and interdependent. Another way to put it is to say the international race to the bottom, where companies continually seek low-cost labor and abandon one country's factories for another's as tax holidays run out, may be at an end in China because its market potential is so large and companies will have to stay there in order to be successful. China is becoming the *de facto* low-cost mass producer and simultaneously the world's largest market, effectively forcing multinational companies to have a permanent home rather than remain as some kind of disembodied transnational entity: The lure of the Chinese market in the future is drawing them back to earth. Thus, while the domestic market consumption driver is the third most important now, it is *the* most important in the future, both to the Chinese economy and to your business venture in China.

Let's look at each of these drivers in more detail.

Exports from AIGO to ZTE

AIGO is the English name for one of China's electronics manufacturers, famous for products such as MP3 players, while ZTE is a mobile phone and telecom hardware manufacturer that may one day rival larger and more famous firms such as Ericsson or Siemens. AIGO is better known outside of China as an OEM, an Original Equipment Manufacturer — basically, a manufacturer that produces for bigger companies on contract. That is probably why you've never heard of companies such as AIGO outside of China, but they are a key part of China's US$1.2 trillion in exports.[1]

In 2007, China's largest trading partners were the EU, the US, and Japan, with US$356 billion, US$302 billion, and US$236 billion respectively in total trade. The total trade surplus (the amount by which exports exceed imports) is large again in 2007, about US$262 billion, adding to China's US$1.76 trillion in currency reserves in April 2008, and may increase by about US$300 billion in 2008 according to the Chinese Academy of Social Sciences.[2] The global interconnectedness that results from trade shows no signs of slowing China down. Even if one of China's biggest customers, the US, enters a prolonged economic correction or recession, it is optimistically thought that this would in fact increase many low-priced Chinese exports even more — an idea that could be moot if high oil prices increase transportation costs for low-priced goods.

Shoes out, dollars in

Despite the Chinese *yuan*'s[†] appreciation against the dollar and other major currencies in the past two years, China's exports continued to grow by about 25 percent in 2007, and are predicted to grow by about 19 percent in 2008.[3] Since the RMB peg to the dollar was scrapped in 2005 in favor of an unspecified basket of currencies and trading band rather than a fixed rate, the currency has been appreciating slowly but steadily, going from approximately 8.27 then to about 7.0 at the time of writing. If one believes American senators, this glacial pace is the crux of the trade imbalance between the US and China, but fast appreciation or revaluation has been ruled out by the central bank of China so that its exporters, one of the lynchpin drivers of the economy, have time to adjust to a new high-RMB environment, as well as to provide time to improve structural problems in the economy such as the wealth divide or labor laws.

[†]The Chinese currency, as mentioned earlier, can be referred to as the *yuan* or the *renminbi* (RMB for short), the people's money. Outside of China, it is usually quoted as the *yuan*, while inside China *yuan* is often used to quote prices, as in "This book is 30 *yuan*." Colloquially, it is called a *kuai*, a piece, kind of like saying "30 pieces," while *renminbi* is used for formal references to money, such as *renminbi duilu*, the exchange rate for the RMB.

The exporters have upgraded production with more efficient machinery and many have focused on innovation as the key to remaining competitive. Compared to 1990, when China classified about 7 percent of its exports as "high-tech," that export ratio is now above 37 percent. Even China's most traditional of industries, silk production, is moving into such non-traditional areas as the production of artificial skin using silk proteins, costing 1/10th of similar products abroad thanks to China's low cost of labor and favorable, even ideal, environment for harvesting silk.[4]

An overdependence on exports is a worry for China, but putting all its eggs in one US-based basket is even more troublesome. The EU's trade with China is technically bigger, but it is not homogenous given the EU's vastly different national markets, so the US is still the single biggest market. From China's perspective, a decrease in US consumer spending could actually help mitigate the US$163 billion trade surplus (or $260 billion trade deficit, if you follow the US perspective, a very different number because of the way the two countries calculate trade[5]), but no exporter in China wants to see a US slowdown. On a macro level, the Chinese government has felt threatened by its bilateral trade dependence on the US, so has sought to hedge its bets by increasing trade with the EU and Japan. Trade with the latter is especially evident in just the last several years as Japan's economy started to recover, many believe due to the strength of trade with China. In 2008, China was also moving forward with a proposal to join the OECD, the organization for 30 of the world's market economies, among an increasing expansion of the grouping which also includes the other BRIC countries — Brazil, Russia, and India.

China's trade with other Asian nations has also increased and it is a major player in turning ASEAN, the Association of South-East Asian Nations, into the world's biggest trading bloc when China joins. A China-led ASEAN free trade zone is still some time off, but ASEAN will in the future be a major balancing force against other multilateral trading blocs such as the (now fragmenting) North

American Free Trade Agreement and the EU.[6] These trends should insulate China somewhat if its largest trading partner, the US, stops importing as much. Yet, the present interconnectedness of trade and globalization as a stabilizing force is important to China's continued development through exporting.

China's impact on the world

Thirty years ago, few would have predicted the extraordinary impact that China has on the global business environment today. Japan looked ascendant, the US and UK were mired in an economic downturn and ideological war with the Soviet Union, and China was mostly closed to outsiders and seemed unlikely to emerge. Yet from the time of Napoleon, who is thought to have once said that China would make the world tremble when it awoke, people have been aware of China's incredible potential, but few would have predicted it could happen so quickly, making the previous rise of Asian economies like Japan, Korea, and Taiwan seem slow in comparison.

Shanghai's Bund Then and Now

Stepping out of the Jean Georges Shanghai restaurant in Wai Tan No. 3 (Bund No. 3), I felt suddenly awakened from Michael Graves' modern design of warm interior colors and romantic lighting, by the noisy bright car lights on the Shanghai streets. How funny it was that Kevin, Marie and Michael, who came halfway across the world to dine with me and my wife, could have the same menu at the New York Jean Georges in Columbus Circle just blocks away from their apartments.

We walked toward the walkway along the Bund, passing the Giorgio Armani store downstairs from the restaurant which displayed almost the same fashion as their stores in New York, London or Hong Kong. The only difference was the 60 percent higher price tags. Strolling along

(Continued)

the walkway following the river, it has been a typical after-dinner walk for many visitors, not only digesting the foie gras and caviar, but also orienting the travelers' sense of time.

On one side of the river, we see the classic buildings in a mixture of architectures such as German Gothic, French Renaissance, Art Deco and others. The Bund started in the 19th century as a collection of buildings supporting the colonial settlements of the English and other countries, and it later become the financial street to the foreign trading houses and banks in the 19th and early 20th centuries, continuing to develop until the mid-1930s when war with Japan broke out and then civil war within China, after which it was turned over to government use. The now fully restored and preserved buildings are artistically lighted at night, displaying their 200 years of history to the foreigners visiting now. Time stops here as you can almost see the Shanghainese and foreign traders and bankers still interacting in the HSBC Building, the Customs House, the Shanghai Club, the Peace Hotel and on the busy streets.

On the other bank of the Huangpu River, one sees quite the opposite: the new Shanghai, gateway to modern China. There is the 88-storey pagoda-inspired Jin Mao Tower housing the Grand Hyatt Hotel, the 468 meter Oriental Pearl Tower, Bank of China, HSBC, and Citigroup buildings, rows of modern skyscrapers that illuminate half of the city with their giant television screens displaying advertising to the tens of thousands wandering the Bund. The new office buildings on the eastern shore of the Huangpu River are almost all related to finance, as the area, called Luijiazui, is China's first and only finance development zone created by the government to promote modernization of China's financial system.

Contrasting with the classic buildings of romantic and memorable Shanghai, the new side of Shanghai extends its earnest invitation to the foreigners to join the fast growth which began only 20 years ago.

Memory brings me back to the summer of 1984 when I first came to Shanghai. After settling in the hotel, I was dragged by my excited wife to the Bund that she had heard so much about from her Shanghainese

(Continued)

father. When the Russian-made taxi reached the Bund, the dark and quiet streets made us wonder if it was the wrong stop. Strolling along all these unlighted dark buildings on the quiet unpaved sidewalk didn't live up to the bustling and lively image of the Bund as described by Natalie's father who lived in Shanghai before 1950 and worked in the Bank of China building on the Bund.

Needless to say, the stroll was not an exciting one. In fact, I had to constantly encourage Natalie to finish the walk. But that did not mean we could return to our hotel; we still needed transportation, as back then a taxi needed to be ordered as there were very few available and which were only occasionally ordered by the foreigners who could afford them anyway. We had to walk all the way back to the Peace Hotel on the Bund and persuaded the porter there to order a taxi for us at the "late hour" of 9 p.m. on Friday night.

— JKY

Billion Dollars a Week: Foreign Investment

How important is foreign investment to China? Since 1978, China has received more than US$2.11 trillion in foreign direct investment. In total, more than 286,000 foreign-funded companies have been set up in China in the past 30 years, with 37,000 companies set up in 2007 alone.[7] Some 480 of the world's top 500 companies are doing business inside China.[8] In 2007, China received a record-setting US$74.7 billion in FDI,‡ pretty good for a former Communist country: Deng Xiaoping would be proud, Mao Zedong would be apoplectic.

---

‡Or US$83 billion in total, if financial portfolio investments in real estate, stocks and so on are included. The amount of portfolio investment as a component of the total is relatively low because China still restricts many kinds of foreign investment in mainland stocks and real estate. Therefore, unlike many developed countries that allow access to their capital markets, most foreign investment in China is non-portfolio investments and used for things such as building factories, providing capital for joint or wholly-owned ventures and so on.

In the 1980s, the joint venture was the preferred model for entry into China, in fact often the only model according to Chinese government regulations designed to ease the economy into capitalism and transfer technology and know-how in the Chinese companies, but these cooperative partnerships were often anything but mutually beneficial, leading to many problems. The 2007 case of France's Danone suing their joint venture partner, China's Wahaha Group, and vice versa, is only the latest and most public spat, but it is indicative of the end of the age of joint ventures in China. Today, the preferred model is a Wholly-Owned Foreign Enterprise (or WOFE for short, a "woofy," though the official term is WFOE, possibly because that sounds more dignified), which gives total control to the owner of the business and no surprises such as showing up to work one day to find your joint venture partner has fled with all the equipment and managers.

Back in the 1980s on the half-empty flights to China, most of the passengers were Taiwanese and Hong Kongese. Any foreigners to be seen were most likely their customers traveling with them to visit suppliers or conduct business. In the 1990s, companies started to come to establish their own factories. Some companies may even have been making money, but repatriation of profits was a problem due to China's currency controls and the idea that profits should be reinvested in the state.

Now, companies come to China for sourcing and outsourcing, and China has become a base of operations for many firms that have relocated their Asia headquarters from places like Singapore and Hong Kong to Shanghai and Beijing. The most favorable areas for investment in China, according to a World Bank report in 2006, are the south-east coastal provinces, consisting of the so-called Yangtze River Delta provinces of Jiangsu, Zhejiang, and Shanghai; the Pearl River Delta province of Guangdong (near Hong Kong and Macau) whose capital is Guangzhou and also includes Shenzhen, Dongguan, and Zhuhai, all special economic development zones; and the province of Fujian near Taiwan.[9] The worst are in the north-west: Shanxi, Sha'anxi, Inner Mongolia, Xinjiang and others, and it is there where you hear about worker exploitation, coal-mining disasters, and social unrest. The current hope of the Chinese government is to slow down development in the better-off areas and shift investment to places like Sichuan and Chongqing, and central provinces such as Anhui.

The influx of FDI creates a need for not only manufacturing facilities, for which funds are typically applied, but increasingly for services. Relocated multinational headquarters have come to expect certain things of any location where they have significant operations: Accounting, legal, auditing and due diligence, human resources, even consulting and investment banking. All of these point to an urgent need for professional services and, therefore, services FDI.

The next wave of FDI in China is related to services, of which China's developing economy needs more, especially in its more developed eastern cities such as Shanghai or Beijing.

It is not just professional services that are growing the services-based FDI; it is also entertainment and dining: Restaurant chains such as Pizza Hut and KFC now dot the streets of China's budding metropolises. In fact, the entire service sector in China, including education, retail, and healthcare, is growing rapidly. In just the first half of 2007 alone, FDI in the service industry totaled nearly US$14 billion, a 58 percent rise over the same period in 2006 and representing more than 43 percent of the total FDI during that time. Clearly the foreign-invested service industry in China is growing, and the Chinese government is allowing more openness in the sector both as part of its WTO entry commitments (which are by now nearly complete) as well as accelerating the opening of other industries such as logistics that will bring in foreign know-how that China desperately needs to keep its development apace.

At the time of writing, FDI continued to pour into China, much of it thought to be *hot money*, funds entering in order to take advantage of the appreciation of the RMB. In the first quarter of 2008, for example, FDI was up 61 percent year-on-year, with US$27 billion in investments from overseas, according to China's Ministry of Commerce.[10]

In terms of the government's preferred FDI at present, polluting, energy-intensive, and labor-intensive businesses in the already developed areas of China are out; high-tech and service industry investments in the cities, and any investments in the underdeveloped western parts of China, are in.

Big Numbers in Future China

Big trends come with big numbers, and China is a country of more than a billion in population, so it's only fitting to have some other amazing statistics. Some of these numbers may be termed irrational exuberance, while other data are just a sign of how much things have changed. Here are some of the bigger numbers:

US$3.5 trillion: The reported size of China's GDP in 2007 (RMB24.66 trillion), making it the world's 3rd largest single-country economy after the United States and Japan, in a virtual tie with Germany for 3rd place depending on the exchange rate. If inflation-adjusted GDP is used (i.e., taking PPP into consideration, the cost of living being significantly lower in China), China's economic size leaves Germany and even Japan far behind, becoming second only to the USA.[11]

US$2 trillion: The value of China's exports and imports in 2007, continuing a pattern of 20 percent plus growth for six years running.

US$2.1 trillion: The total amount of foreign investment China has received since 1978.

US$1 trillion: The approximate market capitalization of PetroChina on November 5, 2007, China's largest oil company, making it the world's first trillion dollar company, double the valuation of rival Exxon yet with only one-half of the profits.

(Continued)

547 million: The number of mobile phone users in China by the end of 2007.

592 billion: The number of text messages those subscriptions sent in 2007, generating US$8.4 billion in revenues.

5 billion: The number of text messages (SMS or short messages) that Chinese sent on a single day — the 2008 Chinese Lunar New Year — to wish each other prosperity, happiness, or to just check if people like them enough to reply. One-day windfall for the telecom operators: US$70 million. This busiest greetings day of the year is about three times the average number of SMSs sent *each day* in China — 1.6 billion.

Hungry Hippo: China's 1.3 Billion Consumers

According to the Boston Consulting Group, China will be the world's number two consumer market as early as 2015, surpassing Japan and Germany.[12] By the World Bank's estimate, this has already happened in terms of PPP-adjusted economic size. China has undergone a series of stages in the development of its consumer attitudes and behaviors which is distinctly different from the consumption patterns of most Western countries, owing to China's unique economic situation. If this can be put into the framework of Maslow's hierarchy of needs, the Chinese consumers in the cities have long ago moved beyond survival needs and are purchasing often for esteem. Young people in the cities desire the latest brand clothing or newest iPod, older consumers want a better car or a bigger house. In the countryside, a different class of consumers exists who are probably looking for security and stability, the second level of Maslow's hierarchy, but are quickly catching up. There is clearly a divided market in China of more affluent city dwellers and poorer countryside peasants. Nevertheless, the modern consumer in China has gone through several stages that are interesting to note for sociological understanding.

The first generation of consumers, now aged 60–80, and consuming prior to the opening of China to market reform in 1978, aspired to purchase the "three rounds and one sound," the so-called "old four": Wristwatch, bicycle, sewing machine, and radio. At this time, China still had strict foreign currency controls, limited imports, and the items in question needed to be paid for not only in their cash value but also by having the right to purchase them using a quota ticket system.

The next generation, at the dawn of China's open-door policy of the 1980s, saw the rise of the "new four things": Washing machine, refrigerator, TV, and camera. Consumer behavior in this period started to include comparison shopping and bargain hunting as people were more free to spend money and competition was heating up. There was no way of stopping the insatiable demand in the cities, and by 1998 there were more than 100 televisions, 91 washing machines and 76 refrigerators for every 100 residents.[13] Penetration rates for goods such as air conditioners, home computers, and mobile phones were still relatively low. These formed the basis for the next generation of consumers of the China Century starting in 2000.

This is the so-called esteem need of Maslow's hierarchy: Urban Chinese consumers have now entered a period of consumption based on quality of life and are quickly adopting the same characteristics that motivate Western consumers: Aspiration purchasing, emotional purchasing, buying for technical benefits, buying based on quality rather than price, choosing status symbols and brands suitable to their incomes, and so on. While the past growth in the consumer market was largely driven by a need for basic goods during the previous stages, the new Chinese consumers are able to buy anything and everything that a global market provides (their country is the one making them, after all). There are growing domestic industries in automotive, construction, and white goods that provide high quality domestic alternatives usually at a lower price than the imported or foreign-branded or even foreign-produced China products.

In fact, new urban Chinese consumer attitudes can often be called brand conscious rather than price conscious: A famous and established brand is a guarantee of quality, safety and effectiveness. As increasing standards of living push up the need for more living space, better cars, more fashionable clothes, and the newest technology in mobile phones and computing, the companies that want to reach these consumers' wallets must now think about differentiation and unique value propositions to consumers. One study found that it is no longer enough to simply sell a product as is, or sell it in the same way as in another foreign country; it requires a selling approach that takes Chinese consumer attitudes and behaviors into account.[14] This is a process we call *Sinofication*, modifying Western products and services to have Chinese characteristics. Some of the world's largest companies are catching on to this idea and enjoying increased success in China as a result.

Another sea change in the way Chinese consumers are being seen by MNCs is as increasingly heterogeneous. Frankly speaking, the Chinese consumers were always so, but for many years after China's initial opening post-1978, the "Chinese Market" idea of a homogeneous consumer prevailed with some minor attempts at segmentation such as targeting the "Little Emperor" children of one-child families. Furthermore, attention was focused on the so-called first tier cities such as Shanghai, Guangzhou, and Beijing, where purchasing power was highest. In the last five years, tier two cities were targeted. Now, with China's new rich being found all over, the relative maturity of the first and second tier markets makes them difficult to compete in. The next frontier in the Olympic Decade is the third, fourth, fifth tier and beyond.

While these cities are more numerous and geographically fragmented, the third to fifth tier cities have more than double the population of the first two tiers, approximately 234 million people versus about 118 milion, representing 43 percent of GDP versus 34 percent, and annual salaries about half of the upper tiers.[15] The urbanization rate in these cities is also high and consumption is growing quickly as these millions of strivers see the better lives and better products in Shanghai or Beijing and want the same.

Multinationals that want to access these new markets have to follow localization strategies for their China business operations: Localize their people, processes, and products to produce more suitable items for Chinese consumer tastes. In regard to these lower tier cities in particular, the MNCs must also improve their distribution and supply chains in order to more effectively compete against local Chinese competitors already in the hearts and back-pockets of retailers. For many manufacturers, this may mean strategies that they are not familiar or comfortable with in other countries: Television shopping, manufacturer-owned stores, creating low-price versions of their product suitable for the local market, and so on.

Primary Growth Drivers

China's primary growth drivers are exports, foreign direct investment, and the developing consumer market. Of these, exports and FDI have historically been most important, while in the future, the growth of the consumer market is critical to China's continued development:

1. Exporting from China is still a viable business opportunity. China's exports are still growing dramatically — 25 percent in 2007. This shows there are still opportunities to operate export-oriented businesses in China. This includes sourcing, contract manufacturing (OEM), assembly or even full production as a JV or WOFE company inside China. Better late than never!

2. The trends within FDI are towards cleaner capital-intensive high-tech manufacturing in the cities, low-tech labor-intensive manufacturing in the western parts of China, and service industry investments just about anywhere but especially welcomed in the cities and in certain industries such as logistics where support is needed to bring China's quality of service up to international standards.

(Continued)

3. China's domestic market is growing very quickly, and consumers are buying quality goods for their social esteem value. Especially in the big cities, brand-conscious consumers look at quality and brand, not price, as primary decision criteria (but they'll still ask for a discount!), and consumers should be properly segmented according to standard marketing characteristics for the best results selling into China's domestic markets.

China's three primary growth drivers continue.

CHAPTER TWO

The Drivers of the Drivers

识天下实势者，　*Shi tian xia shi shi zhe,*
为俊杰。　　　　*wei jun jie.*

"The person who knows the current trends is a person of outstanding talent."

T he Chinese economic drivers are export orientation, FDI, and domestic consumption, as described in the previous chapter. We feel they are still critical to China's growth moving forward, but also that they are too simple to explain the complex development path the Chinese economy is on. China is even trying to move beyond dependence on the first two drivers, exports and FDI. So, to predict the *supertrends*, we need to understand the forces behind those primary drivers. Here, we put forward our premise of the real drivers of the supertrends, what we call the drivers of the drivers, which will complement and in some cases surpass the primary growth drivers to sustain China: *globalization, government policy,* and *Chinese determination.* We represent these with another Chinese saying:

天时地利人和　*tian'shi, di'li, ren'he*

The Right Timing, the Right Place, the Right People

This phrase describes how, with the exquisite opportunities of time provided by the heavens, favorable geographic position, and unity and order of the people working towards a common good, one can enjoy opportunities that are among the greatest in the history of the world. These opportunities are driven by three forces (referred to as the drivers of the drivers) that underpin not only the primary drivers but the supertrends as well.

The right time refers to our current period as defined by globalization: Sourcing materials where they are most abundant, manufacturing goods in the cheapest locations, selling them in the most profitable markets, all while disregarding boundaries such as language, culture, and borders. How does this force drive China's trends forward, both inward and outward? China is arguably both the country most affected in the world by globalization and the source of an increasingly large share of its manufactured products. This process actually started some 30 years before with the rise of the four tigers — Korea, Singapore, Hong Kong and Taiwan — which, together with the developed Western economies such as the US, all at some point began looking for a low-cost labor zone as their own costs began to rise. Situated in the middle of Asia, China was the ideal location for the next *world's factory* moniker. In order to keep up its place in this system, China now has to quickly modernize from low-cost producer to high-tech, high-quality manufacturer without losing its exports to even lower-cost countries as many of the tigers already have to China.

The right place obviously refers to China and its above-mentioned position as the world's current destination of choice for manufacturing, but we take it more specifically to mean the concept of China itself as envisioned by the ruling elite. Issues of concern to China's overall development as exemplified by government policy are at the forefront, such as the decision to follow in the footsteps of the tigers by becoming an export-oriented economy, educating and urbanizing its population, all while solving social problems such as wealth distribution and protecting the environment. Thus, *place* describes a China that is pushed forward overall by the efforts of the government to make it a better country.

Finally, the right people are the characteristics that make the Chinese population a significant driver of everything, from the price of shoes to the emergence of global shortages of key manufacturing inputs, as China's new consumers spend their way to better lives. What motivates them to achieve business success and personal wealth? It is a combination of traditional values and culture, recent historical events, and a desire to reach their place among the ranks of the world's top consumers. This drives an enormous race to prosperity with Chinese characteristics: Relationships, mutual support, and entrepreneurial spirit.

Globalization's Poster Child

China's rapid rise to prominence on the world stage is perhaps one of the most visible manifestations of globalization that causes both fear and awe in developed countries: Fear that one's own job may be outsourced to a cheaper-labor country such as China, awe that a recently poor and backwards country could so quickly dominate certain industries that had been productive in developed countries for decades or even centuries. China is possibly blazing a trail that India will soon follow and, perhaps one day, countries in South America and even Africa will aspire to. Or, maybe not — maybe China is the endgame to the international race to the bottom, so big is its workforce and market.

In many ways, development of the world through globalization serves a greater good, for example by helping the millions of anonymous Chinese factory workers in cities you've probably never heard of, such as Wenzhou or Zhuhai, who can now afford basic lifestyle amenities, better educate their children, or aspire to start their own business. However, the globalization debate in Western countries is often dominated by a few very visible losers such as the United Auto Workers union, a vocal group that has seen its numbers decimated by overseas competition and outsourcing by its own companies.

Inside China, you will hear few complaints about globalization, except maybe how conference calls with the US or the EU always seem to be at the convenience of the Westerners who would rather not get up early or stay up late, or perhaps you might hear some complaints about the high cost of Western labor both inside and outside of China. Indeed, the only major Chinese complaint about globalization is not their own exploitation working directly or indirectly for Western companies, but rather the frustration that the supposedly free markets of the developed world are still in reality protecting domestic business. The US, EU and other countries make full use of their market power to shift the balance and protect certain domestic industries, but one might justifiably wonder whether those industries are still necessary and employ significant amounts of domestic labor in those Western countries: The 2007 EU complaint against China's shoe and textile production; the US's 2007 complaint against various types of paper made in China; and its 2004 complaint against Chinese TV producers TCL, Changhong, Konka and Xiamen Overseas, to name several areas of apparent trade protectionism not for the sake of the populations in general (who are hurt by high domestic-product prices), but rather to protect special interests.

Despite these setbacks, China has been an overwhelming beneficiary of globalization and is starting to assert its rights under the World Trade Organization rules by filing complaints and counter-suits of its own.

Increasing openness to trade and investment

When China officially entered the World Trade Organization (WTO) in December 2001, this was only the latest in a series of steps in the gradual opening of China's markets, following Deng Xiaoping's reforms beginning in 1978. In fact, China's entry to the WTO was phased in to protect vulnerable industries from foreign competition by giving them time to upgrade processes, technologies, and people.

For example, 2007 was a banner year for the finance industry in China: At the same time that three of China's largest banks — Industrial and Commercial Bank of China (ICBC), Bank of China, and China Construction Bank — had graft investigations completed, senior officials ousted, and went public on the stock markets raising a combined total of more than US$40 billion,[1] foreign banks could finally open branches and offer local currency services.[2] HSBC, Standard Chartered, and Citibank were among some of the major banks taking advantage.

While China's original five-year schedule of entry protocols for most industries is now completed,* the Chinese market is now more or less open to the majority of company types.[3] Foreign companies and individuals can operate everything from consulting to couriers, restaurants to retail. As a driver of this book's supertrends, China's continued globalization, adjustment of business laws, and changes in business demand and consumer preference mean that it is an open, if not always level, playing field.

Many of China's industries are still in their infancy and, despite opening up through the WTO, many are still greenfield opportunities.

The issues that remain regarding China's entry into the WTO are no longer absolute barriers, but are more likely to be issues of harmonization and normalization of standard business regulations and

---

*China maintains, as with many developed countries, a list of industries it does not allow foreign competition into, such as in the case of China's many energy-related industries, the telecommunications industry, certain aspects of the finance industry, and others.

practices such as Generally Accepted Accounting Principles, or just simple competitive issues. For example, intellectual property rights enforcement and the counterfeit goods industry, transparency of business applications and administration, and differences in international standards, not to mention finding the right local talent to staff the newly formed foreign-owned companies.

Pro-Business Government Policy

The second driver of the drivers is China's pro-business government policy. The role of government policy in China cannot be understated. From the time of the 1949 People's Liberation when Mao's followers — downtrodden peasants and die-hard Communists — defeated the Nationalist forces of Chiang Kai-Shek, the Chinese economy has been a planned one. To this day, China describes its own economy as a planned market economy, ignoring the inherent contradiction between control and free market. Nevertheless, its chosen path of development has been successful by most international measures: GDP and incomes, literacy and life expectancy are all up, child mortality is down. At present, the growing prevalence of AIDS, pollution, the wealth divide, and relative lack of improvements in the western provinces of China have stymied the central government since the time of the 1978 reforms. It is doing what it can to alleviate even these difficult problems with a coordinated effort of government policy. Where China's policy effectiveness really shines is in one area in particular: Business.

Black Cat, White Cat: Deng's Reforms

In 1978, Deng Xiaoping took the helm of the Chinese Communist Party (CCP) from behind the scenes, not holding an official position but exerting tremendous power through his influence on Party members. He decided to reform the Chinese economy with the force of the CCP

(Continued)

by wiping out poverty and reversing the damage to the country sustained while under the leadership of Chairman Mao and his extreme fundamentalists in the three decades before Deng came to power again (he was once high among the associates of Mao before being purged in a power struggle). The Cultural Revolution had just ended, and many intellectuals who were forced to the countryside for labor re-education returned to the cities and were hand-picked by Deng to the leadership of a new CCP which would undertake the nationwide reforms Deng was envisioning. To Deng, the goal was more important than the method, which he expressed by saying, it doesn't matter if the cat is black or white as long as it catches mice.

First, the government started to liberate the agricultural economy by allowing farmers to give up the farming collectives, manage their own land leased from the local governments and sell it freely in the newly-opened markets. Some of the farmers quickly abandoned the life of fruits and vegetables and established small factories producing daily necessities such as toothbrushes, plain clothes, brooms, mops and kitchen utensils, selling them at small booths or on simple blankets laid out along the streets. Some of the farmers even collected their savings together to start producing larger-scale products, selling them first to their native villages and later to other provinces.

When those early birds saved enough money, they bought a black and white TV, electric fans, and even built larger houses. More and more farmers joined them to do business and, as they increased their quality of life, the small-scale vendor business grew to a larger scale to challenge the state-owned enterprises by having better quality products, faster delivery, and lower prices.

Many Chinese chose to go into business for themselves instead of working for the government or state-owned enterprises. Instead of controlling the people's output as it had for the past 30 years, the CCP accommodated and encouraged this move into private enterprise because it would help to drive economic reform and to release some of the pressure on laid-off workers to find another government job. Seeing the

(Continued)

fast returns and more exciting business life, tens of thousands of state employees who left their jobs voluntarily, or who were forced to by restructuring, decided to join the growing ranks of entrepreneurs.

As the saying goes, "Of one billion Chinese, 99 percent are in business and the remaining 1 percent are waiting for a new opportunity."

A brief history of Chinese economy policy

For those who have not been to China, it is hard to imagine how much the entire country has been fully submerged in a pro-business environment. One can feel the sensation of business no matter where one goes, including government offices. More than half the TV programs shown during prime-time are business-related subjects either commenting on business news, discussion of business trends, or teaching viewers how to do business themselves. Opening any newspaper, book or magazine, business writing dominates the pages, including elaboration of recent Chinese economic policies, real estate, stock trading, and the most promising new business opportunities. Of course, this may all simply reflect what the majority of Chinese people are interested in these days. On the other hand, it also leads one to believe that, in a country where people's movement is closely monitored and mass communication tightly controlled, the nationwide engagement in business is greatly supported, well-promoted, and properly coached by the economically-oriented Chinese government. It in fact aligns well with the country's overall catchphrase for economic reform of "Overcoming Small Difficulties" comprised of attracting foreign investment, exporting more products, and increasing quality of life (as measured through GDP and per capita GDP).

While the Chinese government provides myriad incentives to local people and business, it has not been shy in attracting foreign business to China as well. Knowing their own needs for foreign investment of capital and technology to modernize China, the national and local governments have been extremely accommodating to foreign business needs.

In the 1980s, when the country first opened up, every level of government gave their highest priority to attracting foreign direct investment. Every place the foreign investors visited, the local government rolled out the red carpet to meet them, explain how favorable the local policies are, show them the local facilities, and entertain them with lavish banquets. They had good reason to do so: The performance of all government leaders and their consequent ability to get ahead in the higher echelons of government is keyed to their ability to attract foreign investment, achieve local GDP growth, and export more from their region.

Until very recently, all foreign investments in special economic zones enjoyed a long tax holiday amounting to 100 percent income tax exemption in the first three profitable years and 50 percent tax reduction in the following two years. The effective rates were 24 percent for foreign companies outside the zones, 15 percent inside the zones, and 33 percent for Chinese companies. In order to level the playing field between domestic and foreign companies, this policy will be phased out in steps over the next five years in the mostly developed eastern areas so that Chinese companies and foreign companies will pay the same 25 percent corporate tax rate by 2012. In order to try to narrow 2007's US$253 billion trade gap with the US and discourage low-value export-oriented industries, export incentives will be reduced.[4]

However, in order to encourage more high-tech investments, companies that locate in the development zones and meet high-tech qualifications will still receive a preferential two-year tax holiday and 12.5 percent tax rate thereafter, which is possibly one reason why virtually every major MNC is setting up R&D centers in China at present. Finally, showing that China is making concrete steps to encourage westward migration of foreign investments, the preferential 15 percent rate is available to all foreign investors that go to the central or western regions of China.[5]

In addition, state and local governments, especially those in the west, still have a vast array of incentives to continue to draw foreign investment to their areas. From a steep reduction in value-added tax (VAT), along with lower (or even free) land costs, to commercial loan arrangements, the line between government and business promotion is blurry at best and in many places it is virtually indistinguishable where public interests stop and private interests start. Thousands of acres of farmland have been rezoned to factory and business use, and local bureaucrats developed industrial parks to attract foreign investments and then proceeded to form cities within the zones, with their own administrators running on-site banks, customs, shops, hospitals, and post offices to provide higher quality of service to their foreign investors.

Along with FDI, export growth was highly encouraged by the Chinese government, so it often refunded a major portion (up to 75 percent) of the VAT (17 percent) to the exporting companies. Although this heavy subsidization has been gradually reduced since China joined the WTO, the policy helped elevate exports as a percent of total GDP from 5 percent in 1979 to almost 40 percent today.

Finally, China's intense focus on increasing GDP since 1978 has resulted in a 1998 GDP more than 20 times higher than its 1978 level, a sustained 16 percent annual growth rate, unprecedented in modern economic history. Not content to rest on its laurels, in 2002 the central government set a new goal of quadrupling the GDP by 2020 from 2000 levels, a goal it seems likely to achieve given the last five years of 9 percent or greater growth.

Despite one of the fastest sustained growth rates in real GDP ever to be seen, China's population is still very poor by global standards. China's GDP per capita still remains at a mere 10 percent of US levels today. Yet it is this statistic that is often used by the government as a means of energizing the people. At the closing of the 2007 17th National Congress, CCP President Hu Jintao announced a clear mandate to increase per capita GDP to about US$4,500 per person by 2020, quadrupling 2000 levels.[6] It shows the determination of the Chinese central government to increase national wealth.

This isn't your father's Communist Party

Often, Westerners have a viewpoint on China that is somewhat dated, thanks partly to recent movies which portray China as backwards, even 2006's *Mission Impossible III* in which one minute Tom Cruise was swinging from modern skyscrapers and a few scenes later running through chicken-infested streets complete with canals and stone bridges. Others imagine Mao-suit-wearing people riding bicycles. When it comes to envisioning China's government, most picture Mao Zedong himself and imagine a totalitarian state.

Today's Chinese Communist Party (CCP) is probably best described as Communist in name only, as China the country has not had true Communism for more than 30 years. Instead, CCP could just as well mean the Chinese Capitalist Party for the things they are doing to the economy right now.

No voting for top leadership? This is true, but China's politicians and bureaucracy today, with the CCP as the preeminent political group holding all key positions, are not staffed with *Little Red Book*-toting unquestioning automatons trained in Mao's image. Rather, new CCP members may be the best and the brightest of China's university-educated youth, sometimes recruited directly from China's top universities such as Tsinghua or *Bei Da* (Beijing University). The rank-and-file bureaucracy may be chosen from among more than 600,000 test-takers every year seeking the fabled lifetime government job, of which only about 10,000 or so are offered each year.

Once in the party or civil service, one's *guan'xi* or network may matter more than one's talent, but that is by no means a certainty. In the CCP, people are rewarded for their ability to work hard and get results, being promoted to higher and higher levels, so the best leaders inevitably rise. In this sense, the CCP may be thought of as a meritocracy rather than a democracy, and for now this system is suiting China well. At the lowest levels of government, small townships and so on, the local representative to the party may actually be voted on, but anything higher is usually handled through assignments and promotions within the party.

In the CCP today, the main ideology is not Marxism, or even Socialism: It is wealth-building. China's development depends, in the short-term, on an efficient (rather than equitable, as Communist or Socialist principles would suppose) distribution of wealth, much as what Deng Xiaoping famously said more than 25 years before, "Some must get rich first." Today, trying to bridge the wealth divide between urban and rural people is becoming more important and is more akin to the traditional ideas of equality that characterize Communism, but the ideology of prosperity above all else still prevails. China is a country that needs to get rich fast, and its leaders' main jobs are to make sure that happens. In this regard, they can be amazingly efficient.

One of the things that can surprise people living in China is the speed of change. The close cooperation between government and private business has advantages, one of which is the ability to influence market outcomes. When done in a selfish way, the potential to enrich the few at the expense of the many is great, and there has been a history of what Western critics of big government would call "feeding at the trough," if not outright *stealing* the trough, but as recently as 2007 China has had major graft and influence-peddling scandals which actually resulted in death penalties for those involved. In 2008, Chen Liangyu, the Shanghai CCP chief and former mayor of Shanghai, was sentenced to 18 years in prison for his role in a pension fund scandal.

Clearly the problem of business and government corruption will take more time to stamp out, especially in the less developed regions, but while China has already proven in some ways the effectiveness of a government-led business revolution, it still needs more time to work out the checks and balances.

Determination is the Ancient Chinese Secret

When somebody asks you how you did something but you don't want to say, a popular joking reply goes, "Ancient Chinese secret."

We wrote earlier that there is no such thing. Certainly, when it comes to success and making money, there isn't a magic formula, but in China there is at least a strong determination among virtually everybody, even the so-called Communist government, to get wealthy. This atmosphere pre-dates Deng Xiaoping's famous words, "To become rich is glorious." And it certainly pre-dates Mao's Communist experiment from 1948 to 1978. In fact, it has been a characteristic of China for as long as the Chinese have been traders which, any Chinese will tell you, probably goes back at least as far as China's 5,000 years of recorded history.

During the pre-industrial era and dating back about 2,000 years, Chinese traders are known to have plied the Silk Road, bringing tea, porcelain, firearms and other products to Europe. In the relatively modern times of the past 200 years, Chinese spread to all corners of the world.

There is a word in Chinese for them: 华侨,
hua'qiao, **made up of the characters**
representing China and live abroad.

Those Chinese going overseas left their poor hometowns, sometimes leaving behind but never forgetting family members, to work on the railroads in North America, to become street vendors in South-East Asia, to manage small shops in Korea or Europe. Indeed, these émigrés created overseas enclaves that not only were a platform for trade amongst themselves, but also served as support networks by supplying favors, loans, and cooperation. In many overseas Chinese communities can be seen numerous examples of Chinese entrepreneurial zeal. Well-known professors such as Murray Weidenbaum have called this the Bamboo Network, wherein those overseas Chinese are often in the best position to gain from renewed business ties with mainland China because of their long-standing family bonds, shared language, and common cultural background.

Confucian Values in Modern China

Born more than 2,500 years ago, the philosopher Confucius still has a strong influence on modern Chinese society. This is especially true when it comes to so-called Confucian family values as a possible underpinning of China's determination to prosper while not sacrificing relationships. The philosophy, which emphasizes concepts of benevolence and goodness, the importance of a structured society, respect for family and elders, and attainment of knowledge and wisdom as a form of strength, undoubtedly helps the family to remain strong in the face of hardships by facing problems with acceptance, even in tragic circumstances. Through years of war, endless natural disasters, and being squeezed by greedy rulers, the Chinese have known two things: That wealth is the only power a person or family can hold on to, and that education is the way to change the wealth of a family over a single generation.

Children are taught to value study as a means to prosperity, to live simply and frugally by saving money to grow wealthy, but, above all, to not value material possessions over the bonds of family. The parents save every penny from their hard labor by working from early morning to late at night, while their savings are generously used on their children to educate them. One Western executive who has lived in South-East Asia for decades once commented that local families in places such as Thailand would send their 15-year-old children out to sell flowers to tourists or do other small jobs to bring money home, while Chinese families would spend most of their savings to send their children to the best schools they could afford. The Chinese parents have set goals early in the children's life for them to attend Yale or Oxford even when they just started schooling.

(Continued)

One could say that the Confucian cultural commonality of the majority of the Chinese people is one thing which gives them the inner strength and direction to work together to achieve a common goal of their country's development, which other countries' populations may lack because of too much wealth, materialism, and individual prosperity clouding this sense of family or community spirit.

It is perhaps worth examining in more detail the effect of this culture on China's multi-millennial history as a civilization, and whether Western people might not learn something from it instead of automatically assuming China's backwards development confirms the flawed nature of Confucian philosophy as a basis for life in a society.

After the market reforms of the early 1980s, it once again became possible for the Chinese to actively and, for the most part, legally engage in entrepreneurial activities. The earliest examples were farmers selling their excess produce directly at markets instead of through the government-mandated cooperatives. Some cities, such as the eastern port city of Wenzhou, have become economic and entrepreneurial zones where so-called *network effects* allow all the related suppliers of an entire industry to be located not only in the same geographical region, but also perhaps on the same city block.

Network effects have been responsible for the rise and domination of Chinese companies in the toy, shoe, and soon, low-cost automobile industries globally.

The benefits of a tightly-knit and vertically-integrated local production system are numerous. Transportation costs don't get cheaper than free, and when you need some short-term financing there is often a friend or relative in the same business willing to lend a hand.

But the high pressure to succeed, to become rich, also creates the problems associated with environmental damage, extra-legal and illegal activities, lack of transparency, and government collusion in all of the above. The fast growth and lure of easy money causes damage to society and the environment, with no shortage of people willing to jump in.

High speed, however, wears out the tyres of a car. In China, the workers are most certainly the tyres: The last to leave the ground as the economy takes off, the first to hit when it comes back to land.

Russia, Brazil, and Mexico all had similar drivers to China's, but ended up in one or multiple financial crises or stalled in their development. What is the difference then between those economies and China's? Why can China apparently successfully develop while other countries have difficulty? Of course, there are many obvious differences including the large size of China's economy, the state of the economy in a mostly agrarian structure rather than an industrialized structure (as was the case of the former USSR), and China's current centrally-planned market economy as factors. However, one other possible yet controversial answer exists: Because they are Chinese.

Chinese determination may lead to negative social and environmental effects, but it is largely responsible for the resiliency of the people and the strength of new Chinese companies in global competition.

The Chinese cannot be treated as a homogeneous culture, but there is a determination, an entrepreneurial drive, an emphasis on education and helping the next generation to achieve more than their parents, that, when put together, creates a cultural will to succeed no matter what hardships are required. Whereas Western and even some other Asian cultures may push children out the door to work at part-time jobs and gain real-world experience, a Chinese parent would almost never make their child take valuable time away from studies to make a few extra *yuan*. Rather, the parents work doubly hard to make sure their children have every need looked after and create the opportunities for their children that they never had.

China's bookstores are full of people on any day of the week, filling aisles and sitting on stools, against walls, anywhere that will allow them to read, literally spending hours acquiring knowledge. The Chinese government has long used the bookstores as a place to disseminate information. The largest chain, *Xinhua*, is a government-controlled media conglomerate that also publishes much of the official news in the country, but newer chains are sprouting all the time. In Shanghai's largest, the Shanghai Book City, the aisles are filled not with young Communist party cadres absorbing Mao Zedong thought; they are the youth of today seeking information that will lead to skills to give them a leg up in school or in the workforce.

Books, blogs, and other information media are some of China's fastest-growing sectors.

It could be said that God played a trick on the Chinese by placing all of the major energy sources away from the most easily populated areas, or giving the country the third largest landmass (virtually tied with the US in terms of area) yet with a deficiency in farm land. Thus, China may be called a resource-poor nation whose people in the old days were always in a state of uncertainty over where the next meal would come from. Historically, the country has had warlords and civil wars that created a cultural pragmatism in the people, adaptability to changing circumstances and, perhaps most importantly, roots in family values as the only stable unit in times of change: The family sticks together and supports one another. Family values are also deeply embedded in Confucianism which, when strictly followed, involves filial piety and ancestor worship, but more practically speaking, also explains the emphasis Chinese parents place on education as the path for their children to succeed. It is this driver of the drivers that will possibly be the most important of all.

In May 2008, China's Sichuan region was struck by a magnitude 8.0 earthquake whick killed more than 70,000 people and left millions homeless. It was the largest natural disaster to hit China since the 1976 Tangshan earthquake which killed more than 240,000 people. Following the Sichuan earthquake, the Chinese people came together in an unprecedented show of support and assistance for the region. Billions were raised in donation campaigns.

For China, the people's national spirit is especially strong in 2008. After enduring protests in foreign countries against the Olympic Torch relay, the Chinese people came together to both counter-protest foreign firms such as Carrefour and support the Olympic spirit as the Torch relay continued. At one point, millions of Chinese simultaneously changed their MSN Messenger screen names to include "I Love China."

When directed towards China's economy, this feeling of Chinese solidarity will certainly drive continued growth and development in the future.

The Drivers of the Drivers

This chapter introduced us to the real drivers of the new Chinese economy. In the past, exports, FDI, and growth of the consumer markets were considered to be the strongest drivers of growth, but they do not fully explain what have been the real forces behind the Chinese economy. For that, the drivers of the drivers, and by extension, the drivers of the new supertrends, are:

1. Globalization of China's economy from the inside outward is going to be a new driver of the Chinese economy, as Chinese brands and investments increasingly seek to move outside of its borders.

(Continued)

2. Chinese government planning and policy: The planned market economy takes the form of policy and directives that, if you are aware of them, can be used to chart your China strategy, but always remember that in China there is a big difference between announcement, regulation, and enforcement.
3. Chinese determination and perseverance: This counts for a lot in driving Chinese companies to global aspirations, so do not underestimate Chinese competitors. If you want to do business with China, be prepared to deal with motivated Chinese people as your competitors and harness the productive spirit of Chinese staff in your workforce.

Look for the connection between these underlying concepts and the material in the rest of the book for a deeper understanding of and advantage using the *supertrends*.

CHAPTER THREE

The Supertrends

春江水暖，　*Chun jiang shui nuan,*
鸭先知。　　*ya xian zhi.*

"When the spring river warms, the duck is first to know." — Su Shi, a famous Chinese poet

Where are the greatest opportunities in the Chinese market to be found? They can be found within what we call the *supertrends*. These trends, based on the drivers previously discussed, are the most important during China's Olympic Decade from 2008 to 2018.

What causes a supertrend? A supertrend is a confluence of the drivers of the Chinese economy meeting social change. Recall, a driver is an underlying force present across all industries and sectors of the economy, for example, exports: China exports just about anything and everything, from products to outsourced services, therefore it can be said to drive the economy forward. Our Drivers of the Drivers are the fundamental forces which created the environment for the three primary growth drivers — trade, investment, and consumption — to flourish: The Chinese government's unique political and economic structure and mix of socialism and capitalism that it calls the planned market economy. The supertrends are formed at the intersection where the Drivers of the Drivers power-up the primary drivers, then combine with sociological changes such as new consumerism, demographic shifts, and a booming economy.

Our chosen supertrends are usually industry-focused or cover a certain segment of society, rather than society as a whole, and within the supertrends can be found the greatest business opportunities of the Olympic Decade.

Each supertrend is given a name that is based on its Chinese language equivalent. We group the supertrends into three related categories: Business, Social, and Wealth, each containing several supertrends that are based on new concepts not before seen in China and little understood outside of it, thus forming the basis for a plethora of opportunities in Future China:

- The Business Supertrends consist of the growth of the manufacturing and service industries in China, of which the role of manufacturing continues to be important to the country as a whole (based on the export driver) but is now *Value-adding* and *Innovating* (the first two supertrends), while the service sector is increasingly important due to *Urbanizing*, the process of encouraging people to move into urban areas, creating a need for more businesses *Serving* the people.

- The Social Supertrends refer to the changing Chinese consumer and social structures, moving away from traditional ideas of the Chinese as living to work (for the country) to working to live a life of *Consuming* and *Aspiring* for themselves and their families, while still helping the country to develop. As a result of increased use of information technology, China is leap-frogging ahead of other nations in its adoption of *Inter-networking* social technologies but only now *E-Commercializing* many of its traditional business models.

- The Wealth Supertrends are evident at almost every level of Chinese society: Per capita GDP is rising, the incomes of workers are rising, the wealth of society is increasing, the country is wealthy with trade surplus and currency reserves, and *Affluencing* has become the goal and is the new status quo. At the same time, China is recognizing its own limitations in growth and realizing the impact its rapid development is having on the world, so it is using this opportunity for *Greening* of the country and its businesses.

The Business Supertrends

The two biggest sectors of the Chinese economy by far are industry and services. Agriculture actually employs far more people but produces relatively little value and is mostly for domestic food security, so we disregard it in favor of focusing on the two largest components of China's GDP — industry and services. Industry supertrends concern adding value, upgrading, modernizing, and innovating, while for services, themes of urbanization and servicing are the most important contributors to growth.

Jiazhi hua — Value-adding

While China may be known as the world's factory in some quarters and US politicians are fond of pointing out the number of jobs lost to China, the reality is that China's manufacturing is still on the low end. By value, the US still produces 21 percent of the world's products, while China produces only 8 percent. It is this figure that China has its eye on: Moving from mass-produced quantity to high-value quality. In 2007, China's US$460 billion electronics industry continued realigning itself towards higher value-added electronics, now representing about 37 percent of its exports: Hanging up fixed line phones and fax machines in favor of 400 million mobile phones, 110 million LCD panel TVs and monitors, and 100 million personal computers. Production of those high-tech goods is all up about 25 percent year-on-year, while the manufacturing sector in China grew by 13.4 percent overall in 2007. Revenue growth of the latter technologies surpassed 20 percent, showing China's electronics manufacturing industry is clearly moving up the value chain at the expense of rivals including Korea, Taiwan, and Japan.

This is happening not only in high-tech electronics, but almost every industry, from metals to chemicals to textiles, is moving up the value chain or reaching backward to secure critical supplies. For example, the massive Chinese coal industry, led by world number two Shenhua Energy, is investing heavily in R&D for coal chemistry, liquefaction, gasification, cleaner-burning technologies, as well as eyeing overseas acquisitions to secure more coal. It has increased its output to 28,000 tons per worker, compared with 10,000 tons per worker industry average in the US, but the huge productivity output has not been at the cost of lives as some China skeptics might suspect. Shenhua has accomplished it through the most modern mining equipment available and a safety record that is 0.027 fatalities per one million tons of coal, compared to more than 2 fatalities per ton for the Chinese industry in general, the best in China and on par with global mining firms. Clearly, Chinese manufacturing is cost-efficient and disciplined, but it can benefit from more innovation as the case of Shenhua demonstrated.

Gexin hua — Innovation growing in China

In 2007, China received more than 300,000 domestic patent applications compared with about 50,000 patent applications for foreign entities (seeking a stronger claim to protect their inventions in China), reversing a trend from the previous decade where foreign patents outnumbered domestic applications. Furthermore, the domestic patent applications increased in 2007 by about 27 percent over 2006, compared with 10 percent growth in foreign patents, showing that Chinese inventors are innovating more, or at least seeking intellectual property rights (IPR) protection offered by patents, than ever before. In total, to the end of 2007, China has issued more than two million patents, with the vast majority being domestic.[1]

Far from being the birthplace of all patent infringements it is made out to be, China actually has the third most active patent office in the world after Japan and the US, ahead of high-tech countries such as Korea and Germany.[*]

Enforcing protection of innovations and other forms of IPR in Chinese courts has been more common in the past two years. The courts have recently found in favor of foreign patent, trademark and copyright holders in a series of landmark court cases such as Starbucks suing a copycat coffee-shop called *Xing'ba'ke*, which sounds nearly identical to Starbucks' Chinese-translated name. Unlike in the past when foreign companies were not likely to receive a fair hearing or Chinese laws did not adequately define or prosecute infringement, now laws are both defined and being enforced. What's more, foreign enterprises frequently win, but as there is no punitive damage award under Chinese IP law, only compensatory damages for actual losses incurred,[†] the victories are often symbolic.

IPR protection is getting stronger mainly through enforcement of existing laws, and frequent crackdowns on DVD and software piracy make the news, but China has a long way to go before it matches developed markets in this regard, so this will slow the pace of innovation.

[*]However, on a per capita basis, China is much lower than virtually all of the OECD industrialized countries but still ahead of developed countries such as Belgium, Spain, and Greece.

[†]If there is no basis for calculation of a compensatory award due to lack of information or some other issue, a maximum discretionary award of RMB500,000 (about US$70,000) is allowed.

In order to maintain its place as the world's factory and continue its ascent up the value chain, China needs to do several things. First, it must provide stronger protection for intellectual property, not only to encourage more multinationals to produce higher-value products there, but to help its own manufacturers protect their own investments in innovation as well. Second, it has to produce more capital-intensive goods rather than labor-intensive ones, which is difficult for China to do with its yearly thirst for 10–20 million new jobs.[2] Finally, it needs to focus more on design and branding.

For example, in a study of the iPod value chain, it was found that for a US$300 iPod sold in the US, Apple and domestic retailers captured more than half of the total, while more than 50 percent of what was left was captured by major parts suppliers, most of them non-mainland Chinese, such as Japan's Toshiba for its hard-drive. Chinese companies such as FoxConn that assembled the device and added very little value got, at most, a few dollars.[3] It is in these areas of innovation and value-adding that China desperately wants to improve, and the government has made it a mission to do so.

Chengshi hua — Better city, better life

The theme of the 2010 World Expo to be hosted in Shanghai is *Better City, Better Life*, an idea which neatly encapsulates the current urbanization drive in China. China is urbanizing its population at one of the fastest rates in recorded history. It is building new cities, relocating millions of people for infrastructure projects, and year in year out sees the largest temporary migration of workers in the world. In addition to putting enormous pressure on the transportation infrastructure, China's migrant workforce is straining to cross the wealth divide. By urbanizing so quickly, China hopes to avoid a confrontation between the haves and the have-nots.

While China's percentage of migrant workers (people who leave their traditional and typically rural homes to commute for periods of up to several years at a time) may not be especially high among developing countries, the absolute number surely is. Migrant workers in just ten of China's provinces are responsible for a phenomenal total of almost 100 million moving around the country for jobs. Cities such as Shanghai, Guangzhou, Beijing, and developing second tier cities such as Nanjing or Dalian may see their official populations increased by several million of the so-called *liudong renkou*, the floating population.

Shanghai, for example, grew its migrant workers from 1.3 million in 1985, 2.7 million in 1997, to 5.8 million in 2005 and 6.3 million in 2007 plus nearly 380,000 migrant children; while Shenzhen, the built-to-order city envisioned by Deng Xiaoping as mainland China's answer to Hong Kong, estimated that an amazing 9.4 million people were classified as non-permanent migrant workers in 2006. The capital, Beijing, was estimated to have 5.1 million.[4] Exact numbers are hard to come by as many migrants are working under the radar without any official legal status, but even when they disclose their status they are still granted few of the rights that a permanent resident (somebody possessing an official registration called a *hukou*) has, such as the right to send their children to public schools (rather than to segregated, migrant-children only schools), healthcare, or other city services.

There are more than 100 million migrant workers traveling around China in any given year. They generally go from rural to manufacturing areas such as Guangdong Province.

Unscrupulous employers take advantage of the fact that the workers have unclear or no ordinary rights by using fear to keep them on the job for long hours without breaks or holidays, not providing proper medical care and insurance in the case of accidents, housing them in unheated or unairconditioned barracks, and withholding their pay for months at a time. It is not uncommon to hear of worker riots because of pay being withheld for a year or more and then the company going bankrupt and the owners fleeing the scene. Some workers sadly commit suicide in protest of their poor treatment.

In an effort to clean up the practice of migrant worker exploitation, progressive cities such as Shanghai have moved to legitimize the migrant workers' status and granted them social benefits and rights, such as access to education and healthcare. With more than 33 percent of the births in Shanghai from migrants in 2005,[5] the city also established 18,000 free condom distribution points, as if to say, "Hey folks, stop having so many babies in our city." Also, the new labor law enacted in 2008 grants additional rights to workers in general. These actions begin to acknowledge that much of China's hardest labor (the process of construction and urbanization) is done on the backs of these workers and that they deserve to be treated equally.

Urbanization

China is trying to urbanize (move from the rural areas to cities) more than 50 million people in the next four years. In the next 20 years, it wants to urbanize a total of more than 300 million people.[6] If numbers like this don't sound extremely significant, when you think of it as relocating the population of Canada or Australia twice in five years, or the population of France, Germany, and the United Kingdom combined within 20 years, or the entire population of America — every man, woman and child, moved from their current residence to a new home hundreds, even thousands, of kilometers away — you will get a picture of what a massive undertaking, a heart-wrenching ordeal, this might be. From 18 percent of the population urbanized in 1978 when China opened its doors to the projected 50 percent by 2010,‡ China's urbanization is the largest mass migration in history and is happening faster than most

---

‡China's last major census in 2005 pegged the urbanization rate at 44.8 percent, growing from 36 percent in 2000, according to China's National Statistics Bureau.

people would believe. But one must ask the question *why* they are doing it.

The fact is, the vast population of China is mostly poor and rural. Despite images of modern China sometimes seen on Survivor and America's Next Top Model, the major cities are not where the majority of people live.

For example, in the agricultural sector, China has upward of 700–900 million farmers[7] producing the food for a nation of 1.3 billion. Allowing for some inaccuracy due to the fast pace of urbanization and possibly underestimated population numbers, this means approximately half of the country's population is involved in food production. Compare this with the United States where farmers constitute less than 2 percent of the general population yet produce enough food with so much to spare that the US is also a major agricultural exporter, and one can understand how inefficient some areas of the Chinese economy are.

China, despite 30 years of being open to the world, is still largely a rural and agricultural country. Many of its farmers are still working with manual tools and beasts of burden (sometimes played by the farmers themselves in the extremely labor-intensive rice farming that still dominates the south). Their lives are hard. They do manual labor in a country that doesn't respect that anymore, many of the things they produce are price-controlled by the central government to reduce the potential for inflation, while the production inputs they need, such as pesticides, petroleum-derived fertilizers, even extra hands on the farm, become ever more expensive. They are, in effect, being squeezed from both sides. Yet the Chinese government doesn't want modernization of this sector to occur too quickly lest the labor markets be flooded with farmers looking for new jobs. It is bad enough that their sons and daughters are already migrating to the city, China simply couldn't handle it if many of the remaining farmers *en masse* arrived there too. The government is equally afraid of a "farmers rebellion" as disparities between urban and rural living become greater. Keeping farmers employed is one reason why China only imported about 5 percent of its total consumption of grain-products including rice in all of 2007 (a policy of food security is also important to China's central government).

Getting the rest of those people out of the farms and into the cities is probably China's biggest challenge. China is dealing with this problem in two ways, both of which are a part of urbanization.

China's new cities

First, China is building new cities across the country, but especially in the western areas that have lagged the coastal eastern side. Chongqing is an amazing example, currently one of China's largest cities, and one of only four to be granted a special city-state status to self-govern as a municipality.[§] Once a temporary capital of Chiang Kai-Shek's provisional government during and after World War II, it has grown from a mere 400,000 people to the point where its population has been described by some as greater than 27.9 million, which would make it the biggest city in the world, but this is not really a comparative figure with other world cities since its status as a city-state has allowed it to consolidate surrounding areas, both rural and urban. With the population of the municipality being only about 45 percent urbanized, more conservative estimates of the populace in Chongqing city proper range from 8 to 12 million, which is not as large as some of the world's true megacities. When you visit there, you'll see that it is hardly a sprawling metropolis such as Tokyo, so Chongqing has its own process of urbanization to undergo, whereby four million additional residents will be brought into the city itself within ten years and the surrounding rural populations will be consolidated in satellite towns. Nevertheless, it is still a massive undertaking and part of a civil planning experiment by the National Development and Reform Commission to test a balanced urban and rural development model. This is not the first time China has built a made-to-order city. The prototypical

---

[§]The others are Shanghai, Tianjin, and Beijing.

example is the one that was created as mainland China's answer to Hong Kong.

Shenzhen, the fourth largest city by GDP size, with an official population of about eight million and millions more in floating residents, is within a short commute from Hong Kong. The rise of Shenzhen from a fishing village in the early 1980s with only 70,000 population to a modern city at such an unprecedented speed, is a pioneering example of China's urbanization drive. The growth of Shenzhen in the 1980s and 1990s reflected how China was developing itself on the international stage. Pre-1980, Hong Kong was a major hub for many manufacturing industries. Manufacturing was 25 percent of Hong Kong's GDP in the early 1980s for its well-known export products of textile, toys, watches and electronics. Today, manufacturing represents less than 4 percent of the Hong Kong GDP, much of the industrial and even light manufacturers having long ago moved to the neighboring Guangdong Province's renowned factory cities such as Dongguan, Zhuhai, and of course, Shenzhen.

Shenzhen and Chongqing are just two of the dozens of large cities that are already well on the path to development as international-class cities, but there are literally dozens more being planned and built to accommodate those 300 million new residents from the countryside who will urbanize in the next 20 years.

Transportation infrastructure

China's second tactic to urbanize recognizes that in order to create flourishing cities, they need to be connected together. Transportation infrastructure is one of China's future competitive advantages due to the fact that little or no infrastructure existed prior to 1980 outside of the major cities. In many parts of the country, it has a clean slate to build modern, safe transportation networks without worrying about vested interests.

In many Western countries, infrastructure that is already developed tends to stay in use so long as it is still in operable condition and has not depreciated fully in accounting terms, or the present owners and operators will not let their infrastructure be easily replaced. Furthermore, new infrastructure that needs to be built in the West undergoes rigorous cost-benefit analyses, not to mention requiring strong stakeholder support from the community. The process is a little different in China.

China does away with all of these reasons to retard development by using policy: Transportation infrastructure must be built and updated frequently. If it increases regional GDP, all the better, but financial viability of the asset itself is not usually a pressing concern to those who grew up in the Communist era: With no emphasis on profit and loss during those years of China's development, and the state-owned banks directed to support development projects, new airports, bridges, highways and public buildings get built whether they'll make money or not. When it comes to the question of upgrading or scrapping old infrastructure, useful life and depreciation is not a concept that even reformed Communists or business-oriented state-owned enterprises are comfortable with, so to most it simply does not exist. For these two reasons, many projects that would otherwise be impossible to build on a cost-benefit analysis perspective are built anyway in China. Sometimes they are built for practical purposes, such as Beijing's new Terminal 3 needed to receive the Olympic-sized crowds, which is, incidentally, the largest building in the world (twice the size of the Pentagon is the oft-quoted comparison). Sometimes projects are built at the direction of some government official as a kind of *Field of Dreams* economic stimulus for regional growth: Build it and they will come.

Keynesian economic stimulus policies for state development are quite at home in post-Communist China. State-run banks are directed to lend at low and uncompetitive interest rates to projects deemed important for regional development. Where a new project is proposed to be built, the eminent domain position of the government is hard to stand against because, unlike governments in many countries including Japan or India, the Chinese government doesn't permit residents to hold up an important project with endless debates and lawsuits. Authoritarian, yes, but can China afford the alternative?

In Japan's Narita Airport area, a group of farmers and residents held up construction of a second runway for more than 30 years, whereas when Shanghai needed to build an international airport, it was started in 1997 and completed by 1999 (and with some irony *vis-à-vis* Narita, funded largely by a development grant from Japan). A second runway was built by 2005, a new terminal and third runway are opening in 2008, and a third terminal and two more runways are to be completed by 2015 so the airport can meet its target of 80 million passengers per year and 6 million tons of cargo.[8]

At Beijing's Capital International Airport, Terminal 3 was completed in just four years by 50,000 laborers working 24 hours a day. It opened in February, in plenty of time for the Olympics, without any of the glitches that London's Heathrow International Airport's new Terminal 5 suffered when it started operations in March 2008. The project took two years less and cost half as much as Terminal 5, and was bigger than all five of Heathrow's terminals put together. The concrete had barely had time to set when it opened in February 2008 before discussion begun on a plan to build a fourth runway or start construction of a second international airport for the city, possibly both, to handle increased traffic expected between 2010 and 2015.

Meanwhile in India, the Narmada River Dam projects, the largest dam being the Sardar Sarovar at 138 meters in height, involving a potential resettlement of 1.5 million people, have been off and on again for more than 40 years. Roughly comparable to this is China's Three Gorges Dam, the world's largest hydroelectric project at 185 meters, which began construction in 1993 and was completed almost two years early in 2007.[9]

Those residents who need to be relocated due to large infrastructure projects are usually compensated according to a formula, but there is much criticism of apparent corruption and forced relocations in the process. China's ability to upgrade its infrastructure quickly has been a major success factor in its rise to global superpower and its ongoing urbanization process.

Shanghai's new Yanshan deepwater port replaced the still operable port near the downtown area. This reduced local water and noise pollution and, at the same time, provided a prime location for the 2010 World Expo. Yanshan is expected to become China's largest port in terms of TEUs.¶

In terms of rail transportation, in China, rail is mostly a medium for transporting people rather than cargo. It is the most popular means of travel in China, and the network carries 1.3 billion passengers a year (compared to about 210 million passengers using air travel inside China).[10] During key holiday seasons, a single day may see 10 million people using intercity trains, while 24 million or more will ride the rails to hometowns during the week-long Chinese New Year travel season, as many as five million in a single day. When it comes to travel for many people in China,[11] there are no other practical means to get around besides rail: Cars or buses would take too long and be too expensive on the still-developing and tolled interstate highway system, and airplane tickets are too expensive for the majority of China's rural and migrant populations who are the main ones relying on the trains.

The intercity trains' speeds have been steadily increasing over the last two decades and the fastest intercity trains run at about 250 kilometers per hour now, but the news from China these days is all about 300-plus kilometer per hour bullet trains and Maglev technology — the ultrahigh-speed trains that literally float on the tracks, balanced on a rail of electromagnets, hence the name Magnetic Levitation. This technology is also being developed in Japan and the United States, but Germany helped China build the world's first Maglev train in commercial operation from Shanghai's Pudong International Airport partway to the city, a short eight-minute journey that nevertheless hits speeds in excess of 430 kilometers per hour. While the original project cost more than a billion dollars and probably will

---

¶A TEU is a Twenty-Foot Container Equivalent Unit, a measure of volume in the shipping industry.

never be truly financially viable, the route may be extended to the city center and beyond to nearby Hangzhou in the next ten years.

It is interesting to note that while Japan plans to build a Maglev train to replace parts of the aging *Shinkansen* fleet with a single line from Tokyo through central Japan, it will take until 2025 to construct and nearly US$45 billion to build the 290 kilometer track. Shanghai's Maglev train, with a distance of about 30 kilometers, cost US$1.2 billion, or about US$40 million per kilometer, but what about the Japanese Maglev? The equivalent figure works out to be US$150 million per kilometer. While it is likely incorrect to compare in this manner due to differences in land values and Japan's more stringent feasibility evaluation, it seems clear that China's cost advantage is not just based on labor-intensive industries, but can apply to the most advanced technologies in the world.

Projects such as the Maglev only tell part of the story of China's use of rail transportation. One must also consider China's adoption of municipal subway and light-rail lines, high-speed *Shinkansen*-style long-distance rail links, pioneering tourism by rail, and rail freight to fully understand the significance of China's use of rail infrastructure. It is on par with the importance of the United States' development of the interstate highway system after World War II, except that China is developing one of those as well, at the same time.

Subway and light rail

China's use of subway and light rail has accelerated, with eight cities in mainland China currently using them and an additional eight cities to start using them in the next decade. Shanghai in particular has expanded its system from three lines in 2004 to five lines in 2006, eight lines at the start of 2008, 11 lines and 400 kilometers by the 2010 start of the World Expo hosted in the city, and by 2020 will have 18 lines according to the transit plan. It took New York and London a century to reach the 400 kilometer mark, whereas Shanghai will do it in only 20 years. From 2007 to 2008 alone, the total line distance increased from 145 to 234 kilometers, and the daily passenger flow is expected to increase from 2.3 million to 3 million. Few subway networks in the world can boast as many lines or stations as the future Shanghai network, perhaps only New York, London and Tokyo being comparable, but in fact it is not Shanghai that will have the world's largest subway network in 2020 but actually Beijing, which is working hard to solve the problem of an ever expanding city overwhelmed by cars.

Beijing now has six ring roads circling the city and traffic congestion on the roads is a daily problem, so it is hoped the subway can alleviate the vehicle gridlock woes. Beijing set its standard subway fare from anywhere to anywhere on the network to RMB2, about US$0.25, as a way to further encourage use of the subway rather than cars.

High-speed rail

Japan and Europe have historically led the world in high-speed rail links, but from 2008, to paraphrase Elton John, "That train don't stop there anymore." To be completed within five years, the 21-station 1,300-kilometer line between Beijing and Shanghai will be the longest continuous high-speed rail line in the world and cost US$30 billion. This money has been financed by the Ministry of Railways, local governments where the line passes through, and several Chinese investment funds, including more than US$3 billion to compensate residents needing to be relocated along the route. Once operational, the trains will travel at about 350 kilometers per hour, slightly faster than the operating speeds of Japan's fastest bullet trains or France's TGV trains, and will cut the travel time from Beijing to Shanghai from about 11 hours to just over five. The construction of a high-speed link between Beijing and Tianjin is to be ready before the Olympics, and before 2020, China has announced plans to create about 12,000 kilometers of high-speed track in total.

High-tech and luxury rail travel

Long-distance rail meets high-tech in China's new Beijing–Tibet railway, known as the Beijing–Lhasa Express, opened on July 1, 2006. The 4,000 kilometer line is a three-day journey, reaching the world's highest elevations by rail, as it crosses the permafrost on the roof of the world to reach Lhasa, the Tibetan capital. The train had to be specially designed to accommodate the changes in altitude, both for the passengers and the engines, by supplying additional oxygen inside the cars including airplane-style oxygen tubes that dangle from the ceiling to keep passengers comfortable as they adjust to the altitude changes, especially on the final day when specially-designed locomotive engines from GE are added to the train to pull it up the final leg, the only engines in the world capable of doing so.

The ticket prices are comparatively high but still a bargain considering the distance, with a range of seating and berths relatively comfortable and appointed with small luxuries such as flat screen TVs, but the scenery is so spectacular during the day that they are typically only used at night. If that is not luxurious enough, a luxury train service on the same line to Tibet was scheduled to come into operation in late 2008, until civil unrest in Tibet reduced tourism and travel to the region. When service does start, it will allow two additional days to sightsee, and will come equipped with private rooms with their own bathrooms and a US$5,000 per person ticket price according to the private company investing in the business, about 30 times more expensive than the RMB400–1,200 (US$60–170) ticket price for the Beijing–Lhasa Express.[12]

Rail freight

Finally, China is developing its rail freight network to handle the increasingly large trade within China, targeting 100,000 kilometers by 2020, a figure which is still less than half of the network in the United States, but a large improvement in China where less than 2 percent of containers were shipped to and from ports by rail, compared to countries such as Canada and Australia that have as much as 30 percent of container traffic on rails. In China, trucks are the preferred method for inland container transport, which is not only more polluting but also vastly inefficient given the amount of raw materials and products that are being transported and the poor condition of many roads.

Roads and highways

The road system is probably the least developed and least utilized of all the major industrialized countries, but China has made progress there too and now has the second largest expressway network in the world at 53,000 kilometers with an estimated cost of US$122 billion, a program it started just three decades ago.[13] However, its highway network is 3.4 million kilometers with approximately half of that at a very low level of quality and in need of upgrade, according to a Chinese government official. The same official also highlighted the need to add another million kilometers of road by 2020. China was spending about US$80 billion a year in 2006 and 2007, and the trend is continuing. China's rail network, as large as it is, is mostly meant for carrying people, not goods. If China's roads are to be used for logistics, they need to be improved, which is one reason China continues to make the investments. Another reason to be investing significantly in highways is development of the western regions of China, linking them through commerce to bring prosperity to China's poorest areas and, not coincidentally, reinforcing national unity in China's far-flung and predominantly ethnic regions such as Xinjiang and Tibet.

Fuwu hua — Serving the people

Everywhere you went in China in the 1970s and early 1980s, you would see big billboards such as *"wei renmin fuwu"* ("Serve the People") as were the typical slogans in the old Communist days. The official name of the country is the *People's* Republic of China, the police are called the *People's* Police, some hospitals are called

People's Hospital and so on, to emphasize the Communist ideology of serving the people. But after being established, the absolute opposite of what the slogans and names implied actually occurred: Hardly any people were ever *served* unless they were in a senior position of the Communist Party or in a position that could offer favors to average people. For the common person, there is actually no service, because service has never been a concept accepted by China's population since serving means you are in a lower position, and in the old system known as the iron rice bowl — the state providing all of one's needs — you didn't need or expect service, and people providing the service received no benefits or motivation to work harder or provide better quality, so service was routinely terrible. Modern China is changing quickly, in a process we call *fuwu hua* — serving or servification. Therein exist some of the biggest opportunities of the Olympic Decade.

The Long Train Home

Not long ago, a Western colleague was stranded a few hours outside of Shanghai. Realizing the fastest way home would be by train, he made his way to the nearby regional station and, not speaking much Chinese, went about the process of buying the ticket. Seeing the ticket windows, some with bilingual signage, he lined up and was at first jostled by the crowd who didn't seem to be forming a queue, just pushing to the front. As he neared the ticket window, another traveler simply pushed in front of him, saying nothing. Exasperated, he waited patiently and made it to the front of the line, where the teller looked at him unpleasantly and made a hand gesture to go to the next window. Not understanding why, our friend stood firm and said "One ticket to Shanghai" and endured a barrage of, to him, unintelligible words. But he showed his passport and pushed some money under the window and was rewarded a minute later with a ticket and his change thrown back at him in a pile.

(Continued)

The journey didn't end there of course. He looked around for the right platform, had poker-faced conductors examine his ticket and thumb the direction he should go, again saying nothing to him, not even smiling. Getting on a train finally, he at last felt safe and tried to find his seat, discovering somebody already sitting there. In fact, the whole carriage seemed overloaded and people appeared to be moving randomly about, switching seats and boisterously talking as if they were all old friends. Not wanting to make a fuss, he showed his ticket to the on-board conductor hoping for some assistance and was ignored with a shrug. If it were not for some kindly farmers who, seeing the bewildered foreigner, offered him a seat, it would have been a very long ride home.

Sitting down next to the farmers, who were carrying some buckets of berries to sell in Shanghai, they chatted with the assistance of a Chinese neurosurgeon who just happened to be riding in the same carriage together with the common peasants. In fact, the neurosurgeon, though held in high regard for his education, was paid little more than the peasants he was traveling with. Our foreign friend tried to understand how farmers and neurosurgeons could ride in the same crowded car and not be upset by the conditions, and he wanted to explain how he felt being treated with such poor service, and was met with understanding comments from the farmers and doctor, who evidently endured the same poor quality of service. *"Mei banfa,"* they said, "Nothing can be done…"

In fact, the time of "Nothing can be done" may be coming to an end. On the one hand, you may still encounter poor quality service on China's regional trains, but ride any of the new ones such as Shanghai's Maglev train and you will encounter bilingual, smiling, and helpful staff. When the Chinese government starts something new, they go with state-of-the-art, and they will not accept anything less than international standard service. This is apparent in everything new in China, from bank tellers to building-lobby guides to restaurant hostesses — all will be staffed by bilingual young people eager to provide good service. The opportunity is that these new facilities are a small percentage of the total businesses operating, thus there is a huge potential for upgrading the service in virtually every industry, for competitors with better service to gain an upper hand, and for new service-based business models that have been common in the West but have not yet reached China. The service industry in China grew 12.6 percent to about US$1.5 trillion in 2007, actually trailing overall growth in the manufacturing economy but still responsible for about 39 percent of China's 2007 GDP. In urban cities, it is a different story. Shanghai, for example, expects its current 50 percent share of GDP by service industries to increase to 80 percent services by 2012, with accounting, finance, legal, exhibitions and tourism, and various consulting services to see high growth.

The Social Supertrends

China's diverse population of more than 1.3 billion comprised of 56 ethnic groups and their distinct languages and hundreds of dialects, is spread over the third largest country on Earth[||] after Russia and Canada, making China one of the most heterogeneous countries in the world. For this reason, marketers are finally starting to look at China's unique populations and geographic regions with new understanding and, combining that with Western marketing concepts of customization and personalization, are increasingly starting to see China as 1.3 billion markets of one.

Xiaofei hua, Baofu hua — Consuming and Aspiring

Many people assume that, because of China's modern history as a Communist country, the population is naturally or residually communal and group-oriented, not individualistic. Some look at Chinatowns in every major city and assume that Chinese people are collectivist and xenophobic.

[||]This position is disputed, given that the US is almost the same size and how they are measured can change their relative positions in the rankings.

These are dangerously wrong assumptions. It is true that Chinese abroad do tend to help and assist each other, relying on an inherent trust in their mutual Chineseness which makes them seem to be a group-oriented culture. Indeed, many business textbooks base their conception of Chinese businesspeople on now outdated research such as Hosfstede's seminal cultural study of global IBM managers of the 1980s. Mainland China was not included under the original model, but is often lumped together with Japan and Korea to form an East Asian cultural stereotype. Nothing could be further from the truth.

The reality is that China's diverse ethnicities, languages and cultures are impossible to assimilate (even in China, several areas are referred to as Autonomous Regions). The Communist years in China merely repressed Chinese people's natural individualism but did not eradicate it. While they may argue vociferously and consistently in support of such issues as national unity, modern Chinese are often individuals at heart and, in the newfound freedom of a post-Communist consumerist society, are increasingly expressing their individualization through the things they consume and what they aspire to be.

It is not uncommon to see young and middle-aged Chinese living in the cities consuming conspicuously. Branded items show one's earning power to peers and the opposite sex; items such as a car or even a house may be accoutrements a young man needs before a girl will consider marrying him, and the places one eats, works out, shops, and socializes say much in status-conscious modern Chinese society. It is becoming fashionable to spend money on leisure activities and invest in one's health. Older Chinese are coping with the empty nest syndrome, just as their peers do in the West.

Children born in the 1980s have grown up knowing prosperity is within their grasp. We call them Generation *Yi* (a play on so-called Generation Y and the word *yi*, meaning one, short for one-child family), and they are the first aspirational Chinese in more than 50 years. They are starting companies, traveling around the world, and experimenting with alternative lifestyles. Less people are getting married early, preferring to launch a successful career. Some women are even devoting themselves to work and life alone, leaving millions of men marriageless. These sociological trends are some of China's most interesting, and most potentially profitable, for new businesses to serve their diverse needs. China is no longer a single market willing to take what the state offers; it is now full of 1.3 billion individual markets.

Guanxi hua, Dianzi shangwu hua — *Inter-networking and E-Commercializing*

When combined with the cultural emphasis on relationships and personal networks, information technology becomes a powerful enabler to promote new and effective forms of exchange between people, which is why these are important social supertrends. While the markets for the technology itself (mobile phones, computers, and so on) are undoubtedly very large, many of these products are becoming commodities dominated by large global players. The real opportunity for businesses is the medium of the short messages, the blogs, the social networking websites, and how they can be used to enable more commerce, better advertising, and deeper customer relationships in China. It is useful to understand how the technology platform on which these services are delivered — wireless mobile communications and high-speed Internet, for example — is fundamentally different in China from that found in other countries in several key respects.

Leaping tiger, flying dragon

One of the benefits that China's fast development pace has had is not having to deal with the fixed costs of infrastructure that is already out-of-date in the new millennium. China is in a position to leap over these technologies and go directly to the most modern, cheapest, fastest, or any other superlative you can imagine.

While fixed lines are common in China's larger cities, the countryside is mostly without. China has 63 telephones (including cellular) per 100 people nationally in 2006 according to the World Bank, but the figure for phones in rural areas versus urban areas is much less.[14] Nationwide, the mobile phone to fixed line ratio is about 1.4 to 1, with some 547 million mobile phone users (increasing by 86 million) versus 365 million (a decrease of 2.3 million) fixed line users in 2007, according to the Chinese Ministry of Information Industry.

This continues a trend for the past several years of more and more people using mobile phones for their communications needs. This trend will likely accelerate in 2008 because of even lower mobile usage fees: 2007 saw the advent of free incoming calls for most people, while in March 2008 roaming charges were cut between 54 to 73 percent. Previously, the roaming fees were charged within the same region even on the same network, and could cost as much as RMB1.50 (US$0.20) per minute.[15]

Despite the high initial costs, China's love of the mobile began when it came to wiring the cities and connecting them together: With no existing infrastructure in place, China made the decision to either go with the latest fiber-optic cables instead of copper wire for any distance greater than one kilometer, or skip the wiring entirely and go to mobile communications.

In the mobile space, the Chinese government, in another act of policy, limited competition in the mobile phone market to just two companies, China Mobile and China Unicom, that used different primary transmission systems (GSM and CDMA respectively), effectively turning them into two monopolies. Not only that, nationwide coverage was a priority. So, whether you are in the elevator of one of China's tallest buildings, traveling underground in a subway, crossing the country by train, or visiting a small rural town, you will always have a strong signal even, as was announced in 2007, on the face of Mt. Everest. Your iPod or PC's hard drive may not work at such high altitudes, but your cellular phone will, thanks to China Mobile. As a result, it now has a sophisticated world-class mobile phone network that covers the entire country, even regions sparsely populated.

China is now the world's largest single market for mobile phone users, with more than half a billion subscribers and growing.

China's cellular networks generally use the GSM or CDMA standard, early generation technology, with GSM being the most widely used among subscribers, while neighbors Japan and Korea have invested more heavily in third-generation (3G) networks. China's rollout of 3G licenses has been mired in delays, arising from questions such as how to implement the country's own homegrown 3G standard called TD-SCDMA which allows China to control the intellectual property and avoid paying license fees for other more established technology, as well as how to balance the dominance of market leader China Mobile against the smaller China Unicom and fixed-line firms China Telecom and China Netcom, which are forbidden from offering cellular service at present, putting them in a perilous competitive position as fixed-line subscribers steadily decrease.** China Mobile is so large that its 2007 revenues were almost as high as the other three telecom providers' combined, and its profits in 2007 (US$12.4 billion) were more than double their combined earnings.

Even in monopoly-friendly China, this may be too much power concentrated in one company, so the long-awaited upgrade to the mobile network may have to wait until the round of mergers and acquisitions, announced in May 2008, has completed so that the

---

**China Telecom and China Netcom do not have mobile network licenses, but they offer PHS/PAS technology, a low-range low-cost mobile platform developed in Japan, that is tied into the fixed-line service plans. Marketed under the name *Xiao Ling Tong* or "Little Smart," this platform has achieved nearly 100 million subscribers but is expected to be phased out once the corporate parents are merged or allowed to use 3G technology in the next round of airwave allocations.

power of China Mobile does not again become a monopoly in the next generation of 3G services.

Finally, while China has announced 3G licenses will be issued to the three merged telecom companies — China Mobile, China Telecom, and China Unicom — the need to upgrade to 3G networks is not really apparent, as the maturity of its current networks has yet to be achieved and, for the most part, they suit the needs of consumers who are mostly looking for low-priced ubiquitous service. Some Chinese cities use the popular *Xiao Ling Tong* micro-cellular PHS technology which provides greater battery life and smaller handsets at lower transmission cost (so-called "handy phones" or PHS), but these phones are not very scalable in such a large country as China. Japan's 3G network services such as NTT's DoCoMo are yet to be found in China, but China will again leap-frog ahead by skipping the older 3G standards in favor of the newest and best, or homegrown TD-SCDMA, network systems, whose technology is being developed in the labs of Huawei Technologies and other Chinese technology firms in anticipation.

The China (Mobile) That Can Say No

In the years of Japan's bubble economy, a rising sense of the country's political and business dominance prompted one Japanese politician to write *The Japan That Can Say No*, co-authored with Sony's founder, Akio Morita. There was a copycat book published in China in the mid-1990s and, it is fair to say, both books are about nationalism and government policies to encourage their respective countries to take a larger role on the world stage.

In business, Chinese companies are learning their own power as well, growing up, as it were, in the global economy and having the keys to the biggest house on the block. Apple wanted to introduce its iPhone multimedia mobile communications device in China in mid-2008, but the business model Apple has set for itself puts it not only in the role of

(Continued)

equipment provider, but also as a manager of content and revenue generation for the carriers. This became a point of contention in the iPhone's entry to China.

Basically, unlike other equipment providers, Apple wants a piece of the subscriber fee action, and this was an excellent strategy to shift revenue back upstream to the companies such as Apple that make the phones but don't usually participate in the lucrative services (Canada's Research in Motion (RIM), maker of the Blackberry, is another successful proponent of this model). Since the time of the iPhone's launch in markets around the world, service providers have been falling over themselves to be Apple's exclusive provider. In China, where there is basically only one provider with a big enough user base and technology platform to fit Apple's phone needs, China Mobile just said no.

It is perhaps karmic OEM justice that the country which manufactures the iPhone could also be the biggest market in the world for the device and yet the toughest for Apple to muscle its way into. In January 2008, negotiations were broken off, according to one unofficial source, because China Mobile was not willing to give up 20–30 percent of its user fee revenue to Apple.[16] While Apple is sure to get its iPhones onto the market eventually, it still probably hasn't realized that it needs China, not the other way around. Chinese users are clamoring for the iPhone and without it, they will perhaps start looking a little more closely at some of the new multimedia phones put out by local manufacturer Dopod (a leader in PDA-style smartphones in China), getting a gray-market authentic iPhone that has been imported and unlocked, or, most distressingly for Apple, buying one of the many iPhone clones which are already on the market.

Internet infrastructure

China's Internet communications infrastructure is not as ubiquitous as its mobile phone network, but Chinese companies have also invested heavily in high-speed ADSL and cable-modem Internet access in the cities. With 122 million subscribers on high-speed Internet nationwide, China is quickly catching up and, in fact, surpassing many developed countries: China's wireless and mobile phone Internet access tops 55 million users, and 70 percent of China's Internet users are aged 30 and under.[17] The only country in the world that may match these statistics in the future is India.

China's total Internet users now number in excess of 220 million as of February 2008, surpassing the US as the world's largest online population and still growing, with a penetration rate that is only 17 percent.[18]

The urban/rural digital divide is a particularly important growth trend. In rural areas, the penetration rate for computers is only three per every 100 households with Internet usage of only five percent, while in the cities it is 47 per 100 households with Internet usage of more than 20 percent. However, in absolute numbers, rural users still account for about 52 million at the end of 2007, and the growth in new users added was 40 percent rural, 60 percent urban.[19] Business models which will provide computer and Internet access to the huge numbers of rural population yet to go online or to even have a computer, is an attractive target for microfinance, cheap laptops or other connectivity devices, and online services targeted at the needs of rural users.

A related indicator of China's growing technology usage is the number of registered Internet domain names (i.e., URLs, such as www.yahoo.com.cn) in the country. While for much of the new millennium up to the end of 2005, China's ".cn" website registrations barely topped one million, in 2006 they grew more than 85 percent and by the end of 2007 had reached nine million, making up for lost time.[20] China arrived to the Internet party several years late but has quickly embraced the Internet for business and consumer use, which is undoubtedly driving many of the opportunities described later in the book.

The Wealth Supertrends

While China is far from wealthy on a per capita basis, pockets of wealth and extreme wealth do exist, especially among the entrepreneurial class and within the cities. By global standards, these people are very well-off. At the same time, following the same pattern seen in developed countries, these newly affluent people are starting to think about quality of life and their environment. This forms the basis for the last two supertrends — *Affluencing* and *Greening*.

Fanrong hua — Affluencing

The amount of wealth being generated in China during the last several years, and projected to continue growing in the next decade as China continues its upward trajectory, is staggering. From stock markets to land prices, corporate profits to personal incomes, government tax revenues to government investments, all are up. Yet this sudden prosperity is not without its problems as China's new economy has started to develop wealth bubbles that could be subject to sudden deflation, and China's wealth, spread over such a vast area with varying degrees of development, is unevenly divided. So, the opportunities within this trend are great but so are the risks.

The rich get richer

Looking at the stock and land markets in China, one has little doubt China is in a boom, if not in a bubble. It remains to be seen whether or not there comes another bust, as happened in the mid-1990s culminating in the Asian financial crisis in which the property and stock markets plummeted, while China's currency was relatively unscathed because of its strong peg to the dollar.[21] 2007, when the Shanghai stock markets' main index was the best performing major index in the world for the second year running (97 percent growth in 2007, 130 percent growth in 2006), was the high point of a roll that had been taking place in the stock and property markets since about 2004, when the SARS crisis was resolved and the economy began to speed ahead.

As of the time of writing, the stock markets in China are undergoing a correction that saw them 50 percent off their highs in October 2007, but have stabilized in the run-up to the Olympics.

Recent wealth effects in China have much to do with this current wave of stock market and property booms. Many of the new millionaires and even billionaires owe their Forbes-level wealth rankings to IPOs of their companies, of which there were more than 240 such new listings both overseas and domestically in 2007, raising an estimated US$105 billion. Or, it might have something to do with the US$3.25 billion in venture capital put into Chinese firms in the same year. Fortunes were also made in property development during these boom years of seemingly inexhaustible demand for housing. Whatever the ultimate reason, China's rich are getting richer quickly.

China's rich nearly doubled their net worths in 2007, from US$164 billion to US$280 billion. One of the most interesting trends in the rich lists is that 40 percent of the 400 richest in China were new names in 2007. China has about 66 billionaires, with half of the top ten richest involved in property, including China's wealthiest woman, the 26-year-old daughter of a property developer who received her father's company's shares as a gift. In the IPO for the company, she went home with a cool US$16 billion and for a while was likely the world's most eligible bachelorette until she married in 2007.[22]

China's government gets richer

It is not just the people of China who are getting rich on the booming economy; the government is still the biggest investor around, thanks to its legacy holdings of state-owned enterprises (SOEs). Though the government sold off the vast majority of SOEs in the 1990s and has continued the trend in the early years of the new millennia, it has strategically held onto majority control of about 150 of the biggest money-makers, with combined profits of US$100 billion in 2006.[23] Many of these companies are names that most Western people recognize from various blockbuster stock market listings in the past five years: China Mobile and other telecom operators, PetroChina and other energy-related firms, several Chinese airlines, metals producers, and China National Tobacco, among many others. The most profitable 18 will start paying a 10 percent dividend directly to the government, and an additional 99 will pay a 5 percent dividend, starting in 2008. This will undoubtedly have a long-term effect on the financial performance of these companies, but there is still more than ample demand for the shares as many of those companies are trading at PE multiples above 30.

GINI in the bottle

It could be said that the Chinese government has only one domestic policy goal: To get rich. So, every official's goal is to get rich and to make their people rich. The central government encourages this system by giving its officials three Key Performance Indicators (KPIs): Increase the GDP, increase FDI, and increase the standard of living.

If Chinese officials' rhetoric and businesspeoples' hyperbole were translated into English, one would see their love of "-est" words: Biggest, fastest, tallest, to name several. There is a constant drive to meet all KPIs at the same time, even to the point of overheating local economies by overconstruction of "China's biggest" conference centers or "World's fastest *and* longest" operating magnetic-levitation train, and other pork-barrel projects.

The flow is not easy to stem, thus the central government's constant haranguing of provincial and local officials to slow down spending, and the 2006–2010 11th Five-Year Plan's attempt to refocus development on sustainable industries and reduce energy consumption. Possibly bigger than all these problems, if China continues the uneven development between the coastal and inland areas, the GINI coefficient (a measure of income inequality and wealth distribution in every country) could rise to levels that are thought to indicate the potential for civil conflict between the haves and the have-nots. In fact, this may already be starting to happen.

According to China's Ministry of Public Security, there have been an increasing number of demonstrations and public acts of protest in the past several years.[24] While sometimes directed at companies such as land developers or collieries that exploit and endanger workers, they are also directed at officials that are thought to cheaply seize property or use their power for personal profit.

Chongqing's House on a Stick

2007 saw an iconic image of China's urbanization sweep across the Internet in China and even internationally: What could best be described as looking like a house on a stick, and called the "nail house" for being like a nail difficult to pry out, perched on a 30 meter pillar of earth, around which the surrounding land had been excavated into a vast pit to accommodate the foundations of a skyscraper or perhaps underground parking garage. The precariously-balanced house looked as if it would topple in the first big wind, but, if one looked closely, you could see a banner that had been hung by its occupants: "No violation of legitimate private property!"

A standard redevelopment process in China's cities, for areas covered with many single-storey or low-rise buildings such as *hutongs* (lane dwellings), *shikumen* (four-sided courtyard dwellings) and other less-than-efficient living structures, is for the government to designate areas that require expansion for the *common good*. In other countries, this is referred to as eminent domain and is seldom invoked save for something

(Continued)

like a highway, but even then is fairly compensated and goes through a lengthy court process. In China, again, the process is somewhat different.

Since the concept of private property is still relatively new in modern China, residents of older parts of China's cities frequently do not have any rights beyond squatters' rights to their properties, and so when the government says to move, the residents accept the compensation offered and usually move into much more modern, newly built, low-cost housing on the outskirts of the city.

Mrs. Wu and Mr. Yang, wife and husband, were not such people. Taking their squatters' rights seriously, they occupied their dwelling and refused to accept the compensation offered by the developer which, in Wu's estimation, was insufficient compared to the true property value. This case was seen as a test of a number of issues in Chongqing and China: The level of government collaboration and interference in private real estate transactions, whether squatters' rights could be enforced, the progress of market reforms, and how much the people deserved to be compensated versus the interests of private businesses.

When all was said and done, Wu and Yang accepted compensation and dropped their court case, but the government was found to have been unfairly pressuring them by allowing the excavation to take place before all claims had been settled and, making the situation worse from a publicity standpoint, in warning the people that such acts of private rebelliousness would not be tolerated. The national government reacted harshly against this position and swiftly acted to strengthen property rights with the promulgation of the new Property Law on October 1, 2007.[25]

Ironically, China's GINI index number is close to that of the US's.[26] In other words, China's former Communist country looks more like capitalist America than socialist Europe (all Western European countries tend to have much lower GINI numbers). While in the US, wealth accumulation and the gap between rich and poor is an expected outcome of a free market economy, in China, it is more the result of simple unfairness and lack of a mechanism to redistribute wealth adequately. For example, only in 2007 has China started to actively collect personal tax from higher income earners, and many transactions including property and capital gains are taxed at much lower levels than the US or not at all. The lack of a good legal and tax system to redistribute wealth more fairly is one of the problems that, when multiplied by 1.3 billion people, is very tough to solve, but it seems necessary at the moment to let some get rich first, driving consumption that will bootstrap the rest of the economy. Consequently, the *Affluencing* supertrend is one of the most important for China and potentially lucrative for foreign businesses.

Jieneng, Jianpai — Save energy, Reduce waste

China's 11th Five-Year Plan's key initiative with the strongest environmental impact is undoubtedly the pledge to reduce electricity usage per unit of GDP by 20 percent. As it currently stands, China is one of the least efficient industrialized nations on the planet. Countries such as Russia are worse, but on the other end of the spectrum, countries such as Japan and Germany are hyper-efficient by comparison. China's position on this scale shows that, despite the absolute size of its economy it is extremely inefficient, such as in the large agricultural base relying on manual labor mentioned earlier. In other sectors of the economy, such as manufacturing, China definitely does want modernization and more efficiency as a way to avoid overbuilding the power infrastructure. This trend has a catchphrase in China — *jieneng jianpai*, save energy, reduce waste — and it is the final supertrend: *Greening*.

Government and business coordination

With government intervention as a key driver of the drivers in the economy in general, the environment is no different, with the government playing an active role especially since 2007 when it admitted to having missed key targets set out in the 11th Five-Year Plan. Before the 2006–2010 plan, the attitude of putting economic development ahead of all other considerations prevailed, but on mounting evidence of environmental damage and incidents like the 2005 toxic chemical spill in the Songhua River and the 2007 algae blooms in Chinese lakes, China's government reiterated its pledge to become a green economy. Foremost would be the guidance of the 11th Five-Year Plan to make environmentally sustainable development and reduction of energy usage the new goals, and the fact that China's government officials would now be judged on their ability to govern greenly, not just encourage growth at a cost to the environment.

Before the latest Five-Year Plan, government officials were ranked and graded on essentially the same three primary drivers mentioned earlier: GDP growth, FDI growth, and improvement in the standard of living. While this was great for China's fast development, it was clearly at the cost of quality for quantity, growth rather than sustainability and, above all else, investment in practically anything that would push China's development as an industrial superpower forward, no matter how damaging to the environment that might be. After examining the results of this system, a new grading system was created, one that now judges local officials on their ability to hit the energy-savings target (20 percent overall reduction by 2011), sustainably develop what is left of the environment, and create socially-beneficial harmonious development.

During the five-year term of the Plan, decreasing the power consumption by 20 percent means an average of 4 percent a year. Most of this will come from upgrading of technology and closing of older, less efficient plants, such as cutting steel and iron production capacity by 42 million tons and 49 million tons, respectively, by 2010.[††] In regards to power consumption, China admitted

---

[††]Showing amazing support and coordination between government and industry, the iron industry cut production by 29 million tons, above its target by 7 million tons, while the steel industry missed its target yet still cut 15 million tons. The national planning office and Ministry of Finance assisted by providing incentives and support to the affected provinces to offset lost tax revenue and employ displaced workers.

completely missing that goal in 2006 and 2007. But it is still trying. In 2007, it closed about 9,000 megawatts of inefficient coal-powered generators, saving about 13.5 million tons of coal a year and reducing carbon dioxide emissions by about 27 million tons, but this is actually just a drop in the bucket.[27]

Another way China is seeking to reduce pollution is by acting through its regulatory agencies and instructing them to coordinate with other regulatory bodies or act as *de facto* environmental regulators though their title may be the Ministry of Commerce or the China Banking Regulatory Commission, rather than just the State Environmental Protection Agency (SEPA) working on its own. This cross-agency cooperation is quickly becoming a defining factor of China's environmental policy. For example, in 2007 the Ministry of Commerce cut off exporters who were reported to have evaded pollution standards by refusing to authorize export licenses if an environmental pollution problem was reported by SEPA or a local environmental regulatory body. The China Banking Regulatory Commission started to evaluate loans on the basis of environmental impact, reducing loans by 34 percent in the first half of 2007 to high-energy and high-environmental impact industries such as steel and coal, while preferring loans for larger companies with advanced manufacturing methods and clean technology. Furthermore, the Commission even instructed its banks to recall loans to companies that were polluting the environment.

China's plan also targets reducing inefficient industrial water usage by 30 percent. Considering that many areas of China are in water shortage, this is a good thing. And China furthermore wants to reduce solid waste by about 60 percent by 2010. One Chinese official estimated the market for new environmentally friendly technologies will be worth about US$300 billion in the next four years, with China representing about 30 percent of worldwide demand. China's government has cleared the path for foreign investments that produce environmental technology, use clean manufacturing processes, and allowed a number of other environmentally positive business models.

Protecting the environment

China is also making a number of positive steps towards renewing the environment that has been damaged, and building sustainable cities that will have a small ecological footprint. The consciousness of the youths in China regarding environmental concerns is increasingly positive. These things indicate a sea-change in the attitudes of people and government towards protecting the environment.

Suzhou Creek cleanup

Suzhou Creek, meandering for a little more than 53 kilometers through north-central Shanghai and having a total length of about 125 kilometers, is a tributary of the Huangpu River which eventually feeds into the Yangtze River, China's longest. From the 1920s onwards, Suzhou Creek was one of the most polluted rivers in China because of uncontrolled dumping of industrial waste during Shanghai's development as a business and industrial city, untreated domestic sewage, effluents from shipping such as oil, and poor flow which allowed silting and pollutants to build up. The smell (horrid, by all accounts) and color (black) was too much for residents to bear and a blight on the city's image, so starting in 1998 a program was implemented to clean it up. So far, more than US$1 billion has been spent and an additional US$400 million will be spent in phase three of the cleanup from 2007 to 2009. The cleanup combined building of new water treatment facilities for waste, redevelopment of roads and buildings along the river's edge and, in the last phase, will dredge up to three meters of sludge from along the bottom for much of its length to allow the reintroduction of fish. In 2008, some of the hottest property in Shanghai is along this creek, including converted warehouse office and artistic spaces, residential units with river views, and scenic walkways. That such a project can be undertaken successfully in a decade at a fairly enormous cost is another sign of China's close coordination between government agencies, business, and the public.

Eco-cities

China is embarking on an ambitious program of green development, basically because it must: With hundreds of millions to be moved into cities during the process of urbanization, building unsustainable, inefficient communities will only exacerbate China's already large problems such as water shortages. A second reason it is going green is because it can: Much of China is still underdeveloped, so when the government starts a new city or decides to completely redevelop an area, there are no private interests, or at least none strong enough, to resist going on a sustainable development model. Finally, there is evidence to support that eco-cities will be good business for China to develop a competitive advantage in, as it is able to import and utilize the world's best technologies and develop homegrown industries thanks to its huge potential market.

In late 2007, the State Council, China's cabinet, designated six experimental zones for energy-savings, environmental technology, and sustainable social development, including Shanghai's Pudong New District, Changsha, Hunan, and a handful of others, to focus on developing new models for sustainable social and economic development.

On the international level, Singapore and China are cooperating to create The Sino-Singapore Tianjin Eco-City, and in Shanghai, a local government redevelopment initiative will create a 6 square kilometer central business district in the city's Putuo Area that will use ecologically friendly construction and green urban planning.

Dongtan is perhaps one of the most ambitious of these projects. Established on Chongming Island in the Yangtze River Delta near Shanghai in 2005, Dongtan Eco-City is to be a model to test sustainable development, custom-built from the ground up for half a million people. The initial development is being coordinated by international engineering firm Arup and the first phase will be ready by the 2010 World Expo held in nearby Shanghai. There are to be no gas-powered vehicles, only electric- or hydrogen-powered, and the city will attempt to be a zero-waste city by practicing full ecological stewardship of products made and sold there.

The development is expected to continue until about 2020 when it will be about one-third as large as Manhattan and be home to 500,000, including a bridge, tunnel and subway connecting it together with Shanghai and the booming Jiangsu Province to the north. While the thought of taking the future site of China's hallmark eco-city and an environmental wetland for birds, and then ramming a highway through it does not make much environmental sense, from a regional development point of view it is important to ensure the eco-city develops into the integrated and sustainable economy it is meant to be. One hopes the proposed transportation infrastructure will be built with the same environmentally sound principles that characterize Dongtan itself.

The city has been designed so that every aspect, from energy generation to waste disposal to transportation, is handled in a eco-friendly way and supports a working economy of people attracted to the natural environment and sustainable living. If the model is successful in the early phases, China plans to develop other cities just like it. It could be said that this kind of development will be just a blip in negating the massive environmental footprint that China's other new cities are creating, but the fact it is being attempted will give China a distinct advantage and moral high ground on the world stage when it comes to reducing pollution. Other countries, such as the UK (which invested almost US$100 million of public funds from the British Environmental Transformation Fund), are buying into China's vision and hoping to go along for the ecological ride.

Clearly, the potential for environmental products and business models in China is huge, making it one of the most important supertrends to watch, not only inside China but also globally. China's insatiable demand for energy and the potential for global climate-affecting pollution cannot be understated.

The Supertrends to Watch

This chapter has introduced the *supertrends*, the biggest trends that will contain the most valuable opportunities for you and your business:

1. The Business Supertrends: Adding Value, Innovating, Urbanizing, and Serving the people.
2. The Social Supertrends: Consuming and Aspiring, Inter-networking and E-Commercializing.
3. The Wealth Supertrends: Affluencing and Greening.

Next, we move from the conceptual trends to the actual opportunities that are China's next billion dollar industries.

PART TWO

THE BUSINESS SUPERTRENDS

～商务趋势～

CHAPTER FOUR

Value-Adding to Make Better Things, Innovating to Make Things Better

价值化, 革新化 *Jiazhi hua & Gexin hua*

M anufacturing in China is still growing and in the short-term will not slow down, thus propelling China's export-driven economy to greater heights, but it is facing challenges. A 2008 survey of American manufacturers in China highlighted how perception of Chinese manufacturing — low cost, export-oriented — was changing, and what this meant for the future of this kind of production in China. Nearly 20 percent of the companies surveyed indicated they would relocate their manufacturing base to other countries. 88 percent of those companies said the main reason for doing so was the disappearing low labor-cost advantage and tax holidays.[1]

The Chinese government had recently announced the unified corporate tax, leveling the playing field between foreign and domestic companies. In fact, costs were up for everyone, but for the domestic companies, leaving the country was not such an attractive option. These new challenges have forced China's manufacturers to move up their value chain by adding high-value, high-tech components.

In 2007, the industrial output grew by 13.4 percent while the service sector grew by 11.4 percent, meaning that manufacturing and related industries actually became a bigger part of China's overall GDP, continuing a trend since 2005. For example, in the first quarter of 2008, the Chinese manufacturing economy was 49 percent of GDP, the service economy about 43 percent, and agriculture was about eight percent.[2]

The New Problems of a Factory Boss

It was almost 6 o'clock on an October day in Dongguan, Guangdong Province, part of China's "manufacturing alley" near Hong Kong.

Jin Wang, general manager of NewWear Apparel (a 2,000-employee OEM manufacturer and exporter to the US and Europe), was shuffling a handful of applications in his hands and organizing the interview notes. He contrasted in his mind how last year over 500 job-seekers showed up, whereas this year there were less than 50. Even if he accepted all the applicants, it was far from the 300 people he needed to fill the three large summer orders to be produced by next April.

Starting in early 2007, Wang noted that the workers in his factory had been steadily decreasing. He wondered if it was his apparel competitors poaching his experienced staff. He also noted more and more neatly-dressed young workers in new uniforms from recently-opened technology companies in the neighborhood. One by one, those new technology companies opened and attracted more and more good workers to the high-tech, higher pay jobs, away from the labor-intensive textile and apparel companies.

He also had some factory-owner friends who were moving their 20-year-old manufacturing operations to Vietnam. Times were really getting tough when even the Chinese bosses were moving not to cheaper locations in China, but to completely different countries.

(Continued)

Finally, Wang was facing declining profits. The rising labor costs in the past three years, combined with the strengthening RMB/US$ exchange rate, meant his costs were going up and his prices in US dollars converting to fewer *yuan* to pay his staff.

While continuing to grow, the manufacturing sector itself has undergone a shift since the start of the new millennium, partly at the direction of the Chinese government and partly due to the forces of globalization. These related trends of adding value and modernization will continue for the next decade, and the manufacturers of China will exhibit the effects in several important ways.

First, there is a continuing move away from labor-intensive handmade products, often poor in quality and only suitable for lower-end segments domestically or elsewhere, to more capital-intensive manufactured products. These are world-class products so long as your idea of world-class generally means less expensive and mass produced. The new twist on this trend is that the products are increasingly more technologically sophisticated and with a higher level of value-added within China.

One of the most obvious indications of this is how the Chinese government itself is pushing foreign investment for higher-technology, environmentally friendlier and less hazardous industries. Intel made news in 2007 by announcing a US$2.5 billion semiconductor chipset manufacturing facility in the port city of Dalian, strategically located near the Japanese and Korean buyers as well as being within a Chinese economic development zone with a number of investment incentives. It is Intel's first Asian manufacturing plant with the most advanced technology that the US government allows for export. The *Handbook for Foreign Business People* published for the regions, special economic zones, "new towns" and technology parks has changed from seeking any foreign investors to quality foreign investors, from any business that can improve China's low-level production and help its exports to encouraging only businesses that are on a targeted list of industries such as biotechnology, semiconductors, and other sectors that will make China into a modern industrial nation with competitive technology.

The second effect is increasing costs inside China. This effect occurs even as globalization continues relentlessly in search of the lowest-cost locations to source and manufacture goods. More companies are producing more things in China than ever before and China still has much excess capacity and surplus labor to utilize before its cost advantage runs out, but this, too, is changing quickly with worker migration patterns, inflation, and an end to some tax breaks on foreign investment. However, while the rapid economic growth is truly a miracle, there is no free lunch. The miracle has been built on the backs of the multitudes of labor. China has doubled its GDP more than twice over the past two decades, much faster than other Asian countries such as Japan in the latter half of the 20th century (which took 40 years to quadruple), the US's 60 postwar years, or more than 100 years for the British Empire in the 19th century. Yet in terms of labor rates, the increase over the same time period has been minimal in comparison. According to government statistics, the real wages for general laborers in the Pearl River Delta region, which includes Guangdong Province, where many exporting companies and foreign manufacturers have based their operations, have increased less than 10 percent over the same period.[3]

China's economic growth has been built on the shoulders of the international difference in labor, and its new wealth has not been evenly distributed across all parts of the population. China has realized the problem, and one of the main policy shifts in attracting foreign investment has been to discourage investment in low-tech manual labor (pushing those businesses further to the less developed western regions) and encourage high-tech, capital-intensive industries.

In fact, labor costs are going up in China for skilled workers much more quickly. China raised its national minimum wage in 2007 and on January 1, 2008, a new labor law was enacted with significantly higher protections for workers, such as easier arbitration of disputes and more worker rights. On average, urban wages rose 15 percent in 2006, and when 2007 figures are available, it will surely have risen again.[4]

Additionally, China's urban cities are quickly losing the temporary advantage they had in typical white-collar office or technical and skilled work. Many multinationals are moving to a so-called "China *plus one*" strategy, where the *plus one* refers to another even lower-cost-of-labor country such as Vietnam or Bangladesh, partly as a backup should China's production falter or become too expensive.

Other non-production-related expenses are going up as well, such as environmental and safety regulations. China's equivalent of the EPA, the State Environmental Protection Agency (which was turned into a full ministry in 2008), has already been shutting down the worst offenders or, at least, preventing them from getting further loans through state-controlled banks. Additionally, raw materials costs are increasing globally (partly due to China's own voracious appetites) from basics like iron and copper to plastics. At China's manufacturers, razor-thin margins are being shaved even further. Chinese contract manufacturers (i.e., OEMs) themselves are no longer satisfied with being the sweatshops to the global consumer, so they are doing their best to climb from their position at the bottom on the international supply chain by innovating and developing their own brands.

The third and most recent major effect is a new emphasis on quality. While to some extent every newly industrializing country goes through a period where its products are seen as inferior — think Japanese cars in the 1960s and 1970s until Toyota revolutionized the industry with its Total Quality Management, or how "Made in Korea" used to be associated with poor quality electronics until the likes of Samsung and LG became consumer favorites in high-tech gadgets and appliances — Chinese products have retained an air of cheapness that they can't seem to shake off. This is perhaps justified and best exemplified by the plethora of Chinese products in Wal-Mart at everyday low prices. However, until the poison pet food and lead-tainted toy recalls of 2007, there was no national shame so great as to make front page headlines around the world. These incidents marked a change in how Western consumers see Chinese goods: No longer just cheap, but now potential health hazards as well. So the trend of improving quality is ultimately being driven by Western consumers who will demand quality or stop buying, but there is also significant pressure from the domestic Chinese consumers who, newly flushed with disposable income and faced with a multitude of domestic brands vying for attention against the perceived higher quality of foreign brands, are increasingly looking for quality as a given. These same consumers sometimes ignore the fact that many foreign brands sold in China are actually made by the same Chinese manufacturers that produce the domestic brands, unfairly attributing quality to brand image alone. They are recently becoming more discerning and now have the purchasing power to influence companies to improve their quality.

A reputation for poisoning beloved family pets and endangering the lives of children with toys is serious news to a nation that relies on exports for a large portion of its GDP, so the government is pushing quality even more.

Excuse Me, It's Not Made *in* China, It's Made *by* China

One barrier to innovation in China is that the education system, based on rote learning, doesn't encourage creative thinking. As a Chinese saying goes, the nail that sticks up gets hammered down. It is more important to be part of the status quo than it is to *think differently*. As mentioned in the chapter on China's drivers, China has recently made moves to refocus on research and development as a core competency. It has for several years been trying to develop its own technology for consumer products including video discs and industrial hardware such as mobile phone switching technology, but it has only recently started to achieve some success.

When China first introduced its own standard for a low-density video disc, the VCD, the world barely blinked. Outside of China's own market, it was a dismal failure. At the time, not many Chinese consumers were able to afford the pricey hardware and it wasn't even one of the four must-haves (refrigerator, TV, air conditioner, washing machine), so it was simply absorbed into the functions of DVD players which, as anybody who has recently bought one will know, have been beaten down to the $30–$50 price range at Wal-Mart. Unable to get around the DVD patent restrictions, China's latest foray is into the realm of High-Definition DVD. The battle between Sony's Blu-Ray and Toshiba's HD-DVD may be over, but China (which worked with Toshiba to develop the standard) has one more card left to play: CH-DVD. Short for China High-definition DVD, this format is based on Chinese intellectual property. If China's domestic market can accept the standard (and with an estimated domestic market of 100 million consumers for the product, it just might), the final chapter for Blu-Ray may turn out a little differently.[5]

In the mobile technology space, China's early and somewhat hap-hazard venture into which transmission technology to use resulted in two companies, China Mobile and China Unicom, competing with entirely different platforms, GSM and CDMA respectively, which resulted in a duopoly rather than a competition. Purposely avoiding installing next-generation 3G equipment like that of neighbors Korea and Japan, China has been busily developing its own technology for the next-generation 3G and even 4G networks to be put into use in the domestic market to develop the homegrown standards. The new 3G standard is called TD-SCDMA.* Whether it can compete with foreign standards and ultimately win in the international marketplace is quite uncertain, but again, China is certainly trying to support more innovation via its large domestic market.

Made (chic) in China

While China usually has an image of low-cost and mass produced clothing, it is moving up the chain here as well. Currently it exports

---

*Time Division Synchronous Code Division Multiple Access.

more than US$150 billion of textiles each year, making it the world's largest exporter with about 30 percent of global trade. Clearly this is one of China's most important export industries, but it is not assured of its continued dominance in the next decade wherein new Asian Tigers such as Vietnam, Cambodia, and Bangladesh, not to mention huge Central Asian countries such as India and Pakistan, will increasingly encroach on China's low-cost labor advantage. Raw materials costs are going up, and so are production costs in China as the country modernizes and updates its legal system to protect workers and the environment. In response, some Chinese factories are adapting by designing more, mass producing on contract less.

Chinese factories can now offer the best of both worlds: Low-cost handwork combined with the latest high-technology manufacturing practices to produce smaller runs at efficient cost. This development has resulted from years of working with companies such as Hong Kong's Li & Fung, which in turn supplies the clothes to companies such as Wal-Mart and global clothing companies. After years of producing to exacting standards on-time and at ever-thinner margins, many Chinese factories themselves are now ready to leave the nest. With the addition of some designers to their payrolls, often foreign-trained in places like France or Italy, the Chinese textile manufacturers can offer surprisingly good quality, design, and price.

It's a well-guarded secret in the luxury goods business that increasing amounts of product are made in China, guarded because it doesn't suit the image of a luxury brand to be associated with mass production, low-cost labor and sweatshops. The top brands avoid this fate by producing only parts of the whole products in China, assembling elsewhere with a certain percentage of value to qualify for the treasured "Made in a Country Other Than China" label. But mid-level brands are not so shy, especially when it comes to bags and accessories which China excels in. They may not necessarily come to China just for the price difference (which is neglible in high-quality fashion where materials and brand are the largest components of value), but for reasons of manufacturing flexibility and the ability to meet deadlines.

Unlike the luxury workshops of Europe, Chinese factories take no vacations, running every day of the year. Increasingly, international luxury brands are also manufacturing in China because it is one of their key markets: China is already the world's number three market for luxury goods, meaning that if they are produced here the supply chain is shortened significantly.[6] This trend is, however, counterbalanced by the desire of Chinese consumers to have foreign-made goods: They would rather pay a lot (including a China luxury tax of 20 percent on many popular luxury products) for an imported bag than to get "bargain" luxury products produced in China. Still, adding more luxury manufacturing in China is surely in many luxury brands' plans. The opportunity for smaller brands is clear: Get there first, establish a track record, find the best suppliers and partner up before the bigger players do.

The Shoe is on the Other Foot

The story of how Chinese manufacturers are running away from typical OEM agreements of the past to their own brands is no longer a fairytale — they are *just doing it*. Once in the spotlight as the companies that ran the sweatshops serving Nike and other shoe manufacturers, China's shoe manufacturers are now so competitive on their own that they are subject to trade restrictions in the EU because they are so good and so inexpensive that they are putting what's left of the EU shoe industry out of business.

Chinese-made running shoes have been dominating the Western shoe market for decades. Just as Sara Bongiorni described in her popular book, *A Year Without Made in China*, she tried in vain, going from store to store in her Louisiana town, to find a reasonable alternative to US$10 a pair Chinese-made children's sneakers, and ended up paying US$68 for a pair of Italian running shoes with Velcro straps by mail order.

If you go to Dongguan, a light-goods manufacturing city in Guangzhou Province, you will see gate after gate of Chinese shoe

(Continued)

manufacturers, with millions of running shoes made here being shipped overseas each year at rock-bottom prices and ending up as US$10–$20 pairs of shoes at Wal-Mart.

Like many of his business friends, Henry Yu, a well-known shoe manufacturer, moved his factory from Taiwan to Dongguan in the 1980s when the high labor cost in Taiwan was increasing monthly along with labor shortages due to the fast economic growth at home. The only difference between Henry and his competitors is his keen interest and ability in design. With a Masters degree in mechanical engineering, Henry ran a successful shoe manufacturing business with many repeat customers seeking his ability to continually improve the ergonomic design. With ever-increasing orders, Henry soon found out his margin was decreasing as companies such as Nike and Adidas were constantly driving down the price in negotiations. Facing competition from Vietnam and increasing materials costs, he soon realized that his commodity products would be squeezed out.

Henry started to develop alternatives in high-end specialty markets such as golf and tennis shoes. Using his design expertise and hard work, his shoes soon entered the most demanding — but also highly profitable — market: Japan. Henry hired young engineers, and installed advanced machinery with computer-assisted design to design and manufacture golf shoes under tight quality control that Japanese customers demanded. This was Henry's company's successful transition from OEM, a subcontractor that built to the customers' design specifications, to ODM, an Original Design Manufacturer that created original work to be sold under another company's brand name. The higher profits from this market gave his company the luxury of spending more money on innovative design to become a high-end manufacturer of golf and tennis footwear. But Henry wasn't satisfied with just that.

Henry also spent time and money to develop ice-skates. Every winter, Henry and his assistants went to Europe for trade shows and, while there, they visited ice rinks and handed out €100 bills and free skates to anybody who would try them and give Henry their feedback.

(Continued)

Fifteen years later, Henry's company has become one of the top manufacturers, with its own brand, of premium quality skates that sell for up to US$400 a pair, with profit margins of more than $100 a pair. As Henry commented, "I would still be making US$4 a pair shoes for Nike if I had remained an OEM." As in the old Kungfu movie cliché, the student has become the teacher and, as we all know, the Chinese are pretty good at Kungfu, so watch for more Chinese OEMs moving up the value chain to become ODMs and eventually developing their own brands.

HiPhone and Mini One: iPhone knock-offs, clones, or copies?

The line between knock-off, clone, and copy is thin indeed, especially when you are talking about consumer devices like the super-thin iPod nano or the 2007-released iPhone from Apple. But first, one must define terms: In design, one talks of a knock-off of a fashion designer's haute couture or *prêt-à-porter* ideas as inspiring a lower-end retail line's similar look. In technology, a cloned PC used to be something that was made to mimic the IBM-designed PC's proprietary "BIOS" architecture from the ground up by re-engineering it in an isolated lab, giving the clone PC identical functionality without violating IBM's intellectual property rights. A copy is what many things manufactured in China actually are: An exact duplicate of computer software sold on the street minus the copy protection, a fake DVD (though complete with DVD extras and new Chinese subtitles, often amusingly mistranslated), or a pair of Levi's jeans or Nike shoes that is almost exact in its reproduction (possibly because it was made at the same factory in a phantom shift — an additional shift of workers producing the same products with the same machines in an authorized OEM factory). For example, a phone sold in China through online auctions and other gray-market channels is the HiPhone, a detailed copy of the iPhone from Apple, right down to the box and an ersatz Apple logo (with the bite out of the wrong side).

This is the negative side of China's counterfeit goods industry. A set of fake Ping golf clubs can go for as little as US$150 from an illegal seller, damaging both the brand and possibly the golfer's game. However, a newer kind of product is increasingly being seen in China, with better quality than the original at a lower cost, and only just pushing the boundary between knock-off and copy, not breaking it.

So when a Chinese company launched a line of MP3 players that looked a lot like the iPod designs, down to the popular white color, many wondered what exactly they were — very good knock-offs, or just copies.

The Meizu M3 (since rebranded as the Music Card) was definitely not a clone because, although it looked a lot like the iPod nano, it had completely different internal chipset, and it has no ability to sync with iTunes or anything to do with Apple's operating system: Its technology and software was, in fact, that of a standard MP3 player, of which China makes hundreds of millions a year both for domestic and overseas consumption, including for Apple. The Meizu M6 (since rebranded as the Mini Player) on first glance looked a lot like a cross between the classic hard-drive-based iPod and the new iPod nano released in 2007, with a bigger screen. The M6 was, however, smaller than a credit card and had no hard drive, so it wasn't like the classic iPod, and it had a bigger screen than the new iPod nano. It was, in effect, the best of both worlds, and the two players were definitely knock-offs with respect to design aesthetic.

Did they violate any of Apple's patents in China? It seems not. What seems more likely is that the industrial design itself may be similar enough to confuse consumers, but this issue has not been tested in the court yet as Meizu doesn't sell the players in the US.

This may all change with Meizu's next product, however, rumored to be an iPhone knock-off with large screen and mobile phone capabilities, but on a completely different technology platform both with respect to the operating system (Windows Mobile) and the mobile connectivity standards. Oh, and it will work anywhere in the world on any cellular network, and not be locked to certain providers as the iPhone is in countries such as the US. The so-called Mini One has more memory and is half the price, if rumored information is found to be true. It is, in many respects, *better than* the iPhone.[7] If the product is actually released and is not just vaporware, it will be as a Chinese knock-off product that is on the cutting edge rather than one step behind, following in the tradition of Japanese and later Korean manufacturers who made "cheaper, smaller, and better" into a manufacturing credo which became the foundations for companies like Sony and Samsung. The opportunity here is for the first company to take a chance and distribute the high-tech products of the Meizu's of China. Certainly it may be risking a lawsuit from Apple, but the upside is also clearly there to be at the ground floor wholesaling, distributing or retailing "Made in China" brands before they take off. For product designers based overseas, China is hands-down the best choice to OEM and, increasingly, ODM their products.

The Ultimate Source for Everything

It is sometimes surprising to find just how much China manufactures. China's wholesale markets, such as can be found in the city of Yiwu a couple of hours outside of Shanghai, have tens of thousands of vendors selling hundreds of thousands of products often arranged in highly specific niches with incredible depth. One market, the Futian Market in Yiwu, is like visiting the mother of all markets. If it were open for retail and under one roof, rather than several halls for wholesalers only, it would be bigger than the biggest mall in the world (which is also in China — the South China Mall in Dongguan). Futian Market has 58,000 stalls and is approximately three kilometers long from start to finish, and on a busy day may get hundreds of thousands of buyers. This kind of wholesale market for light manufactured goods is characteristic of many developing countries, where one often finds highly specialized stores for many basic commodities, but no place in the world does this like China's Yiwu. Need some cellophane tape in quantity? Go to the tape whole-saler (actually, there's dozens of such wholesalers to choose from), where you will see literally thousands of rolls of every variety imag-inable, stacked and ready for immediate purchase by the contain-erload if needed.

Basically anything that can be found in a Wal-Mart is probably made somewhere in China and can be bought in a place such as Yiwu's Futian Market, but China also produces high-end electronics. Most laptop computers are already made in China, as are mobile phones and TVs. Companies like Lennovo, Huawei Technologies, and Haier are quickly becoming giants among their respective industries with their own brands and exporting abroad. This has not been the norm so far, with these manufacturers as the exception rather than the rule. China is most often seen as a place for foreign multinationals to source products.

During the 1980s, most foreign businesspeople came to China to export labor-intensive products in large volume; in the 1990s, many came to China to set up joint ventures or, later, their own wholly-owned manufacturing facilities for products sold outside China and occasionally in the domestic market; recently, eight out of ten businesspeople you meet in China are here to source. They source either raw materials for their plants in China and elsewhere around the world, or products to compete more effectively in the global market.

One successful business model that has been adopted by many multinational companies in China is that they will follow the formula to start using, and often import, raw materials specified by their foreign plant to assure their product quality will meet their cus-tomers' requirements. Once their factories in China achieve stable operations and quality, the foreign-specified and imported materials will be replaced with locally produced materials to save costs and transportation time.

Product sourcing, as part of outsourcing, is contracting other companies to manufacture your products for you based on your technology and raw materials requirements. Lower labor cost is only part of the reason. A major headache many manufacturers in the Western world have to face is the constant pressure coming from health, safety and environmental protection (HSE) interests, arising from Western societies' requirements for a better quality of life. Inevitably, this has not only added costs in both initial investment and ongoing operations, but also hindered any new addition of manufacturing capacity at existing facilities in Western countries. The long and tedious approval process in countries like the United States, where special interests can tie up projects for years, or in Japan where farmers can tie up a new airport for decades, has intimidated many manufacturers to move away to other places in the world that welcome them with open arms. Less kindly, this is called exporting pollution. If Western textile manufacturers were attracted by the lower costs of China, chemical-related industries were attracted by the lack of tight environmental regulations and easy approval process. China has historically welcomed all investment and only recently started thinking about its own HSE consciousness with the 11th Five-Year Plan mentioned earlier.

Outsourcing Everything Including the Kitchen Sink

China is not just for outsourcing your basic manufacturing needs, it is increasingly handling more advanced products and services, and even going virtual.

Outsourcing R&D to China

Another trendy outsourcing activity in China is to conduct technology research and development by either contracting local Chinese technical research institutes or universities to work on assigned projects, or establish technology centers in China to work on the projects directly. Foreign companies are creating new R&D

centers in China at a surprising rate. There are three main reasons: First, there is a cost savings for researcher salaries. Compared to the typical annual US$150,000 salary plus benefits (which can be greater than 50 percent of the salary) for a PhD researcher in many Western employment markets, the average total employee cost for their counterpart in China is merely US$50,000 per year — three or four researchers for the price of one, it is no wonder so many MNCs are setting up R&D centers in China. Second, the R&D center in China, being inside the market and staffed by local employees, will be more likely to quickly develop sophisticated products that accommodate the Chinese customers' needs. Finally, the tax breaks for R&D centers in China rival or exceed those of Western countries. Additionally, China's government has pledged to increase spending on homegrown R&D activities from about 1.3 percent of GDP to 2.5 percent of GDP by 2020 in key technology areas such as biotechnology, environmental services, space exploration, communications, and information technology. China's Wuxi Pharmatech in Shanghai is less than a decade old, but already employs 2,500 researchers and scientists.

Meet the New Neighbors

The number of foreign multinational companies doing research in China has skyrocketed in the past three years. According to China's Ministry of Commerce, there were more than 1,100 R&D facilities set up in China by MNCs at the end of 2007.

MNCs typically move their R&D operations to China for several reasons: Cost savings in researcher salaries, facilities costs, and tax rebates; being closer to the market for R&D; and shortening the supply chain between raw materials to manufacturing to distribution. With costs in Shanghai and Beijing rising, a new pattern emerging is for MNCs to have their headquarters in one of those prestigious cities and have

(Continued)

R&D or other operations in second tier cities such as Dalian or Chengdu, or elsewhere.

MNCs either establish their R&D centers as wholly-owned, in a partnership with a local manufacturer (e.g., a potential partner, gaining access to their staff and market knowledge), or with universities on a project-by-project basis. China has ramped up its own R&D spending so there are ample cooperative opportunities.

In 2007 and early 2008, here are some of the American companies that are making big moves into Chinese R&D:

In 2007, GM announced an investment of US$250 million in GM Park in Shanghai, an R&D facility that will include alternative-fuel vehicles as one of its prime research objectives to be a leader in hybrid car technology in China.

Symantec, best known for its anti-virus software, is setting up a US$50 million center in Chengdu, which will eventually host 1,000 staff. By this move, Symantec is possibly acknowledging the growing number of computer viruses and computer security threats originating in China and wants to be close to the action.

Microsoft, already with a large presence in mainland China and an MSN R&D center, announced a further US$280 million investment in what will be its biggest R&D center outside the US. Microsoft wants to double its current full-time research staff in China to 3,000 by 2010.

Biotechnology leader Genzyme is spending US$90 million on an R&D center in Beijing, to host about 350 researchers, only its second lab outside of the US.

Virtual sweatshops

Perhaps it is not surprising that, with just about any and every physical product that can be outsourced being sent to China, it was only a matter of time before China would start manufacturing virtual products as well. The popular and predominantly US-based online game Second Life is based on ideas of community-building and social exchanges, all in an online world. The users of Second Life have the ability to augment themselves (their online selves are called avatars) with clothes and accoutrements, and build virtual houses to live in and stores to do business at. Things, both real and virtual, can be bought and sold, services performed, and online assets, such as virtual real estate in prime areas of user interaction, have become increasingly valuable. Companies such as IBM have jumped onto the bandwagon by setting up virtual offices. The trouble with all this virtual design and development is that building the "things" still takes time and effort. That's where China comes in.

The currency of Second Life is called Linden Dollars, named after the founder, and through a mechanism akin to a central bank, Linden Dollars can be exchanged out of the game for real dollars. The international difference in labor works just as well online as it does offline, so when one online entrepreneur — Anshe Chung, a pseudonym for the real-life Ailin Graef — announced she was the first real-world millionaire as a result of activities based in a virtual world, there was an interesting connection to China in the story. Anshe Chung Studios has set up a real production office in low-cost Wuhan, China.[8] By hiring low-cost labor in China to design and build virtual property that would be rented or sold in an online game popular in the US, Anshe Chung Studios was taking advantage of the cost differential that many MNCs seek when they come to do business in China. That it was achieved in one of the most cutting-edge industries in the world — virtual real estate development — says something about the outcomes possible under China's innovation drive. In this case, it was the real-world to virtual-world and back again currency conversion that turned this business model into a real, rather than virtual, affair, but it was not the first time in China that virtual games made real money for people in China.

MMORPGs[†] have Chinese versions, and Chinese players rank among the top in the world at games such as Blizzard

---

[†]Massively Multi-player Online Role-Playing Games (large-scale online gaming worlds of adventure and fantasy).

Entertainment's World of Warcraft (WoW). WoW has its own online economy though the transactions are often offline: Users can sell their weapons and magic objects on eBay or other auction sites by selling a special passcode for real dollars. Chinese company Giant Interactive and its for-China MMORPG ZT Online suffer from inflation due to the practice of "gold-farming", as do several Western game economies when virtual worlds overlap with China.

In gold-farming, Chinese players, and companies employing vast numbers of "slave players" essentially labor for days online to gain the gold, experience points or items which may then be sold at a premium offline to other players. Buyers from developed countries pay more than the buyers inside China, and with China's own economy being so big (and labor costs so low), there are arbitrage profits to be made simply by hiring some kids in the countryside to sit in an Internet café all day doing the equivalent of online digging for gold. With so many inactive players involved in the virtual labor rather than playing the game for fun, the value of the virtual currency and other items inside the game begins to weaken because of too much supply: Virtual labor in a virtual world creating virtual inflation.

Some of the Fastest-Growing Industries in China

Based on these trends in manufacturing, look towards the following sectors for the greatest growth in the next decade. These are the industries that are rapidly upgrading their production through technology and innovation, casting off the low-quality mass-produced or labor-intensive products of the past in favor of world-class high-tech value-added products. Among them are industries favored by the Chinese government as pillar industries, such as the automotive industry, or sectors that will grow as a result of one or more drivers or supertrends. If you're looking for the next big thing in China, or maybe in the world, look here for some overlooked investment opportunities.

China's Hot Manufacturing Sectors

Here's our list of the manufacturing sectors we think are best positioned for growth based on the *supertrends*:

1. **Energy-related.** With China's massive quantities of coal, look for China to become a world leader in the various coal-related technologies including gasification and liquefaction. With its position as the manufacturer of most of the world's solar panels and having the most solar panels in use, China is likely to start to innovate, but presently the state-of-the-art thin film solar panels are being developed elsewhere, such as the US and Japan. China's companies produce much of the world's wind turbines, and the country is also a large user. Finally, LED lighting, originally developed in other countries, is currently powering China's outdoor advertising industry with huge LED screens on everything from buildings to boats and trucks that ply the rivers and streets.

2. **Designed products with Chinese flavor**. On a superficial level, this might include more red-colored things in our lives and dragon iconography, but these stereotypical ideas are going to be supplanted by companies, MNCs among them, who see product localization as an important strategy to reach China's growing consumer base. KFC's Peking-duck-inspired chicken wraps and Starbucks' green-tea lattes spreading from China, first to other parts of Asia and then globally, are just the beginning.

3. **Innovation.** The business incubators are starting to pay off, but even more growth is going to come out of China's newly formed R&D labs funded by foreign companies. Researchers will, in the Chinese (and not to mention, Silicon Valley) tradition, spin off into their own entrepreneurial ventures taking their best ideas with them. Many of their products will be for the home market first. Additionally, China's promotion of homegrown standards, such as the TD-SCDMA 3G mobile platform, will eventually be adopted in other countries, but first in China's trading partners and then outwards.

4. **Health.** The home of Traditional Chinese Medicine is increasingly becoming a force abroad as those outside China increasingly accept naturopathy, acupuncture and other non-traditional treatments. Look for China's herbal medicine producers, some already listed on

(Continued)

foreign exchanges, to use investment to increase their product yields, lower costs, and innovate effectiveness. The apparent contradiction between healthy natural products and genetically-modified organisms notwithstanding, China's biotech industries are expected to be very active in this area. Finally, China is already one of the world's leading producers of low-end medical devices, so it will likely move up the value chain, producing newer and state-of-the-art medical equipment.

Flying Phoenix, Hidden Dragon

China in 2007 made another leap forward, this time in commercial aviation. While for years China had been campaigning to have Boeing and Airbus produce parts of their jets in China, little progress had been made. There was some concern that as a strategic industry, it was too valuable for the EU or the US to let another country muscle in on.

In what may be termed a factory-for-jets kind of *quid pro quo*, in 2007 it was announced that a joint venture between Airbus and a consortium of Chinese aerospace companies would establish an A320 assembly factory near Tianjin.[9] China currently has more than 370 A320s on order. At the same time, China was moving ahead with its own aviation and aerospace development programs. It was thought that a Chinese aerospace firm, China Aviation Industry Corp. (AVIC), would be a potential bidder in a handful of Airbus factories to be released in a company restructuring, but then in December 2007, the first Flying Phoenix rolled off the assembly line ready for testing. It seemed they didn't really need the factories or technology after all.

The ARJ21 Flying Phoenix is a 90-seater regional jet expected to go into flight-testing around March 2008 and be delivered to customers by September 2009. It has already received more than 170 advanced orders. The really stunning thing about this? The project was started in 2005 and, to date, has only cost about US$800 million.

The Flying Phoenix is expected to be a strong contender in China's domestic market, which is estimated to need an additional 800–1,000 regional jets by 2020, and will enter into direct competition with smaller jet manufacturers such as Canada's Bombardier or Brazil's Embraer SA. While creating jumbo jets that compete with Boeing and Airbus is a long way off, in 2008 China directed its two largest state-controlled aircraft developers, AVIC I and II, to speed up development of jumbo jets by forming a consortium that will also be invested by government entities such as the State-owned Assets Supervision and Administration Commission and the government of Shanghai (expected to host one of the two planned jumbo jet facilities) for a total investment of between US$7–$8.5 billion. Not insignificantly, one of the AVICs is responsible for military aircraft and will utilize the same technology to develop large-capacity military planes. One government official has stated the goal is to have designs made by 2010 and a production line by 2020. This is quite ambitious considering the decades that Boeing and Airbus needed.

It is undoubtedly true that China's advances in aviation are built on the wings (and intellectual property licenses and technology transfers) of foreign aircraft manufacturers, but the trend towards patent independence can be heard in the words of officials who want to reduce dependence on foreign technology, and in practice as can be seen in other heavy industries already. For example, in 2007, China successfully floated its own mid-sized cargo ship, advanced-technology LNG tanker, and 297,000 ton oil tanker, built entirely in China with limited foreign assistance. China has invested US$2 billion in a huge shipyard with a final ship-building capacity in 2015 of 12 million tons.[10]

Baby You Can Drive My *Che*

Regarded as a pillar industry by the Chinese government, and widely desired by the urbanizing and higher-income population, cars are big business in China. China is predicted to become the world's biggest market for cars in 2009 or 2010, overtaking the United States (it has already surpassed world number two Japan). China sold approximately 6.3 million passenger cars (or about 8.8 million vehicles total if commercial vehicles are included) in 2007 with a year-on-year growth of more than 20 percent. The double-digit sales growth is expected to continue in 2008.

China is simply crazy for cars. With over 70 percent of the 57 million vehicles on the road being government-owned, and about 44 cars per 1,000 people (versus 750 cars per 1,000 in the US and 120 per 1,000 globally), China's personal car ownership market is expected to grow quickly in the coming years.[11]

Industry statistics were above 25 percent growth in 2006, meaning in 2007 the market slowed slightly to only 20 percent growth, but certain segments within the passenger car market grew significantly faster, such as SUVs whose growth increased by 50 percent despite relatively high (compared to average incomes) gas prices.[12] Growth may slow further if fuel costs increase, but there seems to be no stopping China's new-found love of cars, or *che* as they are known in Mandarin.

After buying technology and designs from Britain's bankrupt MG Rover, China's car makers ramped up development on domestically-produced vehicles but, in a tight market where imports including GM, Volkswagen, and Toyota are extremely competitive, the locally-produced cars are having a difficult time to compete.

In 2008, this has resulted in American-style "zero interest" car loans and other sales incentives being transplanted to China which, perhaps when combined with the asset-backed securities also being introduced this year, could result in American-style overspending.

China only exported less than half a million vehicles in 2007, but as quality comes up, China will increasingly compete with cars from Korea and, based on the strength of their joint ventures with GM, Volkswagen, and others, eventually challenge the biggest global automotive manufacturers in their home markets by 2020. Growth in consumption within China, as more and more people gain higher incomes, means these manufacturers have a strong domestic market to rely on and develop in before stepping onto the global stage in a big way. It is possible that Chinese car manufacturers will make more acquisitions abroad to leap-frog into key technology such as engines, and establish factories abroad in the next decade as a way of alleviating trade imbalances and avoiding tariffs, much the same way as Japan did in the 1980s to relieve trade pressure with the US.

The biggest of the Chinese players is SAIC, Shanghai Automotive Industry Corp., whose listed unit's profit topped US$500 million in 2007. A multidivision company, SAIC made news in 2007 when it launched the Roewe, its first self-owned model and based on the Rover 75 technology purchased from Britain's Rover Corp. in 2005. The Roewe, incidentally, is known in China by its Mandarin name, *rongwei*, which sounds exactly like Wrong Way. The Chinese name harkens back to when Chevrolet called a car the Nova, or *no va*, meaning "no go" in Spanish.

These Wrong Way sedans would compete with Nanjing Automobile Group's MG series, also based on the same designs from Rover. Aside from the intellectual property issues that apparently arose from the use of the same design by two different companies, both companies again made news at the end of 2007 by announcing they would merge. The Chinese automotive industry is complicated indeed.

The merger of SAIC with Yuejin Motor Group, owner of the Nanjing Automobile Corp., would mean the merged entity will have joint ventures not only with GM, Volkswagen and Fiat, majority shareholdings in Korea's number four automaker, and a number of domestically developed brands, but also compete directly against itself with the Roewe and MG sedans based on exactly the same technology platform. It is perhaps odd to consider the degree to which these joint ventures and domestic branded cars are all competing with each other under one corporate umbrella, but China's government wants consolidation of the industry and to establish at least one industry giant that can compete globally. Fiat and Nanjing Auto almost immediately announced a breakup, and we can expect that more of those joint ventures will have outlived their usefulness (most likely for the Chinese partner) and the new combined entity will develop many more of its own vehicles in the future, having learned from the masters all they needed to know.

Custom-Made for a Wholesale Price

Despite their reputations as mass producers, China's manufacturers are becoming very nimble at the opposite end of the spectrum — mass customization. From dress shirts to wedding gowns, draperies to bed linens, China's textile and clothing manufacturers still use enough manual labor to product exquisite designs at a fraction of the cost of other countries' custom products, but the Chinese manufacturers are taking it one step further by automating the process. After one Chinese manufacturer had success with custom-made dress shirts ordered on the Internet, it quickly spawned a dozen competitors. The cost of a newly manufactured shirt with your monogram on it? US$20 compared to the stunning price of US$150 for a custom-made shirt in New York. A nice bespoke suit in Dong Jia Du, Shanghai's fabric market, can be made for US$60 or a cashmere overcoat for US$80, made to measure and delivered in under a week (if you're traveling in town, this can even be cut to a few days for a small premium).

Quality Control in a Health-Conscious World

After the toy recalls, poisonous pet food and toothpaste, and other quality problems of 2007, China took serious steps to protect the "Made in China" brand. Toy exports, for example, were worth about US$7 billion in 2007, US$3 billion being sent directly to the US, a fairly significant and growing amount of trade. The method and speed with which they reacted to this crisis deserves mention.

First, the quality supervision body of China's government immediately inspected and revoked export licenses of more than 600 toy manufacturers found to have substandard quality. In a nation where there are about 3,000 manufacturers exporting toys, this is a fair number with quality problems, and in a country with tens of thousands of companies that take part in the entire toy supply chain, it could be seen as just the tip of the iceberg, but taking away an export license from what is the top of the supply chain is still a serious step.

While it has since been admitted by Mattel and others that some of the toy recalls were due to design faults rather than production quality problems, the damage to the Chinese industry was done. The Chinese government has again shown one of the benefits of its model mixing business and policy by acting quickly to register the toy manufacturers, inspect them all, revoke licenses where appropriate, and establish new quality control regulations for the industry to follow, all in a period of about four months.

Color Me Red

Pigments are an age-old industry in China. It has been producing pigments for its own use for thousands of years. Lacking strong pollution regulations, China's market for pigments developed with poor quality and lack of environmental manufacturing processes, meaning also they are priced at a fraction of the cost of those produced in Europe or the US.

However, the inconsistent quality and unreliable delivery schedule from many Chinese suppliers still made them uncompetitive on the global market. Scott Ng, a Hong Kong color specialist, spotted the opportunity.

He set up a color laboratory with full quality-testing equipment in Shanghai five years ago. He supplied quality Chinese pigments and dyes with delivery time guarantees to well-known Western companies.

Scott's laboratory in Shanghai hired more than 20 chemists as buyers and quality control technicians. The buyers constantly searched and sourced for "sometimes good" Chinese pigments at absolute low

(Continued)

prices in medium to large quantities. After receiving those pigments in bulk, the lab analyzed the quality and graded them accordingly. Then, each carefully-labeled order was shipped overseas at different prices depending on the grade. With flourishing sales, Scott soon expanded his lab and his business model. Now he has entered into several long-term supply contracts with a few key manufacturers where he also installed quality control equipment and trained their people in advanced manufacturing and quality control procedures.

The opportunities like this one, sourcing from the lot and cherry-picking the best, are still numerous in China, across many industries. With the new emphasis on quality control and ingredients as a result of the problems in 2007, this quality control-related businesses will get even bigger.

High-Tech Manufacturing

While high-tech is usually a way to deliver high-quality and con-sistent standards, it is not always welcomed in tradition-rich China. When the *Quanjude* chain of Peking Duck restaurants announced in 2008 that it would replace its traditional fruitwood-fired ovens and hand-roasting with brand new partly-foreign developed electric ovens, many Chinese cried foul. The price premium on *Quanjude* roasted ducks was not just for the famous brand (which allowed the company to go public in 2007 on China's Shenzhen stock exchange), but also for the hundreds of years of history and hand preparation that reminded people of China's food heritage. The company, natu-rally, believed the electric roasting would standardize taste (at least they were smart enough not to say it would also allow mass pro-duction) and quality, but China's roast duck traditionalists saw it differently.

This is a lesson for foreign manufacturers that feature hand-craftsmanship and traditional practices, to play up that point to the Chinese buyers, many of whom will appreciate the hand-made quality and pay a premium, despite the fact that a mass-produced item or knock-off is available at a fraction of the price in China. Luxury handbag manufacturers such as Louis Vuitton are not the only ones who can use this approach — anything from hand-crafted boats, clothing and foods such as chocolate and wines, have a big potential market among China's growing number of quality-discerning customers.

Going Global

China's manufacturers have started to invest overseas in a big way. For the first 20 years following the opening of the Chinese market in 1978, the capital flow was largely a one-way affair. FDI went in and, if you believe the pundits, not much came out except billions of machined and plastic-molded widgets. The Chinese companies were acting as OEMs manufacturing on contract for multinational companies. Much as Japanese companies started to expand abroad in the 1980s and 1990s, especially in the automotive industry as a way to be closer to their markets and avoid trade imbalance problems, Chinese companies are following suit. For example, the Chinese white goods manufacturer Haier, established just under 25 years ago in the port-city of Qingdao as a manufacturer of refrigerators, has more than two dozen facilities overseas in places as varied as Iran and Eastern Europe, and also in the US, where it makes the ubiquitous "beer fridges" popular with college students there. This is a trend that continues and creates opportunities for those seeking to work with Chinese companies in overseas territories as distributors, resellers or, increasingly, as employees. An employee at a Chinese company overseas needs to be culturally adaptable, able to make inroads in that country, and the best of all, be able to speak some Chinese in order to communicate with Chinese co-workers and the HQ. Chinese companies are paying top dollar for talent that can meet these conditions.

The Top Opportunities in Manufacturing

The manufacturing supertrends are *value-adding* and *innovating*. Doing sourcing or manufacturing in China is no longer about the low-cost mass-production paradigm, so the next phase of opportunities in this sector needs to follow the supertrends:

1. Chinese companies are upgrading their manufacturing facilities. This creates opportunities for expertise in areas such as health, safety and environment (HSE), Six Sigma, Total Quality Management, GAAP accounting standards, ISO 14001, and so on. Within China, both local and foreign manufacturers need people with all those skills, and foreign MNCs especially require people who understand local laws and government relationships, with the ability to articulate and package knowledge for head office consumption. Chinese manufacturers expanding abroad need more executives and managers who can operate in foreign environments *and* communicate with the head office in Chinese.

2. Chinese government planning and policy. The planned market economy takes the form of policy and directives that, if you are aware of them, can be used to chart your China strategy, but always remember that in China there is a big difference between announcement, regulation, and enforcement. The current policy in regards to manufacturing is multifold: High-tech, value-added, R&D-intensive companies will all find welcoming arms in China.

3. Globalization of China's economy from the inside outward is going to be a new driver of the Chinese economy, as Chinese brands and investments increasingly seek to move outside of their borders. Helping them achieve this goal by retailing, distributing, or otherwise supporting Chinese products is akin to being the Honda or Toyota dealers in the 1980s: Perhaps controversial in the short-term, but in the long-term very lucrative as Chinese products mature.

CHAPTER FIVE

Serving Me: Urbanizing and the Service Industry

城市化, 服务化 *Chengshi hua & Fuwu hua*

There is an oft-noted trend which demonstrates that developed countries shift their manufacturing industry off-shore and the service industry rises to take its place. In China's major cities, this is already starting to happen, except that factories are not pushed outside of the country: China is so large, and wants to keep the manufacturing industry at all costs, that the factories are simply pushed further away and encouraged to go to new development zones such as those now being established in the western provinces of China such as Sichuan.

The service industry in Shanghai and other major cities is therefore rising to take manufacturing's place and is booming. China's government has made it a goal to develop the service industry, attempting to move China from the world's factory to a balanced model with services being a larger portion of GDP than industry. This will clearly take some time on a countrywide basis, but the cities have already made some good progress. The trend of Urbanization will bring this goal closer to reality as tens of millions move into cities in the Olympic Decade.

Legal, Business, and People Management

The targets for service sector growth are in high-skill areas, such as legal, advisory and consulting, and people management. It is entirely possible to enter these sectors and serve only foreign clients, as there are so many and the demand for such services is high, but the successful Olympic Decade companies will be the ones that bridge to the domestic market.

Chinese law

Not long ago, China's legal system was often criticized, especially by foreign businesspeople trying to do business in China, for lack of lawyers, underqualified judges, vagueness in the wording of the laws (China's legal system is based on civil law such as that used in France or Japan, unlike the common law of the United States and United Kingdom), and even complete lack of laws in certain areas such as property ownership. When it came to foreign versus Chinese legal action, the Chinese judiciary was thought to be quite supportive of the home team, so to speak. Movies like *Red Corner* starring Richard Gere and Chinese actress Bai Ling reinforced this image among Westerners that China's legal system was tilted in favor of the Chinese, capricious, and undeveloped.

Some of these concerns were perhaps justified, as in 1987 fewer than 20 percent of judges had a university education, and in 1981 there were less than 10,000 lawyers for the whole country. But in less than two decades, 100 percent of judges had post-high school education and there were more than 100,000 lawyers in the Chinese legal association. Either there were a lot of judges going to night school, or the country replaced many of its judges at a rapid pace. Try doing that in a Western country. Also, the stereotype that China was a lawless country, ruled by the Communist Party with an iron hand, made Westerners apprehensive. Without a contract law, how could two parties protect themselves in a business arrangement? Without property laws, how could land be used as collateral for loans? Without labor laws, how could workers be protected from exploitation? In China, legal protection was often subservient to the protection granted from one's *guanxi*, the interconnections which keep the society glued together through mutually dependent relationships. So it is said that no two countries with a McDonald's have ever gone to war, in China no two people with an important connection between them will be fighting for long, as saving face or preventing loss of face is too important. Nevertheless, the lawlessness has been improving: China now has a set of contract laws, property laws* and, starting on January 1, 2008, the new labor law which gives many more rights to workers. In fact, China promulgated nearly 100,000 new laws in just four years between 2000 and 2004, and changes continue.

Finally, in a country that is attracting US$1.5 billion of foreign investment a day on average, there is a constant stream of new enterprises to be established, and millions of contracts to be negotiated and drafted, not to mention the almost inevitable lawsuits that might result. Lawyers, especially those capable of serving foreign businesspeople, will be in big demand in the next ten years.

People people everywhere, but nobody to hire

In 2007 China's turnover rates, the number of employees leaving voluntarily each year, reached as high as 23 percent in some industries, according to a leading Chinese job search website's survey.[1] It's a phenomenon on the increase, up from 15 percent in 2004. Even the manufacturing and service sectors are not immune, where the turnover rates were measured at 22 percent and 15 percent respectively.[2] If it is hard to imagine how to manage a company where 20 percent or more of your workers are replaced every year, you are not alone. Management for the most part is at a loss how to stem the tide.

There are three main reasons for the demand for workers being greater than the supply, especially in white-collar office jobs. First,

---

*Recent property laws even make clear the touchy point of land ownership in formerly Communist China where the people, represented by the government, collectively owned all the land. It has been settled in terms of land grants for 70 years, automatically renewable, though this law is new enough that no test of it has been yet made.

there is a limited pool of talented workers with English capability *and* experience in your particular industry. Second, many of the new office workers are young and restless, thus they look for new challenges, change, and opportunities. If they cannot find them in your company, they will not hesitate to look elsewhere. Finally, there are a lot of choices for workers at this point in China's economic development. Much like the dot-com era in the US when people from all industries could cross-over to new cities, new companies, and new positions, in China there are so many new companies looking for so many new employees that job-hopping is inevitable.

Chinese workers most often want higher pay, more development opportunities, training, and a good work environment. No surprises there. Yet companies, especially multinationals, that provide these still experience low employee loyalty and frequent resignations.

This continues a somewhat alarming trend of job-hopping with impunity. Younger Chinese stay at their jobs for less than two years in a majority of white-collar positions, according to the same survey. So if there are training and other opportunities, and multinationals pay well, why does the high turnover rate persist?

One reason is that many Chinese see foreign MNCs as a proving grounds but with a glass ceiling. So, their attitude may be, "Get in, get your training, and get out." Another reason is that geopolitical events may influence the desirability of working for a certain country's MNCs. For example, working for Japanese firms at the height of anti-Japan protests in 2005 was unpopular, while in 2008 French retail giant Carrefour suffered protests and boycotts after the Olympic Torch Relay protests in Paris. Finally, the employees at MNCs with their perceived better training and communications skills are frequent targets of head-hunters.

In order to keep up with China's 10 percent plus yearly growth, companies need to aggressively expand. With expansion comes the need to manage ever-larger numbers of people and more complex processes, and more management. And the best source for your new management talent? People already trained in other companies.

The head-hunting capital of the world

The large number of foreign companies, 610,000, that have set up in China, when added to the number of new Chinese companies, means there are huge numbers of opportunities for skilled workers. More recently, the trend is to set regional Asia (or these days, even world headquarters) in cities like Shanghai requiring white-collar staff, and establishing global R&D centers near or outside the cities and requiring technical staff and engineers. Also, as China globalizes outwards, firms such as Haier are continually expanding abroad, so they need more people, too. This creates at present one of the most active employment markets in the world, and it also attracts a lot of head-hunting.

Turnover among people with just two to three years of experience is highest, topping 35 percent among this group. This is the sweet spot for training companies, search firms, and employment agencies. When China's entry into the WTO at last made entry into the service sector possible, some of the first entrants were the global search firms such as Korn/Ferry.[3] Yet as many of these companies will relate, finding good candidates for mid- and top-management positions is quite difficult. While poaching employees from other companies is practiced around the world, *guanxi*-rich Chinese society is something akin to an open market, where friends actively introduce friends to new jobs (sometimes hoping to get a cut of the commission or a free dinner for helping find the new job).

Chinese companies have also stepped in to fill this need. Websites such as 51job.com have become as large as their American counterparts such as Monster.com, and also feature a NASDAQ listing.

Won't you please stay with me?

In 2008, salaries are expected to go up, with many employees wanting new market rates to be offered immediately as they change rather than waiting for a yearly or even quarterly review. Otherwise there's any number of companies they could switch to.

And it usually will be an immediate resignation if this happens, as Chinese workers often give little or zero notice. Stories of a foreign manager coming into work and finding the entire sales team or management of the company gone *en masse* are still very common.

With such rapid appreciation of wages, inflation is becoming ever more common, especially in restaurants and stores that cater to the white-collar population. A latte in Starbucks in Shanghai is just as expensive as in the US.

Keeping Chinese staff, then, involves providing them with a competitive salary, but more importantly, training to keep them motivated. What happens when you run out of training to offer? Promotions. Lots and lots of promotions. Some managers reorganize their international-standard organization chart just to accommodate these types of people. In New York, everyone is a VP. In Shanghai, everyone is a manager. Don't be surprised if the rather young and inexperienced salesperson you've just met is a director, manager or a team leader; title is everything but actually means very little in these "departments of one."

Hot job sectors

Manufacturing and retail were the two hottest job sectors in Shanghai in 2007, but positions in manufacturing outnumbered retail and wholesale positions by a ratio of approximately nine to one, showing that much of the Chinese economy will remain focused on manufacturing despite growth in the retail, IT, and other service industries.

Competition with the West for talent

Globalization is a double-edged sword for many economies. As manufacturers move around the world exploiting the cheapest labor, the best labor moves around the world more freely to where the jobs are. China is becoming a magnet for talented people across all industries. Those who want to be on the leading edge, work with the newest equipment, have ample capital to develop new ideas and be rewarded for them, or gain new experience in the world's fastest-growing major economy, are heading to China.

The US, UK, Japan and other markets are in no short-term danger of a massive brain drain similar to what India experienced in the years of the dot-com bubble. Rather, the flow is still so gentle that it could be navigated by turtles, sea turtles to be precise.

Haigui, the Chinese word for the migratory sea turtles known for returning to the place of their birth, has a more modern meaning in China: Chinese educated overseas who are coming home. The *haigui* phenomenon started in a big way after the dot-com bubble burst, when two trends combined to make China more attractive to its people abroad: The lack of jobs, especially in technology areas, in the United States; and the growing number of opportunities in China as the economy ramped up its pace of development in high-tech. The opportunities back home seemed simply too good to pass up.

Still, putting the *haigui* phenomenon into perspective, for every one person that comes back as a sea turtle, there are a handful who never return, choosing instead to stay in places such as *Meiguo* — beautiful country — the Mandarin word for the US, and then there's another handful in China whose goal is to leave. They currently go to countries such as Australia and Canada that have China-friendly immigration policies and large unassimilated Chinese communities, or to the US to chase the American dream.

Not content to accept the brain drain, China is doing its best to stem the tide carrying away its citizens, by encouraging them to come home with preferential policies such as treasured spots for children at top universities. Another key initiative is supporting their businesses when they return. Part of Shanghai's booming Zhangjiang High-Technology Park, the "Pioneering Park for Overseas Returnees," has incubated more than 570 high-tech startups with more than 5,700 turtles participating. By providing these overseas-educated (90 percent with Masters and Doctorates) and multinational-corporation experienced people with support, the program has successfully fostered many multi-million dollar companies in the six years it has been operating so far.

Two Sea Turtle Success Stories

One famous sea turtle is Robin Li, a computer technologist who grew up in China and went to the US for doctoral studies. While in the US, he contributed key ideas through his research to a number of dot-coms, but he didn't make it really big until he returned to China in 1999 and started Baidu.com. Baidu is the major search engine provider in China. With almost 60 percent market share in the country, Baidu is ahead of rival and global leader Google, and it is one of the best performing stocks on the NASDAQ in recent years. Only time will tell if Baidu can become a global rival rather than a regional player, but for now in China, Baidu is the only serious way to reach Chinese Internet surfers through a search engine.

Li Ge, originally from China with a Bachelor degree in chemistry from prestigious Peking University, went to the US and attained a PhD from Columbia University in organic chemistry. He was one of the founding team of US-based and NASDAQ-listed Pharmacopeia, where he worked for eight years before returning to China to start WuXi PharmaTech. WuXi PharmaTech has become one of Asia's most successful pharmaceutical research and manufacturing companies, now handling outsourced work from nine of the world's top ten drug manufacturers. In 2007, it went public on the NYSE after just seven years in business.[4]

Does the loss of people such as Robin Li and Li Ge make a difference to the US economy, which in effect subsidized their education and gave them key opportunities to develop working inside American companies, and then access to American capital markets to boot? If this pattern continues, it definitely will.

Brand and Image

The retail industry grew 16.8 percent in China in 2007, to US$1.4 trillion, boosted by people's rising incomes.

In China, the retail brand-owned store is dominant in certain industries, for example, sports apparel from companies like Nike and Adidas. In the run-up to the Olympics, Adidas is opening an average of two stores a day in China. In a brand-store environment, the choice of the Chinese translation of the foreign brand name is especially important.

When a foreign company comes to China, or when a Chinese company goes abroad, the decision to translate the brand name is always a difficult one. However, the trend for the Olympic Decade is localization, thus Dell is out, *Dai'er* (sounding a little like Chinese white goods manufacturer Hai'er) is in, Nike is *Nai'ke*, and so on. Doing business in China needs a good Chinese name. The proper way to do it is not just sounding out the word in Chinese, but also to choose appropriate characters that lend the name an air of sophistication, whimsiness, or seriousness, depending on the brand image desired.

A company has to be careful, however, in how it picks a name. In 2006 Google decided it was time to go local (some speculated it was either to curry favor with the Chinese government and avoid being blocked by the Great Firewall of China as sites such as Wikipedia have been, or to try to satisfy the Netizens with a Chinese name and appearance) by renaming itself in China as *Gu'ge*, Valley Song, as it might be literally back-translated into English. This name might be a little too whimsical and traditional for the world's biggest search engine, and it has nothing really to do with the original Google "really big number" meaning, which actually upset a great number of Netizens in China, some of whom proposed calling it *Gou'gou* — Doggy, instead. Whether meant to invoke cuteness or scorn as a "running dog capitalist" is not known, but clearly a company must take care to pick its brand name and promote it carefully to avoid just such a fate.

This problem works both ways. Chinese brands face the same trouble when going abroad. *Quan'ju'de Kaoya* is probably unknown to anybody who doesn't speak Mandarin, but if one knew it was Quan'Ju'de' Roast Duck — since 1864, as the official English name of China's biggest Peking Duck restaurant chain has become — one would have a better idea of what it sold, but the name doesn't exactly roll off the tongue like "Burger King" or "Pizza Hut."

This seems to be a great opportunity for marketing and brand services targeted at Chinese companies, for example, helping them to rebrand their identity for sales in foreign markets. In preparation for the Beijing Olympics, poor English has become the target of language watchdogs, correcting such embarrassing menu items such as *chao'mian*, which many Westerners will be familiar with as Chow Mein noodles, but in literal Chinese characters means *fried face* and on some menus for foreigners was actually written that way.

While the world's big advertising players are already in China, there is still a huge opportunity for smaller companies and people involved in branding, brand management, copyrighting, technical writing, translation and public relations to get into the growing market for international services in China.

China's Evolving Service Industry

In the 1980s, if you wanted to buy beef from the butcher at a typical market in China, the owner of the place would likely use a hacksaw to cut off a slab of meat entangled with fat and bones from a side of beef. It was also a rarity to find fresh fish, shrimp and pork at the local market, and supermarkets hadn't become common at that time. Mini-marts like the Friendship Store started to appear in Shanghai, Guangzhou and Beijing to serve foreigners in the mid-1990s, but it was still common for foreign wives to go to the Ritz-Carlton or Hilton Hotels directly to buy quality meat for their families.

(Continued)

Now, in Carrefour and at fashionable restaurants throughout the country's increasingly metropolitan cities, you can buy Kobe beef, Australian beef, and even Chicago-style steaks at Shanghai's Moon's Steakhouse.

In the 1980s, only restaurants at the global hotel chains served food to an international standard, such as at the Beijing Sheraton, where you could find many a foreign businessman with a paperback book eating a lonely meal and trying to strike up a conversation with the not-so-interested waitresses. Or, if you preferred some local fare, you could venture out into the streets and perhaps find a *jiaozi* (dumpling) canteen that served your meal by the half-kilogram on a steel tray.

Now, you can dine at restaurants opened by the most famous of the global chefs, including Jean Georges. At these restaurants, especially the most expensive, the clientele today are much more likely to be local Chinese and buying much more expensive meals than foreign diners, a change from when they first opened.

China has changed so much since the 1980s we could fill a book with reminiscences and stories, but what we really want to tell you is about where the direction is going from here: As incomes and lifestyle choices increase, consumers in China will demand more selection in where and what to eat.

If Only Every China Netizen Bought One Shirt Online...

The so-called China Dream is selling a pack of gum to every person in China or, in the words of 19th century British merchants, "If we could only persuade every person in China to lengthen his shirt-tail by a foot, we could keep the mills of Lancashire working round the clock." This idea of selling some universally-accepted and mass-produced product was a persistent theme in early business writings on China, and may still convince the occasional entrepreneur to head for the PRC, but of late it has been debunked so many times that the

act of debunking has itself become a cliché. But a small company
started in 2005 named PPG may actually have a shot of finally realizing the English merchants' 200-year-old dream.

Invested in by Silicon Valley veteran venture capitalists Kleiner
Perkins Caufield & Byers, and owning no factory of its own,
Shanghai's PPG sells 10,000 shirts a day, three million shirts a
year to China's 220 million Netizens. It has successfully used the
mass customization concept Dell Computers is most famous for to
custom-design, manufacture, and deliver shirts without, practically
speaking, ever touching the merchandise as inventory. Its success
has spawned dozens of competitors.[5] The competitive pressure is so
great that promotion costs reached US$28 million in 2007, recalling
the dot-com mania of the late 1990s when companies would spend
huge amounts on advertising to gain market share.[6]

Altogether, Business-to-Consumer (B2C) companies in China are
selling, based on a 2007 estimate of 182 million Netizens, about US$4
per year each on average on goods bought online. This is up greatly
from 2002, when China's users were spending less than US$150
million online. Showing its affluence, Shanghai's 5.2 million online
users bought about US$1 billion in purchases online, and nationally
consumers spent about US$8.5 billion in 2007, much of this being
Consumer-to-Consumer (C2C) auction purchases.[7] According to
research, people were buying a lot of digital products such as mobile
phones, digital cameras, and laptop computers, and female clothing,
makeup, and jewelry were also popular. Nationwide, C2C auctions
and related business models will grow to about US$9 billion in 2008,
growing about 65 percent from 2007's US$5.7 billion, which had
itself increased by more than 90 percent from 2006, according to one
survey of China's Internet users. Clearly, China's C2C business is
growing quickly.[8]

A measure of online spending in the B2C sector, and which
includes the fees users paid for Internet access, online games, and
other online services, indicated China's 182 million users spent a
more reasonable US$54 billion altogether, or about US$25 per month
on average, in 2007. In 2008, China's Internet users will surpass those

in the United States (with about 221 million users[9]). China's low user penetration rate, only about 13.8 percent in 2007, has far more growth left before slowing down. The US, with a penetration rate of about 71 percent, is growing much more slowly in comparison. It is predicted by the Internet Society of China that total users will top 244 million in China by the end of 2008 and will spend more than US$77 billion in online fees and purchases, a growth rate of 34 percent.[10]

The e-Commerce market in China grew about 30 percent in 2007, with projections for sales growth continuing at 30 percent plus per year. The market will quickly become a significant size and be able to develop industry leaders that will begin the process of consolidation, but as of 2008, it is like 1999 in the US all over again with everyone opening up their own web business and people flocking online to try the latest products by online order or e-enabled service.

Clearly, this is a good time to get into e-Business in China. The market is wide open and many foreign businesspeople have already arrived to establish their own startup business. With extremely low costs of doing business in China, albeit with some restrictions on Internet business models (e.g., no porn allowed), this is the easiest sector for young entrepreneurs to get into.

International purchasing by Chinese

In a country where credit cards were just introduced ten years before, and where it is rare to return purchased goods to merchandisers, it's difficult to see how Internet sales can get popular so quickly, but the Chinese are adaptable and always looking for a way to save time or money. So, e-Commerce purchases to offshore locations are up as much as 25 percent a month. Busy and fast-paced lifestyles in the urban areas for young professionals and a 15 percent appreciation of the RMB versus the US dollar in a short period of time combine to drive overseas Internet purchases up. As the RMB continues to appreciate, look for online bargain shoppers to purchase from overseas destinations, and it's a good time to consider creating a Chinese version of your company's e-Commerce website. If your products are already made in China, think of the potential for drop-shipping inside China as a way to save costs for the Chinese consumers. Pricing in local currency negates the benefits for Chinese consumers and your business would not be able to bill in RMB anyway because of currency controls, so keep prices in US dollars. ← This will become more prevelant since China has allowed RMB to float again.

The Great Malls of China

In shopping-crazed China, where consumption is becoming the most important driver of the economy, it is only appropriate that it also has the world's largest shopping malls.

In fact, in several lists of global mall sizes, malls in China number four of the world's top fifteen. The largest of them all, the South China Mall, is located in Dongguan, the booming manufacturing city of Guangzhou, and also ranks in the world's top ten largest buildings.

These mega-malls of China are overbuilt with expansion in mind, being able to hold 1,000 or more shops.

The South China Mall has room for 1,500 shops, not to mention the usual facilities such as ice rink, movie theaters, indoor and outdoor amusement park, gym, hotels, and so on. It also has more unusual theme areas, each made to look like a certain region around the world: rainforest, Venice, San Francisco, Caribbean, etc. In 2008, it had yet to achieve full usage due to its location, somewhat far from the city center of Dongguan, but it will undoubtedly pick up speed as the region's consumers become more affluent and buy more cars.[11]

Sinofication

Kentucky Fried Chicken (KFC) is big in China. It now has more than 1,200 outlets and expands about 200 outlets per year. Some say it is China's love of chicken that has helped it to soundly defeat McDonald's. Another theory points to KFC's willingness to Sinofy (become more Chinese) in taste, appearance, and style.

Almost from the start of its entry into mainland China, it tried to make its facilities and menu more acceptable to Chinese diners. Where KFC was willing to localize, McDonald's stayed with its tried and tested menu and processes. KFC is now the undisputed fast-food leader in the mainland.[12]

While standardization is the watchword of fast-food businesses, when KFC first entered Hong Kong in the 1970s, its stand-up take-out model and no-utensil finger-licking goodness was culturally odd to the refined Hong Kongese, who wanted to sit down and eat with Western utensils or at least chopsticks. When KFC made its debut in mainland China in 1987 with its groundbreaking location in front of Tiananmen Square, it included a large seating area. Later, it even changed the decoration style to be more acceptable to the Chinese patrons and introduced new menu items such as the Old Beijing Chicken Wrap, which was reminiscent of the taste of Peking Duck and became an instant hit.

While Western diners at KFC in China will still recognize familiar favorites such as the KFC Bucket, there's no buttermilk biscuits, and there are an equal number of Chinese items they've never tasted: Egg tarts, rice congee, egg and mushroom soup, even *fried bread sticks*, a dish normally sold on the streets of China as a popular and cheap breakfast item to be eaten with hot soy milk or, if you live in southern China, together with rice congee. Even KFC's secret blend of 11 herbs and spices was changed to a special flavor intended to be more appealing to the masses outside of the cities that had never eaten at KFC. They will get the chance in the coming expansion of the chain across China. It is this willingness to adapt to the Chinese tastes that makes KFC enormously popular among the Chinese and that, combined with its headstart in China over McDonald's, will make it hard to beat going forward.[†]

[†]KFC outlets outnumber McDonald's outlets about two to one, with KFC having 1,800 outlets at the end of 2006 and more than 2,000 outlets at the start of 2008. Though far behind its rival and suffering from a beef-heavy menu not as popular as chicken, McDonald's will add 125–150 new restaurants a year, building on its Olympic sponsorship to expand more quickly.

Yum! Brands, the corporate parent of KFC, Pizza Hut (there are 250 Pizza Hut outlets in China already) and Taco Bell, may have pushed the Shanghainese a little too far in offering Taco Bell as there is virtually no presence of Mexican food in the city (and a historical lack of immigrants from Mexico), unlike other Asian or global cuisines that have been successfully introduced to the epicurious Chinese. In 2007, Yum! China closed its Shanghai Taco Bell outlet, one of three on mainland China, and replaced it with what may be a symbolically named sign of the times: A completely localized brand made especially for the Chinese market, a restaurant called East Dawning, serving Chinese food.

Westernization

The opposite trend of Sinofication is Westernization, where foreign brands play up their Western origins so that they draw in the consumer who is seeking a status symbol or aspirational purchase. It also covers Chinese companies that adopt a Western look (sometimes copying a Western brand in the process) in order to gain a price premium for what consumers perceive to be foreign goods.

Few can doubt the preeminence of global multinationals when they can convince a country famous for its tea to embrace Starbucks, persuade a people with no fewer than seven distinctive (and delicious) cuisines — *Sichuan, Cantonese* and so on — to consume massive quantities of hamburgers and pizzas, or motivate the makers of a vast majority of the world's clothes to covet wearing foreign-designed fashions from CK, Armani, and Japanese clothing retailer Uniqlo. From bicycles to cars, lane-houses to high-rises, myna birds to miniature pinschers, Mandarins to MBAs, China is Westernizing at an incredible pace. While this undoubtedly upsets the old guards and more traditionally minded of the populace, China's city dwellers at least are embracing an Internationalization trend wholeheartedly, which is good news for companies that have a distinctive place of origin to play up.

Top Opportunities in Services

Services will start to grow faster than industry in the Olympic Decade, especially in the major cities where it is happening already. To be prepared, you should be looking at these opportunities:

1. Professional services such as accounting, legal, consulting, human resources, marketing and brand management.
2. Increasing amounts of retail sales, both in-store and online.
3. Sinofication — creating products to appeal to Chinese consumers.
4. Westernization — keeping a Western brand to appeal to foreign-brand-seeking strivers, or creating a new brand inside China that looks foreign.

Chinese consumers are demanding higher levels of service. Companies that provide it are going to be winners in this growing marketplace.

PART THREE

THE SOCIAL SUPERTRENDS

～社会趋势～

CHAPTER SIX

Health, Education, and Leisure: Enjoying Life as a Market of One

消费化, 抱负化　*Xiaofei hua & Baofu hua*

China's people are healthier, wealthier, and happier than ever before. To continue this growing prosperity, the primary policy tool for China is to realign the economy from investment-driven to consumption-driven through increasing people's incomes. As we saw in the previous chapter, labor rates have been increasing steadily and will continue to do so with the effects of China's new labor law giving more benefits to employees. Thanks to additional reductions in taxes for China's poorest, these policies have begun to bear fruit. Retail spending was up strongly in 2007, further evidence that Chinese consumers have more disposable income and are spending it, not only to buy small commodities but also big-ticket items like cars and houses.[1]

This chapter builds on those ideas but focuses on the new lifestyle supertrends — consumption and aspiration. China's newest opportunities may be found in its changing cultural landscape. Due to the sheer sizes of its population and markets, every demographic trend, every new fad, every market need is multiplied tenfold of even the biggest Western markets, making even microtrends (where just one percent of the population participate) important business opportunities.

As Chinese consumers have more money, they spend more on looking after their health, education, and leisure activities such as travel. What's more, they demand unique experiences tailored to their specific needs. It is the opposite of the old Communist one-size-and-style-fits-all blue Mao cap and jacket. Now, people want tailored and monogrammed shirts, tattoos and, even in ultra-conservative China, dyed hair. They are looking for adventure travel, no longer just traveling in groups, and have the money to spend for premium experiences. In short, they are the largest group of potential customers with the fastest-growing income that you've never thought of before.

Health

China's wellness revolution

In less developed provinces of China, where a youth's only choice may be working in the fields or going to the city to work, increasing numbers of the country's young are choosing the city, leaving behind agricultural jobs for manufacturing work, and, an after-effect, leaving behind aging parents to fend for themselves. Even in tradition-conscious China, there is no way to avoid economic reality and parents often insist their children go off to seek a better life in the city. Such is the plotline of *A Sunny Day*, a new serialized drama co-produced by Starbucks in China, about a white-collar migrant worker and the challenges she faces in adapting to life in the city alone and with people depending on her at home.[2]

When the countryside is depleted of its children, the elderly often become reliant on money sent back from the cities. For some, this will mean a new and better life with a new house. For others, it will mean a full-time maid (often a migrant worker from an even less developed region) to replace the son's or daughter's care. For still more, it can mean poverty and loneliness. A somewhat typical province, Sha'anxi, has 3.75 million people over the age of 60. In a country where it is presumed the young will look after the old, there is a lack of government support for the elderly, a lack of taxpayer funds, and a lack of social work and healthcare professionals who are capable of filling roles in the eldercare industry. Few elderly want to live in nursing homes, making the demand for in-home care quite high.

Senior care opportunities

China's elderly need care and medical services. The shortage of ambulances in places like Shanghai is bad enough that private operators, outfitting regular vans to look and be equipped (more or less) like real ambulances, have been illegally picking people up after distributing their business cards around. The city, in response, will put an additional 500 ambulances into service by 2010. This is just the start of the medical services market for elderly people: Medical equipment for home use, in-home nursing and elder care, medical alert services, diet planning, special meals and meal delivery services should all be in greater demand. The problem of undernourished elderly is so bad that Shanghai built more than a dozen public cafeterias for old people in 2007 providing subsidized healthy meals.

Many Chinese parents will never accept being put into a nursing home, and adults with older parents still remember filial piety and respect for one's elders that includes caring for them at home. But with older people extending life through modern medical care, the burden on the next generation of one-child-family children to look after both parents, or four people in the case of a married couple, will be great. So it is likely that a senior care business model will become increasingly accepted as it has in Japan's similarly respectful-of-the-aged society. Robots looking after one's parents *à la* the latest Japanese home care trends are another matter entirely.

Need a massage? Health and relaxation industries

Cases of work-related stress, chronic fatigue syndrome, lack of exercise, and obesity and concomitant problems such as diabetes are all on the rise in China, especially among white-collar office workers who often work overtime across all industries. It may be unlikely to see a repeat of the Japanese phenomenon of *karoshi*, death by overwork, that was common during Japan's bubble economy years in the 1980s where loyal salarymen would literally work themselves to death for the company. Unlike the Japanese of the 1980s who were part of a lifetime employment system, modern Chinese workers are able to job-hop if they don't see enough value in a company that consistently overworks them without adequate compensation, when they have so many choices elsewhere. Nevertheless, there are cases of unexplained death or suicide among younger workers in China that are being attributed to *karoshi*-like work habits: Long hours, little sleep, lack of exercise, poor diet. In May 2006, a 25-year-old software engineer working at Huawei Technologies passed away from what the hospital said was bacterial encephalitis, but the investigation that followed showed the underlying cause was likely to be the extreme overwork he had been engaging in, following Huawei's "wolf culture" of competitive behavior, up or out evaluations, and aggressive work habits.[3] For nearly a month, Hu Xinyu had been working excessive hours with no time off, making him susceptible to illness which eventually caused his death.[4]

His untimely passing brought new visibility to the problem in China, which is widespread among younger white-collar workers performing unpaid overtime. Trying to alleviate the problem, the new Labor Law enacted on January 1, 2008 specified more rules for better treatment of workers.

Everyone has to work overtime sometimes, and in a booming economy such as China, it is hard to avoid. The opportunity here is then to serve these people with products and services that make their lives easier, less stressful, and healthier.

One sector of the economy that is booming in expat-heavy cities like Beijing and Shanghai is the spa and relaxation business. With the wage differential between the urban and rural areas, migrant worker masseuses and masseurs live and work in the big cities where their skills are more highly valued, especially by the relaxation-loving expatriate community which never seems to tire of US$10 massages. This rate is for a typically Asian style of acupressure massage, but a European-style oil massage can be purchased for as low as US$20, and a high-end day spa experience comparable to any luxury service abroad may cost as little as US$100–$200. The industry in Shanghai has exploded, with one chain being so successful that it is even attempting an initial public offering.[5]

The spa business in China has several tiers. At the lowest level are two kinds — mini-aesthetic salons for women and massage for men. The salons offer basic care such as manicures, facial treatments, and cosmetics sales, and may be part of a franchise. The massage establishments are mostly for men and they are usually undeco-rated functional group rooms with some basic chairs or couches and simple services such as washing one's feet, foot massage, and basic pedicures. Both business models target China's working-class with bottom-end prices to match, and you may find these businesses everywhere, practically one or two on every city block and resi-dential community.

At the mid-tier are spas and salons modeled on Western con-ception of relaxation: Soft lighting, music, professional service and private rooms, offering a wider array of services including facials, aromatherapy, and other services requiring more training of the staff. They may be part of a small chain but not a franchise, and cater to the well-off locals and the value-seeking of the expat community that are looking for a comfortable and clean environment at a rea-sonable price.

At the top tier are international spa chains, franchised interna-tionally or wholly-owned by the parent company, that cater to the wealthy locals or expats on full benefits packages, with international prices and facilities to match.

With the ranks of China's white-collar workers expanding quickly, they are the next target market for this industry and they badly need a place of their own, suitable for Chinese tastes, that is somewhere in between the lower and middle tiers: Professional, clean, and comfortable, but not too expensive. The company that gets this formula right and can franchise or expand it quickly will be very successful.

Yummy: China's vitamins and organic foods

It is an interesting fact that China is both the world's largest producer of vitamins and organic foods, despite its current image as a somewhat polluted country with poor quality controls.[6]

Vitamins started to be produced in China in the 1990s as products ideally suited to mass production, with simple formulations and basic packaging. The domestic market for both human and animal consumption was large as well, so it was thought to be a natural fit for the Chinese business environment.

The biggest boon to China's vitamin industry was when a vitamin price-fixing scandal broke in the US, when global vitamin producers from Europe and Japan were found to be colluding on price and were sued under anti-trust laws. Weakened by the lawsuits, many of these producers were forced to adopt cost-cutting measures and consequently those that could not regain profitability soon withdrew from the market, leaving the Chinese producers in a very favorable position. The Chinese producers themselves were accused of price manipulation in order to undercut prices in the US. Playing on economies of scale, the Chinese vitamin producers quickly dominated the market and today, for some types of vitamins, control in excess of 90 percent of the market.[7]

Despite the increasing demand for vitamins worldwide, they have had a slow acceptance rate among Chinese consumers for several reasons. First, there is a preference for traditional Chinese medicine (TCM) and its natural herbal concoctions for promoting balance of *yin* and *yang*. Also, a number of quality control scandals within China, years before the 2007 tainted food and medicine problems of Chinese producers abroad were in the spotlight, made Chinese consumers distrusting of their own products and brands. In today's Chinese drug stores, it is the foreign brands such as Centrum or Jamieson Vitamins which are considered to be safer. However, they are often too expensive for the general population but recently have caught on with white-collar workers and the affluent, who are looking to maintain and improve health.

This is the opportunity that these brands have already keyed into: Chinese white-collar and well-off consumers will pay extra for premium foreign-branded health products merely because of the perception of safety. A second aspect which is a great opportunity for Western business practices is the way vitamins are sold.

In China, vitamins are sold in the drugstore by people who look like pharmacists but act like commissioned sales people (which, in fact, they usually are). So buyers beware: Go in for Vitamin D, you might end up with a recommendation to buy this brand over that one because "this is better" and walk out with a bottle of Vitamin E pushed on you relentlessly because it is on sale. General Nutrition Center (GNC) and other nutrition centers have yet to find the right niche to reach the new multitudes at the health clubs, but are finding a ready market among stressed out white-collar workers looking to score some health-enhancing Co-Enzyme Q10 or parents trying to give their children that extra DHA-fortified cod-liver oil edge in school. By providing Chinese consumers with a low-pressure, informative context in which to buy health-food supplements such as vitamins, protein powders and the like, more sales are bound to follow.

Health supplements, such as protein and carbohydrate powders, have been introduced into the market, but Chinese are somewhat reluctant to start ingesting muscle-building protein (muscular men are shunned in favor of "girly-man" thinness, and carb powders just don't make sense in a country where the diet is mostly carbs to begin with). This problem of consumer acceptance will undoubtedly change as it has in Hong Kong and Taiwan already, where health supplements are extremely popular.

Innovating the marketing methods and sales channels to reach the consumer are the prime opportunities when it comes to health supplements. Demonstrating that it is the system more than the products that is important in the vitamin industry, the biggest winner of non-drugstore vitamin sales is Amway. The one-on-one sales model with testimonials from your satisfied friend/Amway dealer has been very successful in getting more Chinese to take vitamins.

Health and organic foods

Three subtrends are apparent from the lifestyle supertrends in regard to healthy eating: There are the beginnings of a healthy eating trend in the cities, fad diets are more popular now, and Chinese production of organic foods is increasing.

Although Chinese food is one of the most varied and delicious cuisines in the world, one must be careful not to eat too many fried or oily foods. The standard fare of everyday cafeterias and home-cooked meals is actually quite healthy, despite the impression one might get from eating Chinese food abroad, but young people in China are especially conscious of their diet. Women and men both watch their weight fastidiously, some try to cut down on eating white rice, while others avoid fatty pork and other popular foods.

In China's larger cities, a new trend of healthy food restaurants is becoming apparent as an alternative to either Chinese fare or other Western cuisines such as Italian, also popular, but not especially suitable for those health-conscious consumers. Formerly sparsely patronized and at that only by expats, a number of small healthy eateries in Shanghai and Beijing have been expanding rapidly. Offering more expensive yet healthier Westernized choices (sometimes Western-influenced Asian foods, a new kind of fusion cuisine) with fresh ingredients, typically including fresh juices that might be found in any Western juice bar, these restaurants initially had to overcome a number of barriers to get out of the short-term and unreliable model of serving expats. First, the cost of their fresh ingredients and locations serving Western expat diners meant their prices were out of reach of locals. Second, in China, uncooked vegetables are a cultural no-no, so the salads and vegetarian dishes that are so popular abroad had much difficulty being accepted in the local market. Finally, cold foods such as sandwiches are not common or popular in traditional Chinese cuisine.

For the last several years, a number of these restaurants survived by serving an eager population of salad-starved energy-depleted Westerners until recently, when young Chinese white-collar workers had more income and started to think about their eating habits due to long and stressful work schedules. Consequently, these former expat hangouts have become the new dining trend of China's newly affluent working-class. With so much new demand, several of these restaurants have expanded into chains in just the last two years, with much room in the market, especially in second tier cities such as Hangzhou or Dalian, to grow. Vegetarian and vegan cuisine restaurants are still few and far in between despite the large number of Buddhists in China, and while some Chinese food is vegetarian, it is usually full of oils to "add flavor" and not really suitable for eating on a daily basis. Thus, healthy-eating Western restaurants can capture this growing market as well. Western restaurateurs, chefs, interior designers and food suppliers who understand this model are in high demand in China during the Olympic Decade. Even the Olympic Village has forsaken much traditional Chinese food and serves popular Westernized dishes, sure to be picked up by Beijingers in the post-Olympics economy.[8]

A related trend to the healthy eating lifestyle is dieting. Virtually every young woman claims to be "on a diet," while for Chinese men, thin is in. However, diet methods are typically just reduced eating rather than the diet systems popular in North America. To an extent, cities such as Shanghai and Hong Kong have picked up on Western diet plans such as South Beach, but because the local cuisines are so different from the Western base that the trendy diets are built on, it is almost impossible to stick to them. In the less internationalized cities of mainland China, it is hard to even follow the basics. Want to eat a healthy baked potato? First, Chinese homes don't usually have ovens. Second, they don't buy and eat American-style potatoes, only large red or sweet potatoes which are usually sold by street vendors cooking them in converted oil drums. A skinless chicken breast? Most Chinese people buy meat from wet markets, head and feet still attached — forget about the skin. In short, it is extremely difficult to watch one's diet following Western diet principles, so there is a huge potential industry for either Chinese-specific diet plans or prepared food alternatives to serve this huge market. Switzerland's Marie France Bodyline diet centers are currently making inroads into mainland China by hiring Vicki Zhao, one of China's most popular actresses, to be their spokesperson.[9]

For younger men, eschewing the Western male body image of muscularity equals masculinity, thin bodies and longish hair with a boyish or metrosexual look are definitely popular. Taiwanese and Korean boybands or the popular *My Hero* TV show (where men competed in arts, looks, and personality to be the ideal guy) are powerful media influences driving this trend.[10]

Finally, one does not often think of organic foods as synonymous with China, but the reality is that many foods are easy to produce organically in China because there is little agricultural mass production, farm labor is cheap, and fewer pesticides, herbicides and fertilizers are used because they are too expensive for small-plot farmers to purchase. The traditional growing methods of the ingredients of TCM are accepted and expected. For these reasons, it is relatively easy to outsource production of organic products to China, or introduce organic farming practices with just some minor alterations to the traditional Chinese production methods. So, in addition to supplying the growing local market with healthier foods, China can also become a production base for many organic products, especially grains.

One example of how China is going back to its roots, so to speak, is the practice of organic rice farming. In some rice paddies in China, ducks are used to weed and aerate the shoots, frogs are used to eat flying pests, and fish are introduced to kill larvae and common plant bacteria.[11] These techniques have been used for hundreds of years in China and are only now being reintroduced to satisfy growing demand for organic crops.

Leisure

Gold-medal sports enthusiasm

The biggest driver of health and exercise in 2008 is probably still badminton or ping-pong, perhaps even *tai chi*, but the Olympics in Beijing is undoubtedly playing a part in broadening people's conscientiousness towards sports and well-being. Higher incomes in the cities are also playing a part, following the well-known correlation between income and spending on health and wellness services and products. And it doesn't hurt that China is now the *de facto* manufacturer of all the world's sports equipment.

Chinese people idolize their sports superstars, especially those who have made it big abroad: Yao Ming of the Houston Rockets is king of this hill, but if you haven't heard of Liu Xiang, China's gold-medal men's hurdler, or Guo Jingjing, China's multi-gold-medal-winning women's diving *phoneme*, come the 2008 Olympics you surely will. These athletes are among the first in China idolized not just for their sports prowess, but sometimes even more for their high salaries, media savvy, endorsements, and gossip-column relationships. What has resulted from this amazing confluence of sports trends?

Gyms are popping up everywhere. The US chain 24 Hour Fitness Worldwide has partnered with Yao Ming to create the eponymous California Fitness – Yao Ming Sport Club. It expects up to eight new centers in China in the next two years, but it will have stiff competition from homegrown Will's Gym with eight branches in Shanghai alone, most of them built within the last three years, not to mention well-established chains such as Physical, Total Fitness, and other foreign entrants such as Australia's MOB.[12]

When it comes to Yao's popularity in China, it doesn't hurt that the NBA itself sees the country as a huge new market and has pushed telecasts of games, added three new Chinese players to the league and, in 2008, announced the formation of NBA China — co-invested by ESPN and Hong Kong *uber*-investor Li Ka-Shing's foundation, among others — to promote the sport further. Still, there is the worry that China is becoming a nation of couch potatoes, watching more fake DVDs, IPTV, and sports online rather than actually getting outside and doing something.

Obesity is actually becoming quite a problem in China as the country prospers and the new wealth leads people to ingest more expensive meats and fatty foods, and acquire a taste for Western imported foods such as potato-based snacks that are more expensive (and often less healthy) than traditional rice-based snacks. Among white-collar workers, they have started to eat less balanced meals and more fast foods, in an effort to save time and money in their harried lives. According to the Chinese Ministry of Health, obese people top 60 million in China, nearly twice the entire population of Canada. Diabetes is estimated at about 20 million cases, and 160 million people have high blood pressure, up from 90 million 15 years ago. While many of these problems can be addressed by medical intervention, there are growing opportunities in lifestyle changes such as eating healthier foods both at home and at health-conscious restaurants, going to the gym and exercising more, and taking over-the-counter supplements appropriately, that often can reduce the size of the problem significantly. This is why the Chinese government is using these sports superstars and the Olympics to energize people and get them exercising more.

Stretch yourself

Yoga has taken China's white-collar women to new heights of slimness and flexibility. One of Madonna's famous *yogis* even came to Shanghai to open a center. Indeed, if you are lucky enough to find a place in a yoga class, you're likely to be surrounded by people who have just entered the sport, many that very day. Gyms have always made their money on churning of memberships that most people will use a few times and then give up. In China, where most of the urban residents have never even tried a fitness club, this model is like spandex gold.

Though the yoga craze has more or less peaked in a big city like Shanghai, it has tremendous expansion potential in the second, third and other tiers of China's cities. Yoga only arrived in China in a big way around 2003 with the arrival of international-style health clubs, but the industry didn't expand into specialty yoga studios until about 2005 and since then, the growth in Shanghai has been breathtaking: Indian yoga masters were in sudden demand, and there was a shortage of basics such as yoga mats in the stores.

Journey to the West: Leisure and Business Travel

A famous novel in China, one which virtually every Chinese person knows thanks to countless television and movie adaptations, is translated as *Journey to the West*, or known simply as *Monkey* in one of its most famous abridged translations. It is considered to be one of the classic literary works from the Ming Dynasty (1368–1644). Based on real-life events, but thought by some academics to be a satire or critique of the then-reigning government and situation in China, *Journey to the West* concerns a quest by a Buddhist Monk to go to India to obtain *sutras* (Buddhist religious texts). His several companions and protectors along the way include the Monkey King and Pig, and their journey is thought to represent the seeking of enlightenment and bringing that knowledge back to China. Needless to say, the journey was not easy and he and his companions encountered numerous hardships along the way.[13]

In present day, *Journey to the West* is even known among people outside of China, often children who are familiar with some of the comic or animated versions of the story. Among China's newly affluent middle-class, it is not the desire to travel abroad to bring back knowledge, but rather to bring back duty-free Louis Vuitton bags and Chanel cosmetics, which is an important opportunity for tourism in the Olympic Decade.

Chinese tourism abroad

Chinese tourists are the next wave of international travelers. Already sweeping across Asia to destinations such as the Philippines, Australia and Thailand, Chinese travelers are poised to become the new overseas vacationers everybody wants to woo.

It all started with Hong Kong in 1997 when, upon being returned to the Chinese mainland after more than a hundred years of British colonization, Hong Kong became a possible travel destination for mainland Chinese once again. After such a long wait, mainland Chinese flocked to see the Pearl of the Orient. Macau, another colony maintained by the Portuguese, has also been returned to Chinese control and turned into a tourist destination both for Hong Kongese as well as mainland Chinese, who flock there for the Las Vegas-style gambling and entertainment.

When it comes to Hong Kong, the main attraction for the Chinese is shopping. Long known as the shopping capital of the world, Hong Kong's shops stayed open from 10 to 10 or 9 to midnight every day of the year, and fashion and clothing shops were especially popular. However, the luster of the Pearl of the Orient faded as Chinese tour groups encountered difficulties such as cultural discrimination from the Cantonese- and English-speaking Hong Kongese, and more and more of the luxury brands (Chanel, Dior, Ferragamo, Louis Vuitton and others) which the mainland Chinese desired so much became increasingly common in China's first and even second tier cities. Now it is the Hong Kongese who are coming to China, though they are not likely to buy the luxury products as their own Special Administrative Region status means taxes on luxury goods are lower at home. The Hong Kongese are more likely to be flying to mainland China to work, where their Western education and ability to read, write, and increasingly speak Mandarin are competitive advantages.

The story of the Monkey King, about a quest outside of China, has only been a fantasy for the majority of Chinese today. It is only with the opening of China since the 1980s that travel outside the country became more available, but then only for elite students or people on business. For the everyday leisure traveler, it was simply not possible because many countries put significant restrictions on Chinese tourists — if they even allowed them at all — for fear they would remain in the country and work as illegal under-the-table workers. The restrictions usually included requiring a huge sum of money to cover the conceivable expenses in the foreign country, needing a stable job and ties in China to ensure you would return, traveling in a group with an authorized guide, and so on. Finally, foreign currency exchange was highly restricted and the RMB was unconvertible outside of China, making travel difficult to say the least.

The amount of currency the Chinese residents can convert into foreign money freely has big implications on the travel market. Back in the 1980s and 1990s when travel outside China became more technically possible for non-business and non-study purposes, the amount of cash one could convert to foreign currency was highly restricted. In the early 2000s the amount was about US$8,000 per year maximum for travelers, which was increased to US$20,000 per year in 2006, then increased to US$50,000 a year in 2007. Also in 2007, in a move aiming at further reducing China's then US$1.4 trillion in reserves and possibly to shore up the faltering stock market in Hong Kong, the State Administration of Foreign Exchange announced that any citizen can convert an unlimited amount of RMB to foreign currency if for the purposes of investment in Hong Kong, creating a channel to let money flow from China to the Hong Kong stock markets.[14] While these measures failed to reduce the currency surplus (it had increased to US$1.76 trillion by the time of writing), they did make it much easier for Chinese individuals to spend more abroad when they travel.

At present, the ones traveling to North America, Japan and Europe are generally from wealthy or white-collar demographics, and they will be big spenders on everything from luxury goods (which are highly taxed in China) to authentic clothing (with so many fakes in

China, a chance to buy the real thing abroad is often enthusiastically taken).

Chinese traveling abroad generally prefer to (or must, due to visa restrictions) travel in groups, much as the Taiwanese and Japanese before them, so venues hoping to attract these growing numbers of tourists should do several things: Cater to group sizes and dynamics and work with tour companies rather than trying to attract the rarer individual traveler; provide Chinese guides, menus, and descriptions (preferably in the simplified characters used in mainland China rather than the traditional characters used in Taiwan and Hong Kong, but in a pinch the traditional characters are still readable by most Chinese people); and offer authentic experience-based tours that give a taste of local life and products.

Possibly seeking to gain a piece of the growing Chinese tourism business, in 2007, the US and UK both announced changes to make getting travel visas easier. The UK lowered the cost of its tourist visa application by about 30 percent in a trial program to encourage and support more Chinese travel to the UK.[15]

Another country that is trying to attract Chinese tourists is Japan. Japan is relaxing restrictions on Chinese to get tourist visas. Before 2008, Chinese tourists had to travel to Japan in a large tour group and could not travel as individuals. As a result, only about 800,000 tourists from China visited Japan in 2006, while 3.75 million tourists visited China from Japan. Now, after changing the requirements for the tourist visa, Chinese tourists can travel as a family, or even as an individual, so long as they have a tour guide present. Of course, such a small group with a guide will raise the price of the family and individual tours astronomically, so only the wealthy Chinese will take advantage of this program. This is a good first step for Japan to increase its desirability as a travel destination.

None of these mature markets matches the extent to which South-East Asian nations such as Thailand, Malaysia and the Philippines are reaching out to the Chinese traveler. Low fares and even lower local prices mean the Chinese RMB converted into those countries' currencies is at parity with local living standards or even has greater purchasing power, so Chinese enjoy the extra benefit of getting great deals on hotels and meals when they travel there, unlike the US or Japan, where a typical hotel or train/airport transfer might be half a month's salary for the average Chinese. However, as more Chinese in the cities get higher salaries and the Chinese RMB appreciates further, expect more Chinese tourists throughout the world.

Top Opportunities in Lifestyle Supertrends

Chinese people are living longer through better medicine and health practices, their incomes are up, and they seek new models of Western-style relaxation to combat the ravages of the globalized high-pressure work environment:

1. China's aging population and senior-heavy demographics highlight the need for services to the elderly, including in-home care.
2. Chinese white-collar workers are paying more attention to their health and lifestyles, meaning opportunities for spas and relaxation services, healthier restaurants and foods, diets, vitamins and supplements.
3. The sports enthusiasm in China is being built on the Olympic momentum and a traditional culture of health and exercise such as bicycle-riding and *tai chi*, but is now becoming more Westernized. Chinese are riding stationary bikes and practicing kick-boxing in gyms, as well as a growing number of people taking up yoga.
4. The travel and tourism market is going to be big, in both directions: More Westerners will go to China, especially to see events such as the World Expo in 2010. Also, many more Chinese will go abroad. They are the next high-spending consumers that countries and businesses abroad should want to attract.

CHAPTER SEVEN

Text Me: A Boundaryless Society with Instant Networking

关系化, 电子商务化   *Guanxi hua & Dianzi shangwu hua*

A ctor, singer and Hong Kong media personality Edison Chen could not have imagined what would transpire after his computer went in for repairs: A technician apparently searched his hard-drive while carrying out the repairs and was probably surprised to find hundreds, if not thousands, of X- and R-rated digital photos of Chen and famous starlets, together and individually, in various states of undress, some in *flagrante delicto*. Hong Kong movie star Cecilia Chung and Gillian Chung, one-half of the squeaky-clean pop duo Twins, were both implicated in the scandal, along with a handful of other celebrities. It was reminiscent of any number of Paris Hilton-style "naughty video/picture" incidents, but while these no longer make much of a splash in US media, in celebrity-obsessed Hong Kong, which had never had such an incident before, it was front-page news on major newspapers in Hong Kong and the lead-off story on most news and commentary programs for weeks.

It was perhaps the titillation factor that caused it to grow so large in the public consciousness. At first, small numbers of photos were leaked online to BBSs, the poster apparently somebody who had received the photos by way of the technician, with promises of more to come. As famous actresses' intimate photos were revealed one after another, speculation mounted as to who would be next.

Complicating matters, the government jumped into the fray to try to squelch distribution, in the process appearing to be trodding on people's rights and enforcing censorship, not to mention upsetting open-minded Hong Kongese by their prudish definitions of obscenity. PR agencies and lawyers acting on behalf of various parties waded in, but as Pamela Anderson and Tommy Lee once proved, no amount of lawyering (or pleading) could keep such scandalous materials from spreading. Mainland China also played a significant part in this.

Even before Edison Chen admitted his misjudgment and apologized for the damage he'd caused to so many of the women's careers, thereby implying the photos were real and consenting, the Netizens of China were making up their own minds. A full set of hundreds of pictures began circulating online. It wasn't long before an entrepreneurial DVD producer put them on a disc and mass produced it, flooding the fake DVD shops of China within weeks.

At the same time as his apology, Chen announced he was leaving the Hong Kong entertainment world indefinitely, and the starlets' futures are uncertain. The Netizens who downloaded the photos, meanwhile, spread them to their co-workers, friends, even family (no shyness needed, even older parents wanted to see for themselves what all the fuss was about). It was, in a sense, an unstoppable force of the interconnectedness of Chinese people, made all the more potent thanks to communications tools such as multimedia phones, instant messaging, and BBSs, and what we call the *Internetworking* supertrend.

After literally decades of closed-door policies towards Western technology before the 1980s, China has again opened the door to new technology trends. It has learned quickly, so much so that in the near future, the new technology trends will come *from* China, not the other way around. As China has adopted Western market principles to create "Capitalism with Chinese characteristics," so has the Chinese use of technology been heavily influenced by cultural values of community and networking. As described earlier, China has been able to leap-frog ahead by skipping several generations of now-dated technology and jump directly to, or even beyond, the most modern technologies available at present. The way Chinese will use technology is a huge market in and of itself, but it will also influence the world's use of technology since the Chinese are the ones manufacturing it and will be a main market for it.

In China, at present, the information technology revolution and the influx of foreign capital and IPO funds is enabling massive upgrades to supply chains, to back-office IT systems, and to the web-enabled front-end systems that allow people in China to access data in new ways. China has its own video sites, its own online games, its own auction sites, all with a Chinese spin on the imported Western model. This creates a group of powerful supertrends related to commercializing technology that we call the *E-Commercializing* supertrend.

Together, these two supertrends are changing Chinese society and business interaction.

Mobile Phone Thumb

Joining the world's information technology revolution somewhat late, China has embraced it with enthusiasm, leap-frogging to the newest and best technologies on offer. Whether the adoption of technology for daily life is an expression of making up for lost time, or based on China's cultural characteristics in common with other Asian societies such as Japan and Korea that have also embraced technology, is debatable, but the reality for many Chinese is that the mobile phone (in China, cellular phones are called mobiles, and the literal translation of *shou'ji*, means hand device) is preferred over fixed line. In today's China, people even consider a voice call to be too time-consuming: Many younger Chinese prefer the speed and brevity of a short message, *duan'xin*, known as SMS or texting in the West.

China's mobile users send about one billion text messages a day, and on special holidays the number can more than double with people sending greetings.[1] One reason is the cost. In China, until 2008 when the mobile and especially roaming rates were very high for local users, a short message at a flat rate of one *jiao* (about a penny) per message was much more affordable than a voice call. As well, the immediacy and speed of a short missive allows people to avoid the "How are you doing?" preambles and goodbyes. It is not uncommon to see Chinese people texting anywhere and everywhere, in meetings, movies, classrooms, and restaurants. This is not so different from the younger segments of some Western countries (Japanese youth also have a SMS-based communication preference), but it is the numbers that show the difference: In China, about 90 percent of all mobile users use SMS according to one study, while in the US the SMS usage rate is only 50 percent. The SMSs generated more than US$8.4 billion for the mobile phone service providers in 2007.

The trend is important for marketers who need more appropriate ways to communicate with Chinese customers, and for medical practitioners it has created a new repetitive stress disorder: Mobile phone thumb. Doctors report an increased number of youths with sore thumbs, one or both depending on whether you use a one- or two-handed style. The treatment? Stop sending so many messages. No way, say China's youths, they'd rather switch to a phone with a stylus instead. Sales of smart-phones from Motorola and Samsung that have this feature are booming, not only for carpal-tunnel-stricken teenage girls but also for their grandfathers who can now use a stylus to write in Chinese to communicate with their granddaughters.[2]

Other popular uses of mobile phone messaging is news with multimedia. Every morning, busy white-collar subscribers receive a digital edition of the newspaper, complete with pictures automatically downloaded to this mobile phone, which they then read on the bus or subway on the way to work.

QQ and MSN

If you don't know what QQ is and you think MSN just refers to the Microsoft Network or website, you are not up-to-date on youth culture in China. In the same way that short messages are preferred to talking, instant messaging (IM) is preferred over email. QQ and MSN are the two biggest providers. QQ is an instant messaging platform created by Chinese company TenCent which, the company claims, has 300 million active accounts, making it number two globally.* MSN, in China's cultural context, refers to MSN Messenger, the world's number one instant messaging platform from Microsoft that has been anathema in China to corporate information technology administrators trying to block IM traffic from corporate networks for fear of viruses and lost corporate data. If there is a battle between the IT departments and the users of the world over the fate of instant messaging as a corporate communications medium, China is the front-line.

In China, someone young without a QQ or MSN account is almost like what Westerners would think of somebody without a driver's license. People put their QQ numbers and MSN names on their businesscards: It is not uncommon for high-level executives to have any number of staff, customers, and suppliers on their accounts. 70 percent of Internet users in China use IM, and only about 56 percent use email, with this trend inverted in the United States where only about 41 percent in the US use IM and 90 percent use email.[3]

The ever-practical Chinese think it's just the simplest way to do things, and there's no stigma attached to IM as unprofessional in a society that is just as likely to get a phone call in a meeting and

---

*That this number is actually higher than the number of Chinese Internet users in total indicates most likely that many Chinese have multiple QQ accounts. For example, a person may have separate accounts for personal and for e-Commerce use. QQ is available outside of China but not widely used in non-Chinese-speaking countries.

actually answer while others are talking. Informality is a hallmark of everyday Chinese business and personal interactions. Of course, you wouldn't want to contact your boss over MSN with a trifling "Hi, what's up?" and formal communications still have a place when dealing with certain industries and levels of business and government, but China's younger generations have adapted to the information society by making full use of these tools for fast and effective communication.

China is at the forefront of a new business communication revolution because, for an increasing number of Chinese, there is no line between personal and work time. Having one's IM shut down by the IT department is like having your mobile phone taken away, or being unable to check your personal email while at work for a Western person.

If personal communications were all that was being conducted, one might have a point. But the thing which many Western managers in China don't understand is that many Chinese use IM for work and their all-important *guan'xi* network, so taking it away would actually be counterproductive for a lot of workers. Many an infuriated Western boss has stalked through an office seeing desk after desk of workers with IM services open and cute icons in effect and wondered, how could these people be working? Some IT departments and bosses, citing global network policies, have tried to ban it, but the inventive staff always find a way to tunnel outside the corporate firewall, or, the latest volley against IT and indeed against the company itself, is to just take back control by carrying a smartphone with IM capabilities.

Taking away mobile phones in China would lead to mass defections, so this is one battle that the bosses are not going to win. Rather, the opportunity here is to take advantage of it and embrace the communications medium and all the benefits it can bring to a business in China: Better connected co-workers, customers, and suppliers; speed of response; and one-on-one interaction.

And, with both texting and IM available on newer smart-phones, some people are doing away with computers altogether for their communication needs.

Madison Avenue Comes to Shanghai

One of Shanghai's trendiest streets, Huaihai Road, is dotted with advertising practically from start to finish. From banners hanging over the roads, pennants flying from the streetlamps, to giant LCD screens every few blocks (driving around night and day mounted on the panels of medium-sized vans) shouting out to shoppers, Shanghai has never seen so much advertising clutter. The advertising market grew annually at a rate of 20 percent from 2004 to 2007.[4] Being heard above the din now takes serious effort and money, and this has attracted some of the world's biggest advertising companies to set up their own offices or invest. In the past, many set up as joint ventures, but more recently the trend has been to invest directly or take over local players.

For example, in early 2008 the US-based Omnicom Group invested in Chinese integrated marketing service provider Shunya Communications Group through Omnicom's BBDO subsidiary, while in 2007 France's Publicis invested in Betterway, a Shanghai-based marketing services agency. Meanwhile, Chinese firms such as Focus Media are taking advantage of foreign capital by listing abroad and starting to expand their businesses outside China. These are just several of the more visible investments, but likely to be just the beginning as China's advertising market is now fully opened under the WTO agreement terms since 2003.[5]

One Hundred Million Bloggers

An online journal or web log, popularly known as a blog, is kept by almost 47 million people in China. What's more, many have more than one, including their MSN or QQ spaces, Chinese MySpace or Facebook, and pages on numerous Chinese providers of blog services at virtually zero cost to the user other than their time.[6] Blogs are a big trend in China.

Growth has been very fast, from about 17 million bloggers in 2006 to 47 million in 2007, the number will probably reach 100 million by 2010 as Chinese are going online at a furious rate.

By this standard, China will be the biggest blogging nation on Earth, with implications for writers, audiences, and businesses. By some standards, it already is. Owing to its people power, China's blogs can get an amazing number of visitors. A popular blog post in China may receive 500,000 to 1 million views a day, while the most popular bloggers such as Chinese actress/director/singer Xu Jinglei have accumulated more than 140 million views of their blog postings in just a year or two.[7] What is perhaps more amazing than the fact that a relatively young celebrity can regularly get a million people looking at her blog, is that there is practically no advertising on it — no Google Adwords to be found. We could update the old British merchants' expression for the Chinese market to read, "If only every blogger in China put advertisements on their blog, the click-farmers of Silicon Valley would be harvesting around the clock." Of course, Chinese bloggers are starting to do just that, but the blogo-sphere in China in 2008 still has a kind of pioneering feel and lack of influence from massive media conglomerate pushing out content to the masses. Rather, it actually seems to be real people, sharing their thoughts, their dreams, and their critiques, all without thought of monetization of the same.

Bloggers in China are more likely to be female, about a 57:43 female to male ratio, which is juxtaposed with the online popu-lation in China, which is about 45:55 female to male ratio.[8] This clearly shows that blogs are currently more popular with women, and the uses of blogs reflect that trend: The majority of blogs written are stream-of-consciousness thought-sharing and emotional record-keeping, diaries or hobby sites, that do not overtly seek fame and fortune. Look for this to change as people seek to emulate the previously uncontrived rise of China's online stars.

China's New Media Celebrities

The exploits of early (that is to say, since 2006, since this is still a very new medium in China) online Chinese celebrities, it could be said, were unintentionally hilarious and not entirely premeditated, thus vaulting rather ordinary people to online superstardom through viral emails and BBS postings that they didn't have control over, much in the same way as happened in the US with the Mahir Cagri or the Star Wars Kid.

One of the most famous is Sister Lotus, an aspiring artist and dancer, who started putting her slightly exhibitionist photos online several years ago and, later, videos of her dancing on popular media-sharing websites. She may have been trying to follow the Chinese pioneer of scandalous online attention-getting, *Muzimei*, a possibly fictitious journal of one modern Guangdong girl's sexual conquests and her thoughts on relationships, which attained a mass following. Sister Lotus started posting photos of herself in revealing poses, showing her "S-shaped curves," and became the epitome of online fame and infamy, for too many people considered her to be unattractive and "putting on airs" with her over-the-top photos and dancing. Yet they returned to watch again and again. Showing she was more media-savvy than people gave her credit for, she successfully parlayed the ridicule into offline media fame, appearing in magazines and TV shows.

Another Chinese online celebrity, Qian Zhijun, was really just the victim of one ill-timed photo. He is known as Xiao Pangzi, Little Fatty, a then young boy who had the unfortunate luck of being photographed while overweight and with an expression on his face like he'd been caught with his hand in the cookie jar. Somebody had the idea of Photoshopping his face onto the Mona Lisa and other famous images and, almost overnight, an online celebrity was born.

(Continued)

While Sister Lotus at least had the foresight to capitalize on her image, Xiao Pangzi was caught unaware and too young to realize what was happening. At the peak of his popularity, somebody tracked him down and found him working in a gas station and rather surprised at all the attention. He was just a normal teenager. Since then, he has managed to stop working at the gas station, become a spokesperson for dieting, and has used his celebrity appearances for social causes and not so much for personal gain, though he hopes to host a cooking show on TV someday.

Another Internet usage trend is that blogs and online content in general have become much more multimedia-focused. The biggest reason for reading blogs, according to a 2007 survey, is for entertainment purposes. China has its own versions of YouTube, Flickr and other content sites, but with a much faster-growing, younger, and media-savvy user base, the Chinese versions are getting to be significant players. A Chinese competitor to YouTube called *Tudou* ("potato" in Chinese) claims it serves more content despite the fact it is predominantly a China-only site[†] versus YouTube's worldwide audience and Google ownership.

From animated shorts imported from Korea to spoof videos of Chen Kaige's latest blockbuster movie, multimedia content has turned China into a nation of Photoshoppers and amateur video producers. Flash animations are enormously popular in China and can attain millions of viewers much more quickly than any viral campaign in the West, thanks to the common use of IM and Chinese online forums. Look for this trend to continue expanding, and companies which provide any kind of media content or tools have a huge potential market waiting.

Other blogs act as a voice of popular opinion, so it was with Rui Chenggang, an anchorperson on one of China's national broadcasting stations, who posted his personal opinions on his own blog

---

[†]A brief search by the authors showed that there are also many Western movies, sports, and TV shows user-uploaded complete with Chinese subtitles, but apparently without authorization from the copyright holders.

about the correctness of a Starbucks outlet being inside of China's historic Forbidden City. For Rui, the Starbucks was not aesthetically pleasing and perhaps inappropriate in such a culturally-important monument. The post got noticed, and a chorus quickly developed, with thousands of replies to each update by Rui. The president of Starbucks even wrote a personal response to Rui, which only added fuel to the fire. Whether resulting from the millions of people that read about the story online and had strong views about it, or because the management committee of the Forbidden City grounds reorganized the concession and gift shops around the same time, the end result is that Starbucks is no longer in the Forbidden City.

Numerous foreign companies, from KFC to P&G, Citroen to Danone, have all experienced online campaigns against them, often arising from a single advertisement or a complaint of one Netizen that was not handled well by the company. From that, China's numerous Netizens take over and the story quickly reaches a tipping point in public consciousness.

In January 2008, French automaker Citroen ran into trouble for a newspaper advertisement which it had published in Spain (which was nevertheless seen over the Internet and translated by a Netizen) that used a modified image of the iconic leader Mao Zedong with ad copy parodying a patriotic tone. Citroen, perhaps genuinely apologetic or more likely worried of losing more market share in China, stopped the ad and apologized in a Chinese newspaper (note to advertisers around the world: Don't upset Chinese Netizens).

The behavior of these MNCs certainly does show a lack of cultural awareness, such as Nike's TV commercial of Lebron James battling with a Kungfu master, a flying woman in Chinese attire called a *fei'tian*, and some Chinese-style dragons. While it is debatable if the ad was intended to be controversial for publicity purposes, it was undoubtedly in bad taste for Chinese viewers: In China, dragons are revered as symbols of good fortune and as a character on the Chinese zodiac (rather than feared as they are in the West, thanks to tales such as St. Georges and the Dragon or The Hobbit). In this incident, online furor also played a large part in bringing the ad to the attention of more than just NBA fans who saw it during a televised game.

To cope with online controversy, large companies clearly need a strong online strategy to match, so these incidents point the way to several new opportunities for a number of businesses that have already started to appear in Western markets but are not yet common in China.

This first is blog-related public relations services. As the Starbucks case showed, and many other cases before it, Chinese consumers can quickly amass popular sentiment against corporations online in their BBSs and blogs. So companies in China, whether foreign or Chinese, need blog mediation services to monitor blog postings, respond to them appropriately, do damage control where necessary, and turn the corporate blog into a voice against the sometimes irrational criticism and harsh words the online medium tends to propagate.

Second, there are clearly opportunities to channel consumer sentiment into positive buying behavior if managed correctly. In the US, this is sometimes called trendspotting, and it involves identifying a new thing that target consumers are watching, listening, or doing and then associating that with one's own brand. For example, Xiao Pangzi has announced his desire to have a cooking show on TV and help people lose weight. With so much content online in China, differentiating the good from the bad is a formidable job and will require a large number of companies and experts to sift through it to find the gold in those Internet hills.

Finally, blog marketing will eventually be very big in China. A Chinese-language product support blog or forum, a user's group and so on, can be very effective to build community among Chinese Netizens. And, when any number of blog writers can influence audiences of millions, it would be a good idea to work proactively with key writers to have product reviews, testimonials, and support. Chinese do not accept becoming a shill more than any other online cultural group, so this kind of marketing needs to be done skillfully and ethically, but just one evangelist discussing your product or service on his or her blog could have a much greater impact thanks to China's large number of online users.

Online Mobs

An interesting trend related to the rise in use of the blogosphere in China is online collectivist investigating and protesting behavior. Chinese online culture likes to throw large numbers of people at problems, collectively working to solve a problem, with both positive and negative implications. This is jokingly called the Human Flesh Search Engine and it was even part of an April Fool's Day joke from Google, when it posted an announcement seeking "human search volunteers."[9]

When it is for a good cause, as when bloggers team up to help somebody in difficulty, blog activism works well. In the opposite situation, when bloggers become enraged and want to seek retribution, the medium magnifies sentiments and makes lone voices appear to speak for authority and morality. Several examples of online mob behavior bear mentioning.

One of the first, which happened in 2006, involved an anonymous video of animal cruelty, with no clues other than the unidentified woman on a stretch of shoreline crushing a kitten with her stiletto heels. Enraged Netizens led the search for answers, eventually making some key discoveries thanks to their collective knowledge. The place was located, the likely motive identified, and a suspect found, even matching an e-Bay purchase of shoes to the suspected kitten killer. The case was closed and the people responsible punished, but it would likely never have been solved if it were not for the large numbers of online animal lovers.

The crowd is not always out for justice; sometimes they are out for retribution. In 2006, an apparent foreigner living in Shanghai wrote in detail on his blog about the number of Chinese women he had slept with since arriving in China a year before, even mentioning how he'd carried on an affair with a married woman, women who were his students (he indicated he was an English teacher), and other relationships that

(Continued)

seemed inappropriate at best and insulting to Chinese womanhood at worst. The frank postings on an anonymous blog were an open secret among the foreign community in Shanghai, but word soon spread to Chinese readers. A professor from Shanghai University in particular was upset enough to make an open call to track down this foreigner and boot him out of China. The response was overwhelming, even picked up by offline media, and the hunt was on for ChinaBounder. Threats of violence became commonplace in relation to the foreigner, and teachers who undoubtedly had nothing to do with the whole affair were being looked at suspiciously. The search quickly got out of hand. Perhaps shocked by the fury his letter created in the online Netizen population, the professor called for calm and the offending blog disappeared of its own accord. Nevertheless, the online activism had quickly turned into a lynch mob.

There are numerous other examples. From late 2007, a thought-to-be-extinct tiger was apparently photographed by a peasant in the Shaanxi region of China and a photo published at a news conference. Once the photo hit the blogs, the controversy really began, with Netizens proclaiming it a fake and using all manner of Photoshop techniques to debunk it. Earlier that year, China's moon-orbiting satellite was off the radar for some time and an online conspiracy theory developed that there in fact was no satellite at all.

In April 2008, when the Torch Relay was having difficulty in Europe, Chinese Netizens were up in arms over Western media (particularly BBC and CNN) coverage of the recent riots in Tibet, calling it biased. One portal, Sina.com, put up an online petition on its homepage and, in a day, had more than a million online signatures. An online campaign on MSN Messenger saw millions of Chinese supplement their screen name with "Love China." The Netizens also helped to coordinate a boycott against French retail giant Carrefour with similar online tactics, drumming up support in BBSs and through the transfer of patriotic PowerPoint presentations.

These and other cases show that Netizens in China are not to be trifled with, as there are so many of them but it only takes a few to start a committee, a posse, or a mob.[10]

WoW! China Invaded by Video Games

Online gaming is sweeping the nation and is a US$1.5 industry expected to grow at 39 percent in 2008. Gamers in China are expected to top 59 million by the end of 2008, meaning that China will quickly rival even strong game innovation markets such as Korea and the United States in size.[11] Clearly, the opportunity here is to develop more games for Chinese audiences. Currently, the winner in the Chinese market is World of Warcraft (WoW) from Vivendi's Blizzard Entertainment. Back in 2004, a little known company called The9 acquired the China rights to WoW as well as some games popular in Korea. WoW was a runaway success, achieving one million users in 2007 and helping the company generate revenues of US$1.8 billion. The9 is only number four in China's huge gaming market.[‡]

Following its IPO on the NASDAQ in 2004, The9 has bought rights to some of the world's most popular online games such as Electronic Art's FIFA Online, and also started developing games itself for the Chinese market. With the gaming market set to double in size in 2008, this is an ideal time to port games into Chinese and develop products especially suited for the Chinese players. How about that most Chinese of superheros, the Monkey King? The9 is already doing it, but there are numerous other opportunities yet to be explored.

Buy My *Guan'xi*

Guan'xi is like a good rolodex of business cards: When you have a problem, there is somebody in your file that can help you solve it. In that respect, it is not unlike Western conceptions of a business network, so one would imagine that networking sites would be enormously popular in China. The premise of networking websites

---

[‡]The others being (in order) Shanda, NetEase, and Giant, according to iResearch.

such as MySpace, Facebook, and LinkedIn is to capture your list of contacts in one place and extend it by utilizing the networks of your peers to access their connections, as well as sharing your own connections with them. This should be a true win-win situation for *guan'xi*-crazy Chinese, right?

Wrong. In China, people like to use their *guan'xi* for their own benefit. They don't like to share *guan'xi*, but when they do, it is to act as a middle-person to barter some kind of social transaction. An important part of *guan'xi* is actual physical access to a person. An email address or even a phone number is not enough: People in China exchange business cards spontaneously on being introduced, whereas Westerners may wait until the end of a meeting and even then only give a name card on an as-needed basis. While Westerners guard their mobile phone number almost as carefully as a home address, a Chinese CEO's card may even have a personal mobile phone number.

Real *guan'xi* is about a personal relationship, a connection, a common bond, such as being related, coming from the same hometown, having gone to school together and, most importantly, having a history formed through long interaction and reciprocal favors supporting mutual trust. *Guan'xi* is, therefore, anything but the distant relationships enabled by LinkedIn and other social network website connections with their three or more degrees of separation.

Further illustrating the barriers of online networking sites gaining popularity in China, you would be rude to ask somebody to pass only the contact information of a valued personal connection. Even if you succeeded in getting it, it would be meaningless without the intermediary there to act as a kind of escrow agent making sure both parties hold up their end of the bargain. In a *guan'xi*-enabled favor, the intermediary puts his or her reputation or face on the line: If you violate the trust of the other person in a business transaction, you bring shame not only to yourself but to the intermediary, and it is this desire to protect others from losing face that keeps the whole system going. *Guan'xi* is a coveted resource and a symbol of power: You are who you know. One other thing that makes *guan'xi* different from superficial social networks: People don't like to share their *guan'xi* unless there is something in it for them.

Despite the formidable barrier, therein lies the business opportunity: To find a way to protect the *guan'xi* participants from embarrassment, monetize the transaction, and enable it on a much larger scale than has been possible before.

Several Chinese websites are making an effort at this, but the space is wide open and will be as big as MySpace when somebody gets it right.

A new group of websites featuring *zhi ke*, Job Keys, seeks to put job seekers, of which there are two million plus new graduates a year and hundreds of thousands of people looking for new jobs, together with those who know of a position. This is how the sites work: Have you ever known of a position in your firm, perhaps with a referral bonus or just because your company expects employees to introduce other good people, but you didn't know somebody to fit the bill? What if *you* could troll through Monster.Com or Yahoo! HotJobs looking for good candidates and, if that person was hired you would get a placement bonus? That essentially describes the concept of Job Keys, except the *candidate* pays the bonus and, the more the candidate is willing to pay, the better job they can get, presumably. One Job Key website had more than 5,600 job seekers offering a total of more than US$1.2 million in bonuses. This is enough of an incentive that people can justify using their *guan'xi* networks, and some sites even hold the bonus in escrow, providing the security for two complete strangers to trust one another, acting something like the role of the *guan'xi* middle-person.

Another technique becoming popular to monetize *guan'xi* is called a WitKey, similar to websites such as Amazon's Mechanical Turk or sites that post a job, task or question and an amount of money paid to the person who accomplishes it. The money is held in escrow as well, encouraging those with information to share the information for a price.

What will be the next site to encourage *guan'xi* exchange? This is clearly a business model that has great growth potential in China.

TaoBao: A Chinese e-Bay on Steroids

The online e-Commerce market is set to explode in the next Olympic Decade. China has already gone through several phases of Internet maturity, including portals, online games, and searching. However, Chinese consumers have been reluctant to buy things online until only relatively recently. One reason is that there were few places to buy or sell online and a lack of secure payment methods.

Chinese online auction house TaoBao has started to change all that. With more than 53 million users at the end of 2007 (compared with global leader e-Bay, which is only number three in China,[12] has only 10 million registered users, many of whom were acquired when it purchased the first Chinese online auction site, Eachnet, in 2003 for US$180 million),[13] TaoBao is China's largest auction site and is quickly becoming capable of challenging e-Bay elsewhere globally.

TaoBao was started by the same entrepreneur that launched Alibaba, China's premier portal for foreign companies sourcing in China. When Yahoo! bought a 40 percent stake in Alibaba in 2005 for US$1 billion, the acquisition of the portal was motivated in part by the partial ownership of TaoBao gained in the deal, allowing Yahoo! China to benefit from possible synergies with TaoBao's millions of users.[14]

Since its inception, TaoBao and its founder Jack Ma have been a thorn in e-Bay's China expansion plan by keeping transaction fees at zero and attracting a large number of China's cost-conscious users. According to company figures, TaoBao's transactions totaled about US$5.9 billion in 2007, nearly three times more than the annual sales of Wal-Mart in China. The value of online transactions completed is not a large number compared to e-Bay's greater than US$50 billion in global transactions yearly, but it is growing very quickly inside China — 156 percent in 2007. Despite e-Bay's 69 percent growth in listings in 2006, TaoBao's listings grew at about 300 percent. Possibly in a sign that TaoBao's war of attrition finally paid off, e-Bay's China operation merged into a minority-stake joint venture with HK-based company Tom Online, which is partly owned by, again, *uber*-investor Li Ka-Shing, effectively ending e-Bay's independent strategy in China.[15]

But e-Bay-killer TaoBao itself is hampered by the free transaction fee legacy which it initiated, and has not yet made a profit for its parent company, Alibaba. Also, because the platform attracts mostly cost-conscious young sellers and results in frequent complaints of shoddy goods being sold, it is difficult to monetize those users in a significant way. Instead, the strategy that TaoBao pursues for revenue growth is trying to attract more high-quality and guaranteed B2C sales by creating fee-based services for retailers such as special features and promotions, much as the Power Sellers program does for e-Bay.

Showing turnabout is fair play. In April 2008, e-Bay China announced it would drop fees to zero for a large number of services, just as TaoBao announced it would reinstate trading fees in October.[16]

While credit cards are becoming more common in China, high limits are not, so TaoBao is also exploring financing models that may be unique in the world of e-Commerce, such as a partnership with a "Big Four" Chinese bank to provide trade financing for auction sellers, up to about US$14,000, until their sales receipts held in escrow are released. So long as the vendor has a good credit history and is an active user of TaoBao and its AliPay user-to-user escrow payment service, they can qualify for the short-term financing as needed.

Another reason that e-Commerce has been slow to take off is the lack of availability of online payment methods which, until about 2004, were spotty at best. Thereafter, domestic solutions started to appear in the form of online banking with bill payment functions, escrow payment services, and some mobile phone payment methods. But e-Commerce was still hampered by several problems, notably a distrust in the services themselves as the concepts were new to most consumers and frequent tales of fraud online. Furthermore, many people did not have credit cards at the time, meaning a fairly standardized form of payment on Western e-Commerce websites was not available in China. This led the general population to avoid e-Commerce purchasing. Even after 2006, when online escrow services such as Alibaba's AliPay service were robust and common, online sales would be made on a platform such as TaoBao but then concluded offline in person with an exchange of goods for cash. C2C and B2C e-Commerce needs more time to mature in China, and there are plenty of opportunities still for new entrants.

Enter the Q-Bee

Chinese company TenCent, mentioned earlier as the proprietor and host of QQ, an instant messaging platform that rivals global IM leader, MSN Messenger, claims to have 300 million active accounts (while noting that many people use more than one). In 2007, it had half a billion dollars in revenue, three times greater than Facebook, and is a serious competitor.

TenCent also made waves in 2007 when its online virtual currency, known as the Q-Bi (pronounced Q-bee, a play on the word *renminbi*, the Chinese currency), caught the attention of the People's Bank of China (China's central bank) for possible worries including its potential for money laundering, tax evasion, and even upsetting the money supply as people increased their use of cashless transactions. Not to mention, it was commonly used as a currency for men to pay for online sex acts to Chinese cam-girls who quickly caught on to the concept of C2C e-Commerce.

Q-bee can be bought and sold, converted into *renminbi* through another e-Commerce medium, the online auction provider TaoBao.

(Continued)

The market rate for Q-bee followed supply and demand economics with TaoBao acting as the medium for conversion into real-world value (a ForEx market of sorts). With approximately 66 percent of TenCent's revenues being generated by the sale of online games and digital/virtual products (such as cute avatars for your account, or things bought and sold with Q-bee), they have demonstrated a very important business model in China for how to make money from social networking.[17]

China's technology landscape truly abounds with new models of communicating and doing business online.

Top Opportunities in Networking and e-Commerce

China's adoption and use of technology is rivaling more technologically advanced neighbors Korea and Japan, and will soon surpass them. The Inter-networking and e-Commercializing supertrends mean more information sharing, more communicating, and more services needed to reach these mostly younger consumers:

1. SMS (short messages) and IM (instant messages) are the preferred communications medium for many young people because they are instantaneous and inexpensive. Marketers must learn to use these in a non-invasive way to improve customer relationships, and there are an unlimited number of new business models resulting from this communications trend.
2. Despite the government's supposed control of all online information, blogging is hugely popular in China. Blogs have not become commercialized yet, and can be used by market research companies to understand consumer trends, but be careful of blog mobs (Chinese activist bloggers campaigning against corporate and social wrongdoing).
3. China is where the final battle for social networking sites will take place, as people try to both understand the extent of their communications networks and how to monetize their *guan'xi*.

(Continued)

4. The online game trend is big in China, as is the production of virtual products inside the games, but the market needs its own video games and Second Life type of online communities to really blossom. The next ten years are the window of opportunity.
5. TaoBao is part of the new generation of e-Commerce activities in China: Free, voluminous, and enabling average consumers to do business more easily.

Though these trends have been found in the West for quite some time, they are still new in China and definitely growing. The Olympic Decade of affluence and technological enablement is the best time to get started.

PART FOUR

THE WEALTH SUPERTRENDS

〜 繁荣趋势 〜

CHAPTER EIGHT

Affluencing: China's Accumulation of Wealth and Influence

繁荣化　　*Fanrong hua*

T he China of today can possibly be compared to the Japan of the 1980s: Stock markets and property markets sky-rocketing, an ascendant currency, and fast accumulation of huge foreign reserves. From Japan Inc. to China Inc., has anything changed? Since Chinese computer manufacturer Lenovo bought IBM's PC business, will it soon be buying Rockefeller Center and other US corporate icons? Investing in Rembrandts and Renoirs? Somehow, China seems to be following a different path. Though there is growing prosperity in China, it is mostly retained within the country behind currency controls and domestic opportunities. Will it stay that way? There are signs that China's wealth is spilling over its borders, through a sovereign wealth fund and by way of Hong Kong, but the important supertrend is how it is being spent inside the country.

Where is it Good to be in the Red?

In China, of course, where red is the color of luck, auspiciousness, good fortune and, of course, money: The main unit of currency, the

RMB100 note, is red for this reason. So when the stock ticker goes into the red in Shanghai, don't be surprised if people are pleased: Red arrows and numbers represent gains, while it is green arrows and numbers that upset stockholders.

In China's stock markets, red also refers to red-chips, the colloquial name for Chinese companies that set up overseas listings in the past, usually in Hong Kong, in order to raise capital. China Mobile, the world's largest mobile phone company, is one such business, and it is expected to return to China in the next two years with a mainland listing. When these companies "come home," they can often raise billions of dollars in capital because of the dearth of quality stocks currently on the domestic exchanges.

Stock Market and Land Bubbles — Dreams of Prosperity

2007 was known as the Golden Year of the Pig, according to the Chinese astrological calendar, and for newly born babies (called Golden Pig Babies) it was thought to be auspicious for their future wealth. It was a very good year for China's financial markets as well. Despite nagging concerns about corporate governance, questionable investments, non-transparency and accounting irregularities, China's stocks and major indices could make one wonder if pigs really could fly. During the year, the China Securities Index (CSI) 300 index (a broad measure similar to the Standard & Poor's index charting 300 of China's approximately 1,600 listed firms) led the major global indexes with a 162 percent gain, while the Shanghai stock market closed up 97 percent for the year.[1] In all, it was another stellar year for China's markets following 2006, when the indexes more than doubled.

February 2008 started the Year of the Rat, and one Chinese feng shui master predicted poor performance for the markets. Indeed, the first half of 2008 saw the index decrease as much as 50 percent from its highs in October 2007 and, if this trend continues, China's stock markets may be among the *worst* performing of 2008.[2]

In this booming environment of rollercoaster stock performance, Warren Buffett recommended caution while Hong Kong's land tycoon Li Ka-Shing believed it "must be a bubble." China investors seem to disagree, both domestically and overseas. Many China funds sold abroad — the only way for foreigners to legally participate in the Chinese mainland stock markets — through the Qualified Foreign Institutional Investor program were among the top performers of 2007, with many charting returns of more than 30 percent. While Chinese investors participating directly in China may have lost money, the tales of 100 percent or even 200 percent gains on investment in a few months of day-trading abound. Even, it is said, China's *ayis* (domestic helpers) rushed to pile their savings into the stock markets. This makes one wonder if there is some truth to the old stock-market aphorism that once bartenders and busboys start investing in the market, the end of the bubble is within sight.

One thing pushing the markets higher in general is that Chinese people have limited investment opportunities: Stocks, real estate or savings. Mutual funds, bonds, futures, options and other financial investments are present to varying degrees but, for example, in the case of funds, may be newly or underregulated, recently established and staffed by relatively inexperienced managers, and not improving upon the better returns from seemingly random investment in stocks based on rumor and pump-and-dump promotion. The monkey (or the Monkey King) throwing at a dartboard would almost certainly do as well or better than most fund managers in China. A property market constantly referred to as overheated and subject to capricious regulatory actions by the central government, such as a requirement to pay up to 40 percent as a down-payment for second properties owned in the same family,[3] is not an ideal choice at the current time. With inflation in China in 2007 at 6.5 percent and topping 8 percent in the first quarter of 2008, bank deposit rates of

4–5 percent are nearly half the rate of inflation,* causing investors to shun savings in favor of stocks.

Stocks themselves suffer from a number of problems. In China's two major stock markets, Shanghai and Shenzhen, there are only about 1,600 listed companies *in total*, meaning investors, whether individual or institutional, do not have a lot of choice. The 80/20 rule applies here as well, where the top 20 percent of the listed firms bring in about 80 percent of the profits, so there are good earnings and stability in the relatively few blue-chips and extreme volatility in the rest. Investors in this environment badly need wealth management, funds, and other professional investment alternatives.

IPO Fever

Perhaps with the world's best performance of a major stock index (Shanghai) in 2007, it would not surprise many to know that China was also 2007's IPO capital of the world, as the total amount raised by initial public offering is larger than all the capital raised in the US on the NASDAQ, NYSE, and AMEX combined.

The phrase "IPO" is a bit of a misnomer for many of the biggest companies listing on China's Shenzhen and Shanghai stock markets in 2007: They had already listed elsewhere and were simply *coming home* as sea turtle — *haigui* — companies. Seven of the top ten IPOs in the domestic market were *haigui* in 2007, raising a total of US$39.7 billion† (about 66 percent of the total IPO figure which

---

*Meaning that, in real terms, money in the bank decreases in value because the inflation rate is higher than the deposit rate, giving people an incentive to take money out of the bank and put it into other investments.

†These funds were raised during 2007, when there was a slightly weaker RMB rate, so an exchange rate of 7.2 RMB per dollar was used to convert the numbers in this paragraph into US dollars.

was US$63.7 billion to US$66.3 billion), the largest amount raised globally, edging the US's US$64.6 billion (RMB465.3 billion).[4]

Whether it is the irrational exuberance of the investors driving up the prices of the IPOs, or the quality of the companies getting access to reasonable amounts of capital for the first time and misjudging the market by undervaluing their IPOs, many of China's initial public offerings increased rapidly. For example, the China Quanjude Group, owner of the Quanjude Roast Duck Restaurant chain, up 225 percent in two weeks; Alibaba.com, the Yahoo!-invested TaoBao-owning e-Commerce company, up 186 percent in a month following its IPO; or the best performer of all, China State Shipbuilding, up 575 percent in two and a half months.[5]

To be sure, there were IPOs that are now "underwater" from their original debut price, most notably PetroChina, the world's first trillion dollar company following its IPO in 2007.

Chinese companies listing abroad

Chinese firms are not only listing themselves in Hong Kong and, increasingly, on domestic markets, they are continuing the trend of raising capital abroad. Lest one think that the recovery and strong performance in the domestic stock markets signals an end to the origins of the *haigui*, China's IPOs in the US alone totaled 12 percent of the American total for 2007, bigger than all other foreign country listings combined. Including new listings in overseas exchanges such as Hong Kong, NYSE, NASDAQ, and the occasional LSE or other market listing, Chinese companies raised US$34 billion abroad which, when combined with the domestic total, means Chinese firms raised more than US$100 billion in the public equity markets globally.

These Chinese companies are following in the footsteps of Suntech Power, Mindray, and Baidu by choosing to list overseas rather than in China. For the most part, the Chinese companies going abroad are technology-oriented, which is why they may choose an exchange such as the NASDAQ.

But what about the burn rate?

Survivors of the dot-com boom and bust may be getting a sick feeling in their stomachs reading the numbers and sizes of Chinese company IPOs and wondering if it isn't history repeating itself. Are Chinese companies even now increasing their burn rates, similar to how the dot-com startups were pushed by their venture capital backers to increase the speed of spending to gain critical market share in those early years of the Internet? Will China's large firms blow through their US$6 billion IPOs in a similar way? Will China's stock market bubble collapse in on itself, leaving stock market investors holding the bag? There are two big differences between the China boom and the dot-com boom worth mentioning.

First, many of the biggest IPOs in China are from large state-owned enterprises (e.g., China Mobile, which has become the world's largest mobile phone carrier, listed in New York and Hong Kong for several years, will return for a mainland listing in 2008 or 2009) rather than entrepreneurial startups, nor are they primarily web-based enterprises. They are usually in industries related to infrastructure, energy, and heavy industry. What's more, many of these firms have been listed for years already on a foreign exchange and therefore have excellent GAAP-standard accounting and auditing as well as corporate governance. They may be huge, but they are by no means capricious or foolish with their investments.

Second, China's domestic market driver will sustain many of these companies for years, if not decades, as China develops. Earnings are on an upward trend as these formerly government-controlled firms find new freedom to cut costs (and employees) from their bloated structures, introduce IT systems, and grow revenues with new service offerings based on more aggressive growth models. With the correction in the Chinese markets that took place in 2008 and increasing earnings thanks to domestic growth, P/E ratios are more reasonable but still reflect some exuberance on the part of China's developing economy investors.

Sea Turtle Companies Come Home

Sea turtle, as applied to overseas Chinese people who return home after being educated and working abroad, can also be applied, somewhat jokingly, to companies. When Chinese companies are merely listed in Hong Kong but without having a corporate registration there, their shares are called H-shares. Tsingtao Brewery was the first H-share, back in 1993, and Bank of China and Industrial & Commerce Bank of China (ICBC), the world's largest bank by stock market valuation, started off as H-shares in Hong Kong before coming back to list in China in 2006.

When a HK-registered or other overseas-territory company is at least 30 percent owned by mainland Chinese (usually state-owned) entities as the largest aggregate shareholders, it is referred to as a red-chip, such as China Mobile, one of the most successful red-chip companies. Since a red-chip company is listed overseas, it technically cannot list in China under current regulations, but in 2008 that is set to change. There are 30 such companies in Hong Kong.

Both types of company, red-chip or H-share, can be considered to be *haigui* as here the reference means originally listed overseas (which still includes Hong Kong as there is no financial market linkage with the mainland under the one-country two-systems model) for better access to capital when China's own stock markets were in the doldrums until 2005. As with the human sea turtles, the companies are just as welcome to come home.

Once the boom in the Chinese mainland markets had begun in 2006, it was quickly realized there was a dearth of quality domestic stocks available and many of the best companies were already listed abroad. A solution to this problem would be to have the companies relist on a domestic stock exchange and, not coincidentally, pick up another, much bigger, round of funding even if they didn't particularly need it. Thus, with the market conditions finally right, the *haigui* could start coming home to a domestic stock market for a second, usually much larger, IPO, to take advantage of the demand from inside China for new A-share stocks.

The Trillion Dollar Company

Warren Buffett was an investor in PetroChina, China's biggest oil company with investments around the world and employing more than 400,000 people. Through Berkshire Hathaway, Buffett held more than 10 percent of PetroChina's Hong Kong-listed shares at one point, but in summer 2007 he made news for selling off part of the stake in what looked like a very short-term decision contrary to the long-term investment strategy he is known for. By October the same year, he had sold it all. Buffett stated he made about US$3.5 billion on an initial investment of about US$500 million. By all accounts it was a stellar investment decision, but analysts and investors were confused as to the timing, prior to the planned November 2007 domestic stock listing in Shanghai that was set to raise an additional US$9 billion in capital.

PetroChina is one of the so-called *haigui* companies.

So it was at the height of the stock market peak in 2007 and just prior to the new IPO that Buffett announced the sale. The news that Buffett was selling briefly sent the Hong Kong-listed stock downwards, but in the run-up to the IPO the stock climbed and the IPO was highly oversubscribed, surging 163 percent from the offer price on its opening day. For a few days after the IPO, PetroChina was the world's first trillion dollar company. It also became the biggest company in the world, bigger than both Exxon and Royal Dutch Shell combined.

By most analyses, the valuation made no sense as PetroChina was a bloated state-owned firm that had at one time employed more than a million people. Despite drastically cutting its work-force, closing unprofitable plants, and making profitable invest-ments abroad before the time of high oil prices, it still had only half the profits of Exxon alone.

The overvaluation of PetroChina didn't last long. A few weeks after its stellar debut, the stock began a long slide that shaved 50 percent off its value in just three months, so by February 2008, Buffett was once again looking like an investment genius and had gained new-found respect among Chinese stock-market analysts for correctly advising caution.

Pu'Er Tea Mania

The South Sea Bubble, Tulipomania, the Dot-Com Boom. To this list of famous irrational exuberance you can now add a Chinese variation: Pu'Er Tea.

Highly valued for its ability to aid digestion at long Chinese meals, it has been a staple at dim sum lunches for generations. Pu'er is a variety of fermented tea that is most famously produced in the high moun-tains of Yunnan Province. Thought to help one lose weight and possibly prevent cancer, Pu'er also has the special characteristic among teas that it gets better with age. Much like a fine wine or brandy, Pu'er tea that is kept for years can acquire a higher value than the freshly-made variety. This spawned businesses that aged their teas and tea collectors who kept their favorites properly stored for later use, all quite normal in tea-loving China.

It was not until the boom years that started in 2004 that Pu'er assumed its latest incarnation: Investment vehicle. Starved for places to put their money — between savings, stocks, or real estate, and some of the far-sighted who bought gold ingots — Chinese investors found the bricks of Pu'er tea to be a good buy, appreciating in value by more than 30 percent a year at first but then rapidly increasing as the craze caught on. The tulip-bulb mania that swept Europe in the 16th century was another

(Continued)

agricultural product that was purchased not to plant and admire their beauty as flowers, but to keep for the inherent worth that the bulbs seemed to take on as more and more people from an ever larger number of countries started hoarding them to sell later.

People were buying bricks of Pu'er tea. Not to drink of course, it was too valuable for that. At one point, the value of the tea reached about US$111 a kilogram at the peak in 2007, up from as low as $1 a kilogram three years before.

Perhaps people realized they should be consuming it instead of investing in it, or possibly the tea manufacturers went into over-production when the prices started going up, or it might have been the tea wholesalers hoarding tons of the tea, but when the price of Pu'er collapsed, some people lost everything, tea shops closed, and people went back to day-trading on the stock markets instead. At least stocks had value, even if you couldn't drink them.[6]

The Opportunities

Financial and wealth management services

Surely an important target for any bank, but basically one of the only targets available for foreign banks in China as they lack a retail network, is wealth management and private banking for the super rich. Various rich lists estimate that China has more than 345,000 US dollar millionaires in 2006[7] who are limited in their investment choices the same way that every other Chinese citizen is: Domestic stocks, domestic real estate, or putting their money into savings (or Pu'er tea). While Citi and other banks cannot, in fact, offer much more than those same options for investments, they can at least usually offer these investors more choices through a Chinese government policy called the Qualified Domestic Institutional Investor program, whereby larger domestic financial institutions (which include foreign banks as long as they are registered and capitalized as a full subsidiary) can invest abroad and offer fund products to retail customers based on the investments.

Although thousands of financial managers have been created through schooling or in-house training, the need for qualified and experienced financial managers cannot be more acute. It is not the financial knowledge that the 20- or 30-something young managers cannot master, it is the completely different mindset and lifestyle of their clients that they cannot handle. Only experience will help these managers to develop the investment-savvy and sophistication needed to manage money better than the wealthy can do for themselves.

Foreign banks such as Citi have focused on hiring the best of the best relationship managers for private banking on the mainland and trying to focus only on the super rich (i.e., those with US$10 million or more in assets). They are not alone in targeting the very wealthy; domestic players such as the Bank of China, China Merchants Bank, and China CITIC Bank have all set up private wealth management services. With every bank wanting a piece of this business, there is a lack of qualified private wealth management experts to serve this growing market segment, meaning opportunities for those from abroad with wealth management skills and experience. As yet, offshore banking services are not available, legally, to Chinese customers, so all businesses wanting to target these lucrative clients must be in China with registered offices.

Stock market structural reform opportunities

China's stock markets are still somewhat immature, lacking many of the tools such as options or short-selling that allow Western markets to manage risk. China's Olympic Decade will see the maturing of its stock markets by offering futures, options, and even new exchanges to stimulate China's high-tech economy much the same way the NASDAQ did for the US. In addition to needing experts to advise and set up these systems, the country needs all of the various service companies that are required to support the markets, and it needs traders. Those who are willing to come early and work in the wild west of China's markets will undoubtedly enjoy a huge advantage in the next decade.

China's golden years

China's future retirees need more financial planning services for the future. While China has a pension plan for the former workers of China's massive state-owned enterprises who are now entering retirement age, the payouts are sometimes much less than the admittedly low salaries they received in the first place. The iron rice bowl, as it was once called, where the state looked after every need, is little more than a rusted container these days. For the generations to come, there is a growing consensus within China that the pension system cannot cope with future demands.

Due to China's One-Child Policy, the current generation is already supporting the larger generations before them. The problem is exacerbated by the fact that birth rates are at an historical low in China, particularly among the high-earning urban population, meaning that they will only have one child (or at most two, under the revised terms of the One-Child Policy whereby a husband and wife who both come from single-child families can marry and have two children).

The rising standard of living and inflation mean that the meager required contributions today will hardly be enough to support a future retired life to which the young people are becoming accustomed. This creates an incentive for many young people to start saving for retirement but, lacking programs like 401(k) plans and RRSPs, they must start doing so now on their own. Retirement planning and consulting services are in great demand for those people.

Barbarians at the Great Wall: Venture Capital in China

Since the ending of the dot-com boom in the United States, a number of funds have been increasingly looking to China as the next big thing. After Chinese IPOs of portal and game provider NetEase.com, search engine and future Google-rival Baidu.com, and the NYSE-listed Suntech Power and Mindray Medical (a Shenzhen-based manufacturer of medical devices) all performed well over the past two years, the race was on to find the next Chinese pre-IPO firm that would make millions for its venture capital (VC) backers. The pickings, however, have been somewhat slim, and venture capitalists appear to have gone beyond their typical comfort zones to make large investments in non-standard business models and under trying conditions.

The VC industry in China has been a mostly foreign affair. Though there are some larger Chinese funds, such as the Shenzhen Capital Group with a fund of more than US$300 million, most of the firms come from outside of China.

The first problem that venture capitalists encountered on arriving was the amount of competition for good deals. It was a case of too much money going after too few quality firms, and with P/E ratios of Chinese companies in general being very high because of the booming stock markets, pre-IPO valuations were expensive and competitive.

China is awash in cash — from a trillion dollar currency reserve to billions a day in FDI, from state-owned banks giving loans to state-owned enterprises, family members investing their stock-market profits in an uncle's new light-manufacturing business, or young Chinese entrepreneurs starting online ventures on even more of a shoestring budget than the stingiest of Silicon Valley entrepreneurs. The typical multi-million dollar investments that VCs like to make in non-seed capital investments were, well, not needed, thank you very much.

(Continued)

Part of the reason behind the refusal to accept VC money was the strings attached. Many Chinese firms are true command-and-control organizations, with the president making all the decisions and not beholden to a Board of Directors. Corporate governance is still catching on, and a sense of building shareholder value may be difficult to foster in many smaller firms. So, the typical North American venture capitalist's focus on growth rather than profits, board seats or even control of the board, shareholding majorities, buyout rights, lock-in periods, and other typical items on any term sheet, were unappealing to the typical Chinese *laoban* (boss).

Finally, the legal system and corporate structures for doing business in China are not as transparent as VCs are used to having. For example, contracts with key suppliers or customers may be done verbally based on *guan'xi* relationships, legal structures of a company may be convoluted or near non-existent, and accounting practices may not follow GAAP. In practical terms, this means that understanding the inner workings of a company takes far more effort, and the security and stability of the company may be below comfort levels.

Despite these barriers, VCs are still making their best efforts in China, and several have had notable successes by participating in companies such as Alibaba which went public on the Hong Kong stock exchange in 2007, Suntech, and FocusMedia, one of China's top advertising companies going public in the US.

In fact, the amount of money being invested by VCs and the number of projects is steadily increasing. After relatively flat growth from 2003 to 2005, 2006 and 2007 were huge, seeing investment triple from 2005 to 2007, to US$3.25 billion on 440 deals, showing that they have finally found their footing in China's turbulent markets.[8]

What are the VCs investing in? Shirt factories, organic farms, restaurants, hotels, and of course the usual VC staples — high-tech and Internet startups. With China aiming to set up its own NASDAQ-like venture exchange, 2008 promises to be a very exciting year for them and still offers room to grow for those not in the market.[9]

Chinese M&A: Globalization is a two-way street

The reason globalization is a driver of the other drivers is that it is not just about opening up China's markets to foreign goods; globalization is also — to some — a double-edged sword, meaning that the price for open access to China's 1.3 billion consumers is opening up one's own market to China. And Chinese companies have, in the last three years, been very active indeed, expanding abroad quickly but following their own game plan.

One characteristic of Chinese companies is that overcapacity in the domestic market leads to intense price competition at home. There is so much overcapacity in some industries that, if a global slowdown were to occur, China would experience deflation. In such a competitive domestic environment, surprisingly, foreign markets are often these companies' only source of profit and, contrary to the approach taken by Japanese companies of using their home market as a profit center and selling (some would say dumping) products abroad more cheaply, the Chinese domestic market prices are among the lowest in the world, so much so that foreign consumers gladly pay a higher price and still see it as a bargain compared to other countries' goods.

A second aspect of overseas strategy that Chinese companies utilize is akin to surrounding the most valuable areas and biding time to build up strength, then sweeping into the prime territory. Companies such as China's Haier and TCL are already doing this. This is a very long-term strategy but, as any China watcher will tell you, Chinese have a long-term perspective and a very long-term historical memory. So many companies elect to enter markets in Eastern Europe, South America, or South-East Asia before they will be ready for the biggest EU regions, North America and Japan. This is what it means to use the countryside to surround the city.

Chinese companies are already becoming active in overseas mergers and acquisitions as both a way to gain technology and, in many cases, to gain just a brand name. China's TCL merged with Thompson of the Netherlands. China's PC giant Legend rebranded itself Lenovo, and quickly acquired IBM's computer business, sales network, top staff and, most importantly, the ThinkPad notebook PC brand.

Then in 2005 there was the aborted attempt by the China National Offshore Oil Corporation to acquire US-based Unocal, and 2007's attempted takeover of 3Com by China's Huawei Technologies (a telecommunications equipment manufacturer) and Bain Capital Partners. The Unocal bid failed due to intense political opposition, while 3Com voluntarily withdrew its application to the Committee on Foreign Investment when it became clear the national security concerns would lead to formidable difficulties.[10] Despite the fact that both deals failed due to political opposition, they still indicate how rapidly China's companies are growing up. These are only the most visible of China's overseas M&A activities; in fact, hundreds of Chinese companies have quietly bought up brands, technology, even entire factories. This is very big business for overseas investment banks and advisories, probably for years to come.

In 2007, Chinese M&A reached its most sophisticated level yet, with a number of key investments in overseas private equity and venture capital firms, the biggest being by the Chinese government's China Investment Corporation, a US$200 billion sovereign wealth fund created in 2007. Its first two investments — a US$3 billion purchase of a nine percent stake in the Blackstone Group, and a US$5 billion investment in Morgan Stanley for about ten percent — seem to be a way for China into the US financial industry.

In this way, globalization is turning out to be a boon for the Chinese companies that were previously limited to domestic markets, OEM agreements, and lack of brand power. It is no mistake that many of these activities including the investment in Blackstone were led not by the invisible hand, but by the hand of the Chinese government.

RMB Revaluation Issue

From the time of the Asian financial crisis in 1997 up to 2005, China believed strongly that its stable RMB policy was good for China, and for Asia and the world. Many believe it is what kept China safe from the effects of the crisis and prevented further losses in neighboring countries since China was acting as a breakwater against the tide. The American government believed that the official peg rate, 8.27 RMB to the dollar, was too low, artificially devaluing the true strength of the RMB and, by making Chinese products appear cheaper than they should, grew a large trade imbalance with the US.

China's position on the trade imbalance is not to blame the managed RMB versus the dollar exchange rate, but rather to look at differences in the business environment which make Chinese products unnaturally cheap. The government points out that it has a trade surplus with some countries and a deficit with others, so before acceding to the demands of the US because of the extremely large trade surplus China has, it wants to focus more on structural problems.

Two areas are labor costs and environmental controls. Since the cost of labor in China is so low, the theory goes, it makes the Chinese currency appear weaker than it should be. The support for this argument is that China has a trade deficit with a number of countries and that the Chinese RMB's purchasing power abroad at the current exchange rate is about right.[11]

The second structural weakness which undervalues Chinese exports is environmental controls, of which there are many but which are seldom enforced. So, in order to correct the trade imbalance with certain countries, environmental laws should be enforced more so that costs of production increase in line with international levels. Until China has corrected these structural problems, it will resist efforts by foreign countries to speed up the pace of revaluation lest they overshoot the mark, so to speak, ending up much as Japan did in the 1990s with a period of *en-daka* — high yen — that hurt Japan's exporters.[12]

On these fronts, in 2007, the Chinese government introduced a new set of labor-related laws that went into effect on January 1, 2008 and also increased the minimum wage. On the environmental side, the country cut off exporters who were reported to have evaded pollution standards by refusing to authorize export licenses if an environmental pollution problem was reported.

Making money from the RMB appreciation?

The RMB appreciation since 2005, when adjustments were first started on the 8.27 RMB/US$ rate that had been in place since the time of the Asian financial crisis in 1997, has not been any-thing spectacular, but it has been consistent, amounting to about a 15 percent decline to 7 RMB/US$ at the time of writing. From 2005, the strengthening against the US dollar has continued unabated, though the appreciation rate has been faster in 2008 and will likely continue to rise under the intense inflationary pressure present in China. A growing number of economists are predicting, if not sug-gesting, a further 10–15 percent revaluation is in order, the sooner the better to discourage more hot money from flowing into China on the expectation of currency gains.[13]

The start of the Olympic Decade will likely see the Chinese cur-rency appreciate further, meaning asset valuations inside China will increase in dollar terms. By how much? Nobody really knows, but looking at the appreciation of the Japanese yen from the 1980s bubble economy years until the bubble collapse in the early 1990s, the yen almost doubled in purchasing power abroad, which is how the Japanese came to own so many Renaissance paintings and large foreign companies.

It is dangerous to compare in this way two unlike economies (the main difference being that China's currency is not allowed to freely float), but virtually all economists agree on one point: The RMB must appreciate further in order to reach a more natural equilibrium that will reduce the trade imbalance and satisfy increasing calls from countries such as the US for China to stop using the RMB to under-value China's exports.

The Chinese Government Goes Shopping

China Investment Corporation (CIC) — known as a sovereign wealth fund because of its government-linked ownership — is in a position to help the Chinese economy by diversifying its foreign currency reserves, stocks, bonds and treasury bills into investments that will spread risk, and the hope is, generate a higher return. The size, US$200 billion, is quite large but not exceptional among global sovereign wealth funds. It is managed by a team of Chinese financiers who, by their own admission, are taking it slow and learning as they go. This can be seen as an opportunity for the West to source from a much larger pool of investors, be an alternative to some of the largest funds from Dubai, Norway, and Singapore, and be a place where Western investment banks (or investment bankers) can find new projects and opportunities.[14]

While many countries have sovereign wealth funds, including some that are much bigger such as Norway's US$380 billion pension fund, any investment made by CIC will be looked upon suspiciously by Western democratic capitalist societies as a little too much like Chinese government intervention in markets or, worse, speculation that the Chinese have some hidden agenda. Although CIC is not yet active as a fund, having only made two major deals (the Blackstone and Morgan Stanley investments), the precedent for anti-Chinese investment sentiment was set in 2004 when a Chinese government-connected entity, the CNOOC oil group, made a bid on US-based Unocal: It was rebuffed by the US Congress for fear, perhaps, the Chinese were trying to get American oil. The accusation had little more merit than denying the Dubai Ports Corp. permission to control American ports because it was from an Arab country. Forget that Dubai is one of the few US-friendly Arab countries, it was the political impression that mattered, and so it will happen with CIC as every deal it makes (especially in the US) will be gone over with a fine-tooth comb.

That makes the first deal CIC made all the more surprising. In 2007, it was announced with much fanfare that CIC was buying into then privately-held Blackstone Capital just prior to its IPO. Blackstone is perhaps symbolic of American capitalism at its most pure and brutal extreme: A private equity and leveraged buyout firm, Blackstone specializes in buying other companies, cutting out the fat (whereby fat often means jobs) to increase efficiency, and then running the firms as cash cows or repackaging them for sale. What could be more Gordon Gecko capitalist than that? And here was China, the Communist and now market-planned economy, buying in. CIC put down US$3 billion, a sizeable amount but nowhere near a controlling interest as it didn't even purchase voting-class shares. When Blackstone had its IPO, perhaps it was just bad timing in the markets or, if you believe conspiracy theories like those proposed in China's 2007 bestseller *Currency Wars*, part of a cabal of Western bankers controlling the world economies. But in any case, the shares quickly lost value following the IPO and, at one point on paper, China Inc. was out US$1.5 billion. Maybe learning as they go is not such a good idea after all. It makes the case stronger for providing quality investment advice to CIC and its sister funds in the future. This is a US$200 billion fund that badly needs advice and opportunities from the Western investment strategists it seeks to emulate.

China's Own Subprime Crisis?

Credit is being extended in China so quickly that, in 2007, the central bank thought it necessary to raise banks' reserve ratios ten times, and by June 2008 it reached a record high 17.5 percent. It usually trickled out the increases a half percentage point at a time, but by the end of 2007, realizing it was having hardly any effect on slowing down liquidity, tried to unsuccessfully shock the system with a full percentage point increase. However, the collective shrugs of the banking sector could not be mistaken for surprise. 2008 promises more increases to the reserve ratio, but as long as the stock markets, trade and currency surpluses continue to increase, the pace of money entering the system will remain faster than the central bank can take it out, raising the pressure on inflation further.[15]

It was in this environment that, almost quietly, China's first asset-backed securities were announced: A US$270 million pool of auto loans was packaged by the Chinese joint venture of the US's General Motors Acceptance Corp. (GMAC) and China's SAIC, and resold in the interbank bond market. This has perhaps opened the door to any number of derivative products which, due to structural or legal reasons, currently do not exist. Will 2008 see repackaging of housing loans? It is doubtful, but China is trying to launch a full-scale futures and options market, so Western-style financial innovations are likely to be increasingly common in China and financial players should be poised to take advantage of this opportunity (or run from it, depending on their current perspective on loan-backed securities instruments).

In 2005, China underwent a correction in its real estate prices resulting from some government moves aimed at cooling the property sector. At this time, newspapers were full of stories of investors who simply walked away from their properties when the mortgage appeared to be worth more than the value of the property. Those investors are probably regretting that decision now as property prices have recovered with a vengeance. That said, China will not have any Western-style subprime mortgage issues for several reasons: Loans in China are not resold to other financial institutions, fixed-rate short-term mortgages are more common, and China's government has moved to restrict property for investments by specifying higher minimum interest rates and down-payments for second and third homes within the same family, so the land bubble seems to be coming under control albeit slowly.

Top Wealth Opportunities

China's increasing prosperity and influence also create opportunities to make money, but in the current global climate of financial uncertainty, one must be careful where and how to invest. China is getting richer via accumulated foreign reserves, an appreciating currency, and growing

(Continued)

wealth from the stock markets. Clues for how to prosper in this environment can be found by observing the trends:

1. The Year of the Pig was a great year for the markets, while the Year of the Rat promises much uncertainty for investors.
2. Global investment banks and real estate funds have made major real estate investments in China, but the government is trying to cool speculation.
3. Venture capitalists are investing in everything from shirt factories to restaurant chains and organic farms.
4. China's own companies and its sovereign wealth fund, CIC, have become active in overseas investing.

CHAPTER NINE

Red China Goes Green: Saving Energy, Reducing Pollution

节能, 减排   *Jieneng & Jianpai*

C hina has been an industrial nation for the last 50 years. Starting under the leadership of Mao Zedong, the country attempted to emulate Soviet-style industrialization while upholding Marxist principles of Communism: The means of production were in the hands of the people. The country went through several aborted attempts at large-scale industrialization, notably the Great Leap Forward, a program aimed at vastly improving agriculture and jump-starting China's production of industrial goods such as steel. The impact on the environment at that time was not in proportion to China's already massive population.

China was, and still is to a great extent, an agrarian population struggling to modernize. Farmers were trying to create small-scale steel mills in the countryside — small furnaces that took cutlery and farm implements as their inputs and turned out mostly slag. The Leap was a leap backwards for many, using excessive amounts of coal to produce minor amounts of poor-quality steel, sometimes melting down their only tools in the process, taking away their means of producing sustenance. No exact figures are known, but it is speculated that millions died of starvation.

The trouble with China's early programs of industrialization was that, unlike the Soviet Union's economy, at the time of the 1949 revolution China was an agrarian economy with no industrial base on which to build a more balanced social economy. Thus, farmers in the fields tried to become factory workers and disaster followed.

The failure of the Great Leap Forward from 1959–1961 led to the reinstatement of more moderate policies and marginalization of Mao's boldest initiatives, but his dissatisfaction with the pace of change led to the Cultural Revolution of the 1970s — an attempt by Mao and his close circle to regain control of politics and society by purging all perceived negative influences of religion (the only acceptable beliefs became atheistic, and churches, temples and religious symbols were destroyed) and cultural imperialism (music, books, art were all destroyed in the name of cultural purification). Even people who espoused old ways of thinking (everyone from artists and academics to businesspeople, landowners and even their descendants) were, at best, publicly shamed, and at worst, sent to re-education camps, killed by mobs, or executed by the state. During this time, China took another step backwards and remained largely an agrarian economy with little impact on the global environment.

It was only with the market reforms and opening of China to the outside world by Deng Xiaoping in the late 1970s that China's economy took major steps towards building a manufacturing economy. Unlike previous attempts, there was a small industrial base by that time, mostly supporting the military complex, but lessons had been learned about the power of the market and people were allowed to take their businesses into their own hands for the first time in 40 years. The people embraced the new freedom with enthusiasm. For the last 25 years, growth has largely been non-stop at a compound annual growth rate of 15 percent per year.*

---

*Calculated from 1977 to 2007, compound annual growth rate calculation of GDP in RMB.

The unchecked growth came with some unexpected conse-
quences for the environmental commons of land, air, and water,
both domestically and internationally. Perhaps nowhere else in the
world was the pillaging of the commons so great as in China, where
an entire generation saw everything as owned collectively by the
people of China and therefore, in some way, theirs to do with as
they wanted yet with no individual responsibility: Everybody's
resources, nobody's problems. The impact on the environment, in
terms of industrial inefficiency, electricity and water waste, pollution
of lakes, rivers, and air, was unprecedented. Save for some environmental laws which are rarely enforced, the past two decades
have seen unchecked damage to the domestic shared environment
and, in the 1990s and 2000s, it was increasingly noted that China's
industrial activity was also polluting the world. There was factory
fallout in places as far as Denver, on the other side of the world.
The environmental harm of China's growth could no longer be
doubted.[1]

In China in the last three years, multiple algae blooms appeared
in some of China's most picturesque and historical lakes, plagues
of rats ravaged farms, and a major river spill in northern China's
Songhua River effectively shut off the water for millions for several
months. It is in this context that the Chinese government formed its
11th Five-Year Plan which, among other initiatives, put environment
and sustainable development at the forefront. As well, the pressure
of the world's eyes on China during the 2008 Olympics was a shame
too great to risk and China is trying to turn this situation around
by becoming one of the world's leading producers of green-tech
and enforcing policies that put developed countries' environmental
policies to shame.

Nevertheless, China is not willing to put the environment ahead
of its economic development. It relies on the argument that Western
developed countries are imposing their post-development standards on developing nations, China included, forcing them to in
effect foot the bill for the decades of pollution Western countries

put out during their own industrialization. However, China is trying to find a fragile balance.

On the issue of energy in particular, China is in a conundrum. The nation needs massive amounts of electricity to fuel its factories and has limited energy options. It has huge reserves of coal and, consequently, legions of coal-powered generators which supply just under 80 percent of China's electricity needs (versus about 50 percent in the US). Yet the pollution from this form of energy is arguably the worst, combining carcinogens released in the atmosphere (many generators are said to turn off scrubbers when regulators are not looking, to increase profits) with tons of carbon dioxide which remains in the atmosphere for centuries and travels around the world, contributing to global climate change. China also uses crude oil and natural gas for a large part of its remaining needs, with hydroelectric a very distant third.[2]

China is home to two of the world's longest rivers, the Yellow and the Yangtze, and has built dozens of large hydroelectric dams, most notably the world's largest, the Three Gorges Dam project that has so far resulted in the relocation of more than a million people and may eventually force six million in total to urbanize because of unplanned effects from erosion around the edges of the reservoir. China is damming its rivers in increasing numbers, thereby possibly damning them to problems including silting, flow reduction, and loss of natural flora and fauna including its fabled *Baiji*, the freshwater white dolphin.[3] But it needs the power for newly developing areas such as Sichuan's Chengdu and the massive city-state of Chongqing, which is estimated to have more than 28 million people thanks to amalgamation of nearby townships. Therefore China is, in effect, dammed if it does, and damned if it doesn't. Nuclear power is a viable, less polluting alternative than coal or oil, but with so much coal available, China is unlikely to make large investments in this form of power generation in the short-term.[4]

Water supply is a big problem as generation of electricity uses a lot of fresh water, as do China's inefficient agricultural and manufacturing practices. Finally, there is the 1.3 billion thirsty population. Many parts of the country are already in a permanent state of drought due to desertification and depletion of the water tables, and other parts of China contend with yearly cycles that see rivers dry up and the population subsisting on water trucked in. Sichuan, home to the Three Gorges Dam, is ironically one of those places.

With such visible examples of polluted environments and resource shortages, several opportunities from the *Greening* super-trend will result.

Alternative Energy Generation, Products, and Services

There is a push for alternative forms of energy generation for three reasons. First, China wants to reduce its dependence on foreign oil, the lack of which would grind China's economy to a halt as it has little natural reserves of its own. China's foreign policy in the past several years has been dominated by its quest to secure resources, of which oil is the most important. Despite what may be termed successes in getting foreign countries in the Middle East, Africa, and other conflict-prone regions to agree to supply China's oil needs, the dependence is still bothersome as it must be transported long distances by sea or pipeline. China's lack of significant naval power means supplies by sea are difficult to secure. Thus, China is actively seeking to become a major producer of alternative energy sources, currently solar, wind, clean-coal, and hydrogen, for energy security and long-term energy independence.

Another reason is that, by acting quickly, China can become a leader in these new technologies. Despite the fact that they've all been developed abroad, China is looking to become a world leader in certain enviro-tech. Companies such as the NASDAQ-listed Suntech are leading the way in the solar market.

The last but still important reason for the government and the people is the positive impact the technologies have on the environment. Living with pollution is grudgingly accepted even by China's highly educated white-collar workers as the price of growing prosperity. Their new apartments need air-conditioning and heating, their new cars need gas, so they all realize that embarking on a green revolution too soon would stymie growth rather than promote it. Some rural and agricultural areas of China have no power at all, but with the exception of these farmers choosing between having electricity or not and who don't particularly care where it comes from, the government, business and the people in general all favor cheap coal-powered energy from the grid over clean energy. While it cannot be said that there is a willingness to hurt the environment, most people in China would rather make money by selling solar energy equipment than to try to save the world from global warming with it. This means there are a huge number of opportunities in Chinese manufacturing for green technology.

Cleaning up the Mess

The second major opportunity arising from the *Greening* supertrend is cleaning up after decades of environmental damage. The Chinese government is trying its best to clean up some of the most egregious pollution problems: Polluting factories dumping into rivers, wasted electricity in the form of inefficient production, and highly visible pollution such as that in cities that are gateways to China: Beijing for the 2008 Olympics and Shanghai for the 2010 World Expo. It is perhaps surprising that Beijing is the more polluted of the two, but cleanup activities in Shanghai have been extremely efficient and effective: It has a smaller area, and does not have to cope with the smog-causing dust storms that plague Beijing and other northern cities. It remains to be seen how much the Beijing environment can be cleaned before the Olympics, but the government is not short on ideas. This creates new opportunities in environmental services and consulting, pollution-reduction equipment, and green products. In fact, it is not too much to say that China will become a world leader in this field as well because it has to; we believe it will happen in as little as ten years. Thus, this is a big opportunity, but it must be acted upon now.

The Environment vs. Development Tradeoff — China's Environmental Gamble

The Chinese leadership is in a tough spot. On the one hand, it needs further development to continue to supply new jobs for the millions of new workers entering the workforce each year. On the other hand, the combined effects of manufacturing to the global market, urbanization of China's people, and consumerism driving even greater quantities of production and electricity needs, have increased the manufactured pollutants, concentrated them more in the cities, and led to greater energy needs than ever before. To impose greater environmental controls could mean slowing down the pace of development, losing jobs, and increasing prices. The effects of this conundrum can be seen everywhere. Chinese cities which are the most developed, such as Beijing and Guangzhou, experience smog that make Los Angeles in the polluted 1980s look pristine by comparison. For example, in 2007, Guangzhou experienced 131 hazy days, while a neighboring city in Guangdong province, Dongguan (home of the world's largest shopping mall), experienced 213. A non-hazy day doesn't necessarily mean blue skies: In the summer, the climate is naturally humid and overcast, trapping the smog and preventing the sun from burning off at least some of it. In the winter, the climate is dry and has low air circulation, allowing dust to linger.[5]

China's State Environmental Protection Agency (SEPA) (from 2008 upgraded and now to be called the Ministry of Environmental Protection), until recently has not had much ability to stop the pollution, and the courts were no better, largely ignoring citizens' pollution concerns and refusing to accept many court cases. According to environmental groups like China's All-China Environmental Federation, less than one percent of 100,000 cases in 2007 were allowed to proceed.[6] Most failed because of the burden of proof requirements falling on the citizens making the claims. It is too early to know how the upgraded Ministry of Environmental Protection will impact these kinds of concerns.

While China did join the Kyoto Protocol (which it regularly chides the US about when environmental issues are raised between the governments), its pollution since ratification has increased. China hosts 16 of the world's 20 most polluted cities.[7] Yet it has stricter environmental laws on the books for everything from car emissions to allowable quantities of certain chemicals in consumer products.[8] This reflects the weak enforcement of environmental laws, by choice it seems, in order to keep the economy growing.

Occasionally, the laws are used opportunistically, as when in 2005 P&G's SK-II brand of cosmetics was found to contain levels of certain potential irritants. This caused a huge scandal when Chinese consumers arrived *en masse* to SK-II cosmetics counters and demanded refunds for unsafe products. It was widely reported that SK-II was originally a Japanese brand and the timing of the quality inspections was at a key moment of tense relations between Japan and China. The company insisted the products were the same as sold in other countries with the same formulations, but China's quality control watchdogs saw it differently.

Changes seen starting in 2006 and 2007 after the Songhua River pollution and Tai Lake algae blooms include enforcing the laws more strictly, upgrading SEPA to Ministerial status, and making environmental improvement as one of the parameters used in evaluating provincial officials.

On the bright side, blue sky days are supposedly back in certain Chinese cities that have pushed manufacturing away and made environment a priority. One such city is Beijing, which has experienced an increase in blue sky days of 246 days in 2007 from 100 days in 1998, even as foreign journalists based in the city looked out their windows and saw mostly grey. The campaign was started in an effort to clean up the air for the Olympics, and Beijing has spent more than US$17 billion on the project so far.[9]

One Billion Roofs — China's Solar Initiative

China's use of solar energy is more than 80 million square meters, making it the single biggest solar user in the world and about half of the world total installed capacity. Much of this is solar-powered water heaters that are ubiquitous in China's smaller cities and agricultural communities, often the only source of hot water for farmers.[10] China is also the world's third largest producer, after the EU and Japan.

As part of its renewable energy strategy, China is making solar a key priority by not only producing but also using. China's solar industry, however, has a critical structural weakness. All of the main patents and technologies in solar are foreign-developed, such as the technology to make polycrystalline silicon (PCS), a key and expensive ingredient in both computer chips and solar cells. What's more, a new technology being developed, thin-film solar cells, threatens China's dominance in the traditional glass and PCS panels, so some consolidation of this industry is expected as thin-film technology becomes more widespread. It appears that both Nanosolar of the US and Sharp Electronics of Japan are close to commercializing their separately-developed thin-film technology, and it remains to be seen whether China can develop its own or whether technology transfer of the patents will occur.

Green Energy Solution — Sun Power

With revenues of nearly US$1.4 billion in 2007, Suntech Power is one of the world's three largest solar cell manufacturers, together with Sharp of Japan and Q-Cells in Germany. The Wuxi-based company, the first privately-owned Chinese company listed on the New York Stock Exchange, posted profits of US$80 million for the third quarter of 2007, up 115 percent from a year earlier. The company's revenue has also

(Continued)

been growing rapidly for the last three years. The company's founder and chairman, Shi Zhengsong, envisions his company's sales will reach US$13.8 billion (RMB100 billion) by 2012, overtaking both its rivals.

It's hard to imagine how a newly-established company can fly so high and so far within seven years. After spending more than ten years in Australia for his doctorate degree and research in thin-film solar technology, Shi came back to China to start his own company, Suntech Power, manufacturing silicon solar cells and modules. With the support of the Wuxi government and investment from several local enterprises, Suntech was formed in 2001 with 20 employees.

Financial difficulties in the first few years persisted, the demand for solar energy not being as great as it is at present. Shi had to purchase second-hand equipment from overseas, which cost only one-third of his earlier-purchased new equipment. Despite the financial difficulties and the bleak photovoltaic market in the early 1980s, Shi remained convinced of solar energy's future, even when Suntech did not have money to pay wages.

As the solar-energy sector began to take off, Suntech's sales shot up from just under US$21 million (RMB150 million) in 2004 to US$111 million (RMB800 million) in 2005 and US$167 million (RMB1.2 billion) in 2006.

China is a large solar cell and module manufacturer, and there is great industrial and consumer demand in China for alternative forms of clean energy to supplement its overreliance on polluting coal. The market potential for solar energy is huge if solar power can be introduced extensively to commercial and residential areas. The main barrier is cost versus other forms of power, especially coal. In China, solar energy costs about US$0.70 (RMB5) per kilowatt hour to generate, eight to ten times the cost of coal-fired electricity. But with the advent of thin-film solar technology, the cost of sun-generated energy is expected to be competitive with coal and Suntech Power is sure to be an important player in this new technology.[11]

Coal Gasification — More Than Just Hot Air

China's coal consumption is the highest in the world, yet it also has huge reserves, so it has historically been a net coal exporter. That is, until early 2008, when China experienced a power shortage due to lack of coal in 13 provinces including the prosperous southern province of Guangzhou. In fact, China's supply of coal was sufficient — the problem was getting the coal to the places that needed it because of logistical problems. Overall, China's power grid has a surplus but due to poor interconnections between regions, some parts of China still experience power shortages at key times such as summer when air-conditioner use peaks together with production for the Christmas season.

2008 will likely mark China's transition from a net exporter of coal (a trade surplus of just 2.2 million tons was recorded in 2007) to an overall importer. Growth in coal imports topped 30 percent in 2007, which is indicative of a trend that China is not scaling back use of coal but is actually using more and more. This is undoubtedly bad news for those worried about climate change. But it's good news for any companies that produce coal-related technologies for mining, scrubbing and filtering, and environmentally sounder clean-coal technologies like coal gasification, such as China Shenhua Energy Co., China's largest coal producer.

Shenhua has the second largest reserves of coal globally thanks to its preferential access to the Chinese market, and has gained more than 50 percent in market value since its initial public offerings in two separate stock markets, Hong Kong and Shanghai. Originally listed in Hong Kong in 2005, its stock was not available for purchase by most mainland China investors so, when it announced it would raise nearly US$9 billion in the world's largest IPO in 2007, the stock in Hong Kong shot up and the value on its Shanghai IPO nearly doubled the subscription price and has remained strong amid the rising demand for coal. With a vested interest in coal generation, Shenhua is likely to be active in clean-coal technologies and has allocated a large portion of its IPO funds to acquisitions.[12]

Feng'Shui — Wind and Water

China's water quality is poor in many regions for two reasons. On the one hand, pollution is a persistent problem in virtually every lake and river because of uncontrolled dumping of factory effluent; but on the other hand, water which has ostensibly gone through treatment and purification may still not match the quality of developed countries' water systems because of poor-quality treatment equipment and obsolete pipes that may have been installed 30 or 40 years ago.

It is typical in many parts of the country to have significant scaling, and deposits of calcium and minerals, on pots after just a few uses. The strong chlorine smell and, sometimes, muddy water from the faucets force many residents to choose bottled water. Bottled water is popular, and multinationals such as Nestlé have jumped into the provision of water supplies with deliveries of large bottles on the backs of laborers on pedal-powered tricycles. Chinese people are green tea drinkers, making hot water dispensers quite popular. Another solution is filters, which are becoming more popular. But in order to really satisfy the needs of the entire population of tea drinkers (and personal water users as well), better treatment facilities and equipment are needed.

Supplying clean water, filters, and water treatment products is a growing business in China, which world water leaders Nestlé, Veolia and GE Water are already jumping into.

Water pollution

Tai Lake (*Taihu* in Mandarin) was formerly one of China's most picturesque bodies of water, being written about in centuries-old poetry and still a popular tourist destination, until 2007 when Blue-Green

Algae blooms made the lake unnavigable, undrinkable, and unappealing as a travel destination, much less a subject of poetry.

The blame was placed on a combination of warm weather and too many nutrients in the water, but the root cause was the lack of control over factories that dumped effluents in nearby areas which seeped into the water tables, or often directly into the lake itself. The disaster required millions of dollars to clean. Afterwards, questions were finally being asked: How did this amount of pollution get into the water? Why were there no controls?

While examples of outright dumping of toxic chemicals are rare now in China (the Songhua River chemical spill in northern China was blamed on an accident), it is still quite common to have factory water (used in cleaning, cooling, or other industrial uses) simply dumped untreated. Milky, murky, even black water is sometimes dumped into rice paddies.

Financial incentive (i.e., avoiding treatment costs) and lack of government enforcement of regulations are the primary reasons significant amounts of pollution still happen. Much as Western, Taiwanese, and other countries' factories sought out China because of its less strict environmental management laws and hence lower costs, so Chinese companies themselves seek to reduce costs as much as possible by skirting, bending and even breaking the rules by moving around within China to a place that will tolerate them. With competition in China being intense due to overcapacity, any cost reduction counts. And often, a company that evolved under state ownership would lack government oversight since they were, in effect, agents of the government and therefore beyond reproach. The entrepreneurs of the past 20 years would simply see this as a hassle cutting into their profit margins. The attitude in China among older generations that grew up in a shortage economy, that you take what you can while you can, still prevails.

From the government perspective, officials were rewarded for development, not clean environments (until 2007, at any rate, when environmental GDP growth became one of their key performance indicators), so the financial incentive of attracting foreign direct investment and factories to one's region to push up GDP was great. Even industries which were polluting were welcomed, but in retrospect the areas that accepted such factories for the sake of investment are now paying a very high price. Many foreign factories, seeking to escape environmental legislation and costs in their home markets, moved to China in the 1980s and 1990s to escape, in effect exporting their pollution to China.

The sheer number of factories in the vastness of China's lands makes it difficult to police everyone, and the financial incentives for factory owners from cutting corners, and for the local government in tax revenues and sometimes in the form of bribes from owners to officials, were too hard for many to pass up. Thus, pollution became institutionalized.

SEPA was able to catch significant numbers of polluters but, as a federal agency, had little power to enforce directives at the provincial and local levels. The fines that it could impose were often so small that it was cheaper for factories to pay the fines and keep on polluting rather than clean up their acts. The situation changed in 2007, when both the national government and SEPA acted in conjunction with the major banks to create a polluting-firm blacklist. Firms on the list were not supposed to receive additional financing and had their applications for public listings suspended.[13] There was also increased cooperation between state and local government to shutter polluting factories in Heilongjiang and Shanxi provinces and Inner Mongolia. In one city, Wuxi, suffering from the effects of the Tai Lake algae bloom, this resulted in 1,340 factories being closed immediately or in the short-term.[14]

**The best opportunities in these regions are
pollution reduction and treatment technologies:
Filters, scrubbers, desalination (for providing
fresh water for factories),
treatment chemicals, and other water treatment technology.**

Water shortages

China, despite its large geographic size (it is the third largest county after Russia and Canada, but is larger than Canada in terms of usable land area), has an absolute shortage of water, and an even greater relative shortage of water once its population is factored in. More than 400 cities in China have a more or less constant water shortage. According to research in China, the water supply in China is approximately 2.8 trillion cubic meters, or about 2,300 cubic meters per person, one quarter of the world per capita average.[15]

While China's increase in desertification is hard to quantify due to a lack of reliable data, the first official government estimate in 2005 pegged China's desert area at about 1.57 million square kilometers. With the water shortage being dire in that area, top soil simply blows away, resulting in some of the worst dust storms globally that regularly see particulate matter traveling thousands of kilometers. Nearby cities such as Beijing have sandstorms several times a year that coat everything in a layer of dust.

China's main defense against this is a kind of Green Wall of China: Reforestation efforts along the northern parts of China to stop the southward desertification trend. The magnitude of the effort would probably make such a wall one of the greatest ecological projects ever undertaken.

What's more, water is unevenly distributed, with the southern parts of China receiving a disproportionate amount, while in the north per capita availability is only 500 cubic meters per person (just five percent of the global average) despite the fact the north is much larger and agricultural land more spread out. China's north is dry and receives much less rainfall, so there have been many droughts there and it is easy to see the changes taking place. Some bridges, such as the famed Marco Polo Bridge over the Yongding River, are no longer strictly necessary as the water flow is minimal, if not dry, all year round.[16]

The Yellow River, the north's main source of fresh water, is China's second largest river, but its average flow rate per year is only 58 billion cubic meters, one-sixth that of the largest and more central Yangtze River, and only two percent of the total river flow in China. Its namesake comes from the fact that it picks up the largest amount of sediment in the world, 35 kilograms per cubic meter, from the Yellow Earth Plateau. It is a river that is historically noted for flooding, yet in many places it remains untamed today because of this sedimentation. Aside from the fact that this makes it much harder to utilize the water for drinking or production, the sediment also continually settles and raises the riverbed. In some places the river is higher than the surrounding cities, supported by dikes and levees, which in the past have flooded more than 1,500 times. On the other hand, the river stopped flowing altogether at least 20 times between 1972 and 1999 and a total of 74 days between 1991 and 1997.[17] With such an imbalance, China is trying desperately to reduce the north-south water differential problem.

An ambitious south to north water redirection plan will move more than 44 billion cubic meters of water per year by 2050 using a system of pipes and aqueducts at a cost of more than US$62 billion. China will need huge amounts of plastic linings, reinforced PE and PVC pipes, fittings, pumps, and metering systems for this project.

With frequent shortages and the water available being polluted, water recycling and water saving technologies are in great demand in China.

Saving Money One Flush at a Time

The owner of a kiln in a small village several hours north of Shanghai was faced with a dilemma: For years he had successfully managed his company as a supplier to some of the world's largest producers of toilet

(Continued)

bowls, but the combined forces of growth and competitive pressure resulted in reduced margins.

An American standard-sized toilet may use six liters per flush, while a Chinese model may use as much as nine liters of water. With China's strong push to reduce water consumption, the factory turned to innovation and designed a toilet that used only 4.2 liters per flush.

Business is booming from Western Europe, Japan, and the US, but in a sign of the water-shortage times, sales in China and other developing countries are also increasing quickly.

Air Pollution

With air quality in China being poor almost by definition (14 of the world's 20 most polluted cities are in China, according to the World Bank in 2007), a lot of foreigners who move to China for work end up leaving, sometimes with pollution being the main reason for their departure, especially if their children suffer from asthma. Some people in Beijing were understandably skeptical that the city could be awarded the Olympics based on its poor environmental record. When it was campaigning for the appointment back in 1993, the city appeared so clean when the Olympic Committee were visiting that some expatriates joked that residents and companies must have shut down all the coal burners. Whenever there is a major event held in China, such as when it hosted the APEC meting in 2001, various temporary traffic and manufacturing controls may be announced. The problem in the past was often due to small coal-powered burners that residents used to cook their food and burn coal in the winter for heating, while today it is more likely due to the number of vehicles on the road or factories.

It is more useful to look at steps that are being taken to correct the problem. Between 1998 and 2002, the Beijing government used about US$6 billion to clean the air and reduce sulfur emissions by controlling auto registrations, improving the coal burners, and relocating factories. In 2002, resulting from these changes, particle mass became about 167 milligram per cubic meter, only about 1.7 times that of the comparatively pollution-conscious Japan.[18]

For 2008, the Beijing city government has set especially strict goals for the year to ensure a clean Olympics. First, in terms of reducing carbon dioxide through energy generation, the energy consumption per unit of GDP must fall by five percent, which is one percent higher than the national target set under the 11th Five-Year Plan.[19]

In terms of air and water pollutants, emission of sulfur dioxide, one of the chemicals responsible for acid rain and a gauge of air pollution, is to fall four percent. And the chemical oxygen demand (COD), a key measure of water pollution, should drop by 10 percent. Finally, as a combined measure that also includes the effects of traffic and smog, there should be an increase in "blue sky days" — days when the air quality is fairly good — to 70 percent or about 256 days, 10 days more than in 2007.[20] In order to ensure clean air for the Beijing Olympics (as well as to reduce traffic congestion), the city government has announced a plan to have only odd- or even-numbered car licenses on the road on alternating days.[21] By setting these targets, the government is making it known that failing to do so when the eyes of the world are on China would result in a loss of face.

When it comes to China's overall carbon footprint, these kind of improvements in just one major city are actually minor, but it becomes increasingly difficult for developed countries to accuse China of doing nothing about the problem. While a new 2008 ranking from the Netherlands Environmental Assessment Agency puts China as the world's largest CO2 emitter, official statistics still rank it as the second largest producer of carbon dioxide in the world after the United States, producing about 13 percent versus the US's 23 percent of the world total. But China joined the Kyoto Protocol climate control treaty, while the US did not.[22]

Wind Power

China is also a strong user of wind power, with 91 wind farms with more than 5,600–6,000 megawatts of generating capacity. China is assisted in this area because it is also a major producer of turbines for wind power, and one of China's largest wind companies, Goldwind Science & Technology Co., went public on the Shenzhen stock exchange and bought into a German wind-turbine manufacturer. China requires foreign investments in this sector to use 70 percent local production, and the national targets for 2015 and 2020 have been set at 10,000 megawatts and 30,000 megawatts respectively, but an industry spokesperson said the goal could be revised to as high as 100,000 megawatts by 2020 which, based on current growth rates, would give China the largest installed capacity in the world.

China's Ministry of Finance is also encouraging more imports by refunding value-added tax and tariffs for key turbine components, so growth in this industry is very likely to be strong should these goals and incentives stay in place.[23]

Efficient Construction

China's market for green buildings and construction materials is growing rapidly because of mandates for China to cut its overall usage of electricity per unit of GDP by 20 percent, decrease its use of water, save land, and so on. This translates into an initiative to create all new buildings from 2008 with at least 50 percent more energy efficiency, and Shanghai has further promoted the goal of 65 percent less energy used.

One of the biggest opportunities in this area is construction materials, not necessarily even green construction materials, just *better* materials. For example, in much of Shanghai and especially in the areas south of the Yangtze River, insulation in buildings has been practically non-existent. Most construction in China is concrete high-rises; even houses are built from concrete. However, when the properties are sold to home buyers, they typically do not include any kind of interior design. Basically, buyers take possession of a concrete box and then build the rest themselves through a general contractor. This is also a great opportunity for interior designers, of whom there is a shortage with Western design and technical experience.

When interior design and decoration is done, typically insulation is left out, as are double-paned windows and energy-efficient doors. Insulated floors are rare: It is much more common to put some wood flooring directly on top of the concrete. In most concrete-structured buildings, large holes are drilled through the wall to the outside for the air-conditioner's uninsulated pipe to the heat-exchanger.

Furthermore, there is usually no central air-conditioning or heating system in older buildings, and even in newer residential buildings it still may be left out, allowing residents to make their own decisions on air-conditioning and heating. When this happens, usually wall-mounted units are placed in every major room, and certain places such as the kitchen or bathroom are not climate-controlled at all: Cooking dinner can be like working in a sauna, while taking a shower in the winter definitely wakes you up as soon as you stand on the cold tile floors.

Green building technologies have big potential markets in China as it seeks to lower its energy consumption: Lighting, insulated doors, energy-efficient appliances, simple home automation and energy monitoring systems, and so on.

Alternative-Energy Vehicles

It is said that world oil supplies could not handle the demand of every Chinese family owning a car. The Chinese government believes the roads couldn't handle it either, putting high license fees in place to discourage mass consumption of vehicles.

The World's Most Profitable DMV

In a bid to keep Shanghai's high-spending consumers from flooding the roads with cars, Shanghai has instituted a cap on new license plates at about 5,000–7,500 per month, which it sells at a monthly auction.

(Continued)

In 2007, the monthly vehicle license plate auction generated about US$500 million in revenues, probably making the authority the most financially lucrative Department of Motor Vehicles in the world. Most of this money was used to improve local public transportation facilities and subsidize public transportation costs.

In the monthly auction during the last two years, demand appeared very high and prices for plates have been steadily rising since the system was introduced in 2000. The price of a plate can be as much as 8–16 months of salary for a typical office worker, yet consumers seem willing and able to pay up to US$8,000 on average for a license plate in December 2007. Sixes and eights are important in Chinese numerology, so plates with auspicious numbers such as 888 are even more expensive and can go for astronomical amounts.

With the cheapest cars in China selling for as little as US$5,000, the license plate often has more value than the vehicle it is attached to. This may in fact have an unintended consequence for the environment which is that, with the license plate costing so much, many consumers use that as a justification to get a more expensive car which will likely have poorer fuel economy and greater impact on the environment. Still, it's a good way to keep Shanghai's streets from getting too clogged up.

Shanghai being able to limit itself to 60,000 new cars on the road in 2007 is probably a good thing, considering the country itself purchased about 8.5 million vehicles in 2007. Without the controls on new plates, Shanghai would become overwhelmed with cars, much the same way Beijing already has. What once was a city of bicycles in a country of bicycles has now become a city of cars.

It is with an understanding of these trends that companies in China are rushing to develop alternative-fuel vehicles that will be cheaper to run and help reduce the smog that envelops many Chinese cities around rush hour (which is basically all day in Shanghai and Beijing). Chinese-made hybrid cars appeared in China in 2008 and every auto company, from Toyota's Prius (now being produced near Guangzhou) to GM, is introducing its hybrid in China. GM, despite very strong sales growth of 19 percent in 2007 and sales of more than a million units, is not growing as fast as competitors such as Volkswagen and Toyota, growing 28 percent and 62 percent respectively. Toyota's growth is especially impressive given that many Chinese consumers have an anti-Japanese product bias due to lingering sentiments over their war history. GM is looking to improve its growth prospects with new or updated models such as the Buick LaCrosse Eco-Hybrid, a localized update with new interiors and features designed in China, turning it from a grandpa car in the US into a hot executive ride appealing to a much younger demographic in China. GM's new US$250 million R&D center has alternative-fuel vehicles as one of its prime research objectives and is part of its strategy to be a leader in hybrid car technology in China. Hybrids and alternative-fuel vehicles appear to be the most likely candidates to form the next generation of vehicles on China's roads.

Getting ready for the 2010 World Expo being held in Shanghai, the city is setting up the infrastructure to run 1,000 hydrogen fuel-cell vehicles. With only three stations nationwide and just a single hydrogen fueling station set up in Shanghai's neighboring "Car Town" Anting (also close to Shanghai's iconic F1 racetrack, shaped as the *shang* Chinese character in Shanghai), the city has only two and a half years to reach this ambitious goal, but there is a strong push to achieve it.

However, with 20,000 buses on the road, half of them more than three years old and regularly spewing black diesel smoke onto the streets, correcting the air pollution of the buses in service is probably an important first step. There are also the ubiquitous diesel trucks, delivering anything from bamboo to a load of migrant workers, which are an unchecked source of pollution. Shanghai is addressing this problem by creating an inspection task force with the power to take polluting vehicles off the road immediately if they fail a spot emissions check.

As well, Shanghai's subway system is being expanded rapidly and as soon as routes on the subway and the buses are redundant, the transportation authority pulls the bus routes. While this has left many on overcrowded subway cars, it is undoubtedly better for the environment whenever these pollution-prone buses are taken off the road.

Shopping Bags Be Gone!

China will follow several other countries' lead to reduce free plastic bags from June 1, 2008. While one may say this is just following the green trend, China uses so many plastic bags that it sets a strong example for other developed countries to follow by actually banning free bags. It has also completely banned the use of thin plastic bags which have no possibility for reuse because they break too easily. The main producer of these bags, China's Huaqiang, which makes about 250,000 tons of bags a year, almost immediately closed the factory and laid off 20,000 workers when the announcement was made.[24] The measure affected small-scale bag manufacturers as well. One Shanghai manufacturer producing about 50–60 tons of bags a year put up a "For Rent or Sale" advertisement on the Internet soon after the measure was announced.[25] This has created a huge opportunity for biodegradable plastic bags, reusable cloth pages, carriers, and other environmentally sound solutions.

Biofuels

China has a potential biofuels industry, mostly based on sugarcane in the southern areas like Hainan and rapeseed in other parts of the country, but the rapid inflation rise which had started in 2007 made the government restrict biofuels projects that use staple food products as feedstocks, in order to avoid adding to upward inflationary pressure.

One Austrian company, Biolux, is attempting to move into this sector in China in a big way with a US$115 million processing facility near Shanghai. It will not only handle biodiesel production from rapeseed feedstocks from China, but also from neighboring countries such as Japan and Korea and places as far away as Canada and

Australia, as China does not currently produce enough high-quality feedstock to supply a biodiesel refinery of that size.[26]

While projects like this have been slowed down significantly, it is part of China's goal to have 10 percent renewable energy resources by 2010, and 15 percent by 2020,[27] so this sector is likely to grow once inflationary pressures have been reduced.

Efficient and Ecological Production

With China already being the source for many low-cost commodities, attention should now be turned to not just looking for alternatives, but to make existing products better in an environmental or green way. This could be done by modifying products to use less power, or by changing the materials to be less energy-intensive or easier to recycle.

When it comes to those commodities, the list is endless. Since China makes a lot of textiles out of unsustainable petrochemical fibers, why not provide the organically-grown cotton to the manufacturer directly? Or take the multitude of petroleum-based plastic products and upgrade their production using ecologically produced potato starch? Add a thin-film solar cell coating to a knapsack or briefcase so it can recharge your electronic devices. The potential product ideas are only limited by the imagination of the designers and the willingness of Chinese manufacturers to produce. The latter's willingness is often never a problem, as many Chinese factories are faced with overcapacity and are in a competitive price war with other suppliers, so they are usually very flexible and open to new ideas.

The driver of this trend will be green-aware consumers looking for reasonably-priced environmental products, large corporate purchasers with a mandate to buy and sell green, such as Wal-Mart and GE, and government regulations which state that new products must have a certain percentage of sustainably-produced materials, a higher energy efficiency, or be completely recyclable at the end of its lifetime, as became the norm in the EU when it implemented new Restriction of Hazardous Substances (RoHS) and Waste Electrical and Electronic Equipment (WEEE) directives which had wideranging implications for Chinese products being sold in that region.

For visionary product designers with a willingness to get beyond China's image as a polluting and labor-exploiting country, China's manufacturers present a wealth of opportunities to produce the next green thing.

Top Environmental Opportunities

This is the final chapter in the book for a reason. Of all of the supertrends mentioned so far, none are as big or as important as saving energy and reducing pollution. China's development puts enormous pressure on world resources. When visiting China, you can easily see the problems of pollution first-hand. It is a relief that the Chinese government is being proactive in solving the dilemma of balancing growth with sustainability. These opportunities promise to be the best of the Olympic Decade:

1. Solar and wind power are widely used in China, and its manufacturing sector leads global production of related technologies. If your business is solar or wind, China's market or China's production are your opportunities.
2. China needs more water and air pollution reduction processes and services. Water treatment, desalination, and air purification are all huge and growing business opportunities.
3. China will lead the way with alternative-fuel vehicles such as hybrid, electric, and hydrogen.
4. Better construction and environmental buildings are a huge new market in China. Eco-cities like Dongtan are being built from the ground up, using the latest green technologies and sustainable living practices and will be the first of its kind in the world.
5. For product designers, China's manufacturing base combined with your sustainable designs is an ideal match.

The future of red China is green indeed.

PART FIVE

CONCLUSIONS

CHAPTER TEN

Become a Gloriously Rich
Businessperson

These opportunities are like a US$100 bill on the ground, and China is a country with thousands of such bills scattered everywhere. But while we all can know that such opportunities exist, the difference is whether you can be the one to pick them up before somebody else does.

In this book, we've told you how the Chinese economy became rich through the drivers of its economy such as exporting and accepting investment from abroad. We've discussed how the drivers still continue throughout the Olympic Decade under the heavy influence of the *drivers of the drivers*, some old and some new ideas about how China is achieving the critical mass to generate wealth on its own, especially through its consumer market development. One might argue that a China decoupling from the world economy is possible under this scenario, but it is not likely. We live in a global world where no country is an island (except literally) in the sea of information, culture, capital, and people that travel around the globe. We have shown how the drivers lead to new *supertrends*, which we called the business, social and wealth supertrends, which in turn lead to the opportunities of China's Olympic Decade.

We've shared our opinions on what the best opportunities within the trends might be, but we picked those with which we had some personal experience, knowledge or intuition that we know will grow. These are not the only opportunities. To extend the analogy above, the US$100 bills on the ground do exist, but they are constantly being blown around by the wind, washed away by the rain, picked up by passerbys. New opportunities are falling from pockets all the time, misplaced by people who are too careless to notice. This is, in fact, only the beginning of the Olympic Decade, which represents another huge growth phase for China that will see its GDP double again in just seven years if China continues at the pace it set in 2007.

This book does not allow us to get into the specific details of starting businesses that take advantage of these trends, so for that we have created an online forum to continue discussion with our readers.

The latest information and updates, commentaries and discussions, and questions and answers about this book, and details of living, working and succeeding in the new Olympic Decade can be found at the official website:

www.chinasupertrends.com

We invite you to visit and look forward to seeing you there.

Notes

Preface

1. Wen reportedly first said in a November 2003 interview with the Washington Post, "Any small problem multiplied by 1.3 billion will end up being a very big problem, and a very big aggregate divided by 1.3 billion will come to a very tiny figure…" Thereafter this became a common talking point, covered in numerous locations, one of which is here: http://english.people.com.cn/200403/04/eng20040304_136505.shtml

2. McDonald's China website (www.mcdonalds.com.cn) lists more than 750 store locations, including 693 24-hour outlets and an unspecified number of other outlets, including McDonald's by delivery. Forbes Magazine in a recent article in February 2008 puts the total are more than 875 outlets in China. http://www.forbes.com/markets/2008/02/25/mcdonalds-china-pricehikes-markets-equity-cx_jc_0225markets04.html

Introduction

1. The many tales of Marco Polo were initially thought to be so far-fetched that few of his countrymen believed them. Nevertheless his book at the time was one of the most expansive accounts of the then-Mongol Empire, and later examinations showed Polo's stories to be at least partly factual. A good summary can be found at http://www.silk-road.com/artl/marcopolo.shtml

2. In China's fast-developing aviation field, there is much conflicting information from carriers, manufacturers, and regulators. An official report from US and Chinese officials following economic talks, as

reported in Reuters via USA Today and other sources, on May 23, 2007: "Under the new agreement, the number of daily round-trip flights will jump to 23 from the current 10 within five years." http://www.usatoday.com/travel/flights/2007-05-23-us-china-flights-deal_N.htm

3. Boeing's estimate was reported in a number of locations, such as this Asia Times Online article, October 23, 2007, "Foreign Firms Fly High Leasing Planes": http://www.atimes.com/atimes/China_Business/IJ23Cb01.html

4. The Civil Aviation Administration of China (CAAC) projection 2007.

5. Foreign students studying in China increased 20 percent in 2007, according to China's Ministry of Education: "The number of foreign students studying in China reached a record of more than 195,000 last year, up 20 percent year on year, latest figures from the ministry showed." Reported on China Economic Net, April 24, 2008, "Bid to attract foreign students gears up." http://en.ce.cn/National/Politics/200804/24/t20080424_15259516.shtml

6. Data from the Shanghai Federation of Trade Unions, as reported in Shanghai Daily, May 6, 2008, "Foreigner influx doubles in five years.": http://www.shanghaidaily.com/sp/article/2008/200805/20080506/article_358456.htm

7. Author estimate based on tabulation of data from numerous sources. Note this figure includes Hong Kongese and Taiwanese classified as foreign residents, which may differ from official statistics.

8. Author estimate. With Shanghai and Beijing alone being home to up to 500,000 foreigners each (again, including Taiwanese and Hong Kongese) the other major cities of Shenzhen (large Hong Kongese population), Dalian (large Japanese population), Guangzhou (numerous foreigners from a variety of countries), and others are quite large.

9. The annual Mercer Human Resource Consulting Cost of Living survey is widely used by human resource professionals to determine expatriate pay packages. The 2007 version can be found at: http://www.mercerhr.com/costofliving and downloaded at http://www.mercerhr.com/attachment.dyn?idContent=1262535&filePath=/attachments/English/COL_Ranking_Top_50_Final_07.pdf

10. The ECA International Cost of Living survey, found at http://www.eca-international.com/Asp/ViewArticle2.asp?ArticleID=199

11. Also from Mercer, the annual World-wide Quality of Living survey ranked Shanghai and Beijing at 134th and 166th respectively, far below

other regional business centers such as Singapore or Tokyo, http://www.mercer.com/referencecontent.jhtml?idContent=1173105

12. The report, On the Development of Chinese Talent in 2006 conducted by the Chinese Academy of Social Sciences, said that a million students had gone abroad between 1978 to 2006, as quoted in the following article: http://www.cbc.ca/news/viewpoint/vp_metz/20071105.html

13. The slogan, "Some must get rich first." was attributed to Deng many times starting about 1978, at the time of the first economic opening reforms, sometimes in reference to places, sometimes in reference to people.

14. The two-year campaign to improve safety in the mining industry resulted in thousands of small mines being closed and more than a billion dollars was spent upgrading facilities and equipment for safety. See the following article from Forbes, which includes sources from the State Administration of Work Safety and Xinhua: http://www.forbes.com/afxnewslimited/feeds/afx/2008/01/13/afx4524639.html

15. Wanting people to be able to better adapt to the eight percent inflation at the start of 2008, Guangdong was not the only place that raised its minimum wage. As reported on MarketWatch, February 27, 2008, "China raises minimum wages to calm consumers": http://www.marketwatch.com/news/story/china-raises-minimum-wagescalm/story.aspx?guid=%7BB120D814-3C01-468A-9C11-B7596BCE1-A35%7D&print=true&dist=printTop

16. More information about wage and price inflation, and the McDonald's wage increase in particular, can be found in this Asia Times Online article, August 8, 2007, "McDonald's Raises Wages in China": http://www.atimes.com/atimes/China_Business/IH08Cb02.html

17. More information from Mercer regarding the Chinese market can be found here: http://www.mercer.com/referencecontent.jhtml?idContent=1268900

18. Economists and China-watchers may be divided as to what is China's biggest threat currently, but the government is unanimous: The Chinese Premier, Wen Jiabao, following the announcement of China's 2008 first quarter economic performance, said in a statement that inflation was China's biggest threat (http://www.bloomberg.com/apps/news?pid=20601087&refer=home&sid=aKWZ_ IFAP3c4) and the Deputy Premier Wang Qishan labeled inflation the biggest economic problem in China and reaffirmed that the government would

maintain a tight monetary policy, according to an article in the International Herald Tribune, May 9, 2008, "Producer Prices on the Rise": http://www.iht.com/articles/2008/05/09/business/yuan.php. Economists are divided on whether the inflation is monetary or supply-side in nature. Food commodity prices have increased rapidly, while efforts to reign in China's money supply have been insufficient as of early 2008.

19. This figure for China's savings rate is widely reported, here in an article from the Cato Institute on June 8, 2007 as "...a dizzying 55%." (http://www.cato.org/pub_display.php?pub_id=8272) The US savings rate is essentially zero or below zero because it imports more than it produces.

20. Figures vary depending on the source, the Chinese National Bureau of Statistics has the 2007 increase in pork price as high as 48.3% (Reported via Xinhua at http://news.xinhuanet.com/english/2008-01/30/content_7527600.htm) while other sources were lower. One thing is certain, China's overall inflation increase was due in large part to increases in food and agricultural commodities.

21. For more information about China's GDP to 2050, there are a number of options: China's internal projections from the National Development & Reform Commission, or external sources such as Goldman Sachs' Global Economics Paper No. 99: Dreaming with BRICs: The Path to 2050, found at: http://www2.goldmansachs.com/ideas/ brics/brics-dream.html

22. These types of predictions are often made by China's leaders in relation to achieving some other target such as, in this case, Wen Jiabao aiming to double the per capita GDP by 2010: http://www.chinadaily.com.cn/china/2006-03/05/content_534421.htm

23. Shanghai is reported to be the city most-affected in China by land subsidence, according to the Chinese Ministry of Land and Resources, reported via Xinhua, February 10, 2007, "Chinese Cities Suffer Land Subsidence": http://china.org.cn/english/news/199613.htm

24. The World Bank's new Chief Economist, Justin Lin, an esteemed academic from China, recently calculated that as early as 2030 China's GDP could be 2.5 times the size of the US's and its per capita income half that of the US's, compared to about 1/20th now, in the May 2008 Chinese-edition of Harvard Business Review, as referenced in China Daily, May 3, 2008, "GDP could be 2.5 times that of the US by 2030": http://www.chinadaily.com.cn/china/2008-05/03/content_6657813.htm

25. With exception of three years when growth of GDP was 5.2% or less, China has maintained seven percent or greater growth (sometimes as high as 15%) for the last 30 years: http://www.chinability.com/GDP.htm

26. Despite missing that goal in 2007 (China's GDP grew as much as 11.9% in 2007), Wen reiterated the same goal at the end of the 11th National People's Congress in March 2008, setting the GDP growth target at 8 percent, reported via Xinhua, March 5, 2008, "China's parliament starts annual session, sets GDP growth at 8%": http://news.xinhuanet.com/english/2008-03/05/content_7719856.htm

27. More information can be found about the Olympics through press releases and other details on the official Beijing Olympic website: http://en.beijing2008.cn/

28. The World Expo will be hosted in Shanghai in 2010 and the city has spent billions of dollars preparing. More information can be found at the official Shanghai World Expo site: http://en.expo2010china.com/

Chapter 1

1. Data from the Chinese Ministry of Commerce: http://zhs2.mofcom.gov.cn/aarticle/ie/statistic/200802/20080205367271.html

2. As reported in the Shanghai Daily, April 4, 2008, "Forex reserve reaches US$1.68 trillion": http://www.shanghaidaily.com/sp/article/2008/200804/20080412/article_355658.htm

3. Prediction by the Asian Development Bank, as reported by Xinhua, April 3, 2008, "ADB: Chinese economy to grow 10% in 2008, inflation at 5.5%": http://english.people.com.cn/90001/90776/90884/6385740.html

4. As reported via Xinhua, October 7, 2007, "Chinese Exporters Adapt to Rising Yuan": http://news.xinhuanet.com/english/2007-10/07/content_6839128.htm

5. The US figure was a trade deficit of US$ 256 billion in 2007 (http://www.census.gov/foreign-trade/balance/c5700.html#2007) while the Chinese figure was US$163 billion, according to China's Customs Statistics, as reported on US China Business Council: http://www.uschina.org/statistics/tradetable.html

6. NAFTA was once thought of as a strong three-way partnership between the US, Canada, and Mexico, wherein Mexico played the part of factory. The three countries were each other's respective

largest trading partners. Now, Mexico has lost its cost advantage to China, and China has surpassed it as the US's second-largest trading partner. At the time of writing, Democratic presidential candidates Barack Obama and Hillary Clinton were openly criticizing the NAFTA agreement on the basis of lost jobs.

7. See the following article on the increase in foreign direct investment in the first quarter of 2008, increasing dramatically because of the hot money effect, reported in China Daily, March 3, 2008, "Wu: More hot money to flow into China": http://www.chinadaily.com.cn/bizchina/2008-03/10/content_6523605.htm

8. As reported by China's National Development and Reform Commission, referring to the period between the opening of China in 1978 to 2007, as reported on the government's official website, May 6, 2008, "Official: most of world's top companies invest in China": http://english.gov.cn/2008-05/06/content_962250.htm

9. The World Bank report, titled "China Governance, Investment Climate, and Harmonious Society: Competitiveness Enhancements for 120 Cities in China" October 8, 2006, can be found at: http://siteresources.worldbank.org / INTCHINA/Resources/318862-1121421293578/120-cities_en.pdf Also, see a related report, also from the World Bank, "Improving the Investment Climate in China" March 2003: http://www.worldbank.org.cn/english/content/investment.pdf

10. Data from China's Ministry of Commerce, as reported via Xinhua, April 11, 2008, "FDI up 61% in first quarter": http://english.people.com.cn/90001/90776/90884/6390549.html

11. The World Bank's calculation uses PPP, purchasing power parity, to estimate the true size of an economy after the effect of exchange rate is taken out. GDP is customarily reported internationally in US dollars, meaning that GDP magnitudes can be distorted by exchange rates. The World Bank's new Chief Economist, Justin Lin, an esteemed academic from China, recently calculated that as early as 2030 China's GDP could be 2.5 times the size of the US's and its per capita income half that of the US's, compared to about 1/20th now, in the May 2008 Chinese-edition of Harvard Business Review, as referenced by China Daily, May 3, 2008, "GDP could be 2.5 times that of the US by 2030": http://www.chinadaily.com.cn/china/2008-05/03/content_6657813.htm

12. The BCG report was widely quoted in Chinese media, such as this story in International Business Times, October 22, 2007, "China to become the world's second-largest consumer market by

2015": http://www.ibtimes.com/articles/20071022/china-consumer-spending.htm

13. See research from China Center for Economic Research, Justin Yifu Lin, February 2004, "Is China's Growth Real and Substainable?": http://www.ccer.edu.cn/download/3024-1.pdf. Also, "Consumer Durables Ownership [in China] 1990–2002": http://www.chinability.com/Durables.htm

14. Many books and China strategy papers talk about localization tactics for the Chinese consumer market. One report by Boston Consulting Group and Knowledge@Wharton, "Selling in China", can be found here: http://www.bcg.com/publications/files/Selling_in_China_Final.pdf

15. Data source, China's National Bureau of Statistics. More information can be found about China's second, third and fourth tier city business expansion in the following articles: China Daily, via Xinhuanet, June 29, 2007, "Real estate focus turns to China's secondary cities": http://news.xinhuanet.com/english/2007-06/29/content_6306920.htm. Also, see Xinhua, February 22, 2008, "Global Retail Giants Battle for Market Share in China": http://www1.cei.gov.cn/ce/doc/cen3/200802211738.htm

Chapter 2

1. The IPO amount total is somewhat difficult to calculate because of exchange rate differences and greenshoe allotments, but the 2006 Bank of China listing in Hong Kong raised US$ 9.7 billion (11.2 billion with the greenshoe over-subscription), the 2006 ICBC dual listing in Hong Kong and Shanghai raised US$22 billion total, and the 2007 Construction Bank Shanghai stock exchange listing raised US$ 7.7 billion (57 billion RMB converted at 7.2 RMB/$). Construction Bank was a *haigui* company, with a previous listing in Hong Kong in 2005.

2. For more information on China's accession to the WTO, a summary of the terms negotiated can be found on the US Trade Representative's official website: http://www.ustr.gov/Document_Library/Fact_Sheets/2001/Background_Information_on_China's_Accession_to_the_World_Trade_Organization.html For more information on China's implementation of the banking reforms in particular, please see this article from the International Herald Tribune, September 5, 2008, "China Tries to Limit Access for Foreign Banks": http://www.iht.com/articles/2006/09/05/business/chibank.php

3. For information about China's compliance with WTO accession obligations, see the US Trade Representative's annual report to Congress, December 11, 2007, "2007 Report To Congress On China's WTO Compliance": http://www.ustr.gov/ assets/Document_Library/Reports_ Publications/2007/asset_ upload_file625_13692.pdf

4. In part to appease US trade negotiators and reduce the amount of the trade imbalance, China cut or abolished a number of export rebate programs in 2007, and reduced the number of low-tech labor-intensive products it sells to the US via export limits. This article from Bloomberg summarizes some of the changes, July 25, 2007, "China to Limit Exports of Labor-Intensive Products": http://www.bloomberg.com/apps/ news?pid=20601080&refer=Asia&sid=a9c64IDUkhpo

5. The latest information on China's tax incentives and mitigating policies at the time of writing are summarized at the China website of PricewaterhouseCoopers here: http://www.pwccn.com/home/ eng/chinatax_news_mar2008_2.html A lighter summary of China's new unified corporate tax, effective from 2008, and the associated policies to reduce the shock to foreign companies that were previously attracted by low tax rates, can be found via China Daily, December 30, 2007, "Policies to cushion impact of new corporate income tax law": http://www.chinadaily.com. cn/china/2007-12/30/content_6360500.htm

6. For more information about China's GDP, GDP per capita and other economic statistics, we used the National Bureau of Statistics website at http://www.stats.gov.cn/english/and the China Statistical Yearbook published by the NBS.

Chapter 3

1. The State Intellectual Property Office published a good summary of the state of intellectual property and parents for 2007: http:// english.ipr.gov.cn/ipr/en/info/Article.jsp?a_no=198450&col_no= 102&dir=200804

2. There is no official figure for the amount of new jobs that need to be created, but typical Chinese government announcements in the last several years for urban jobs needed are between 8–10 million a year, while an additional 10–14 million yearly are needed for rural residents. These estimates are based on the number of new graduates

from universities and high-schools, the number of expected layoffs from inefficient state-owned enterprises, modest population growth, the amount of migrants moving to the cities (i.e. urbanization rate) etc. See: Speech by Chinese Ambassador to the UK Fu Ying's speech to the Royal Society of the Arts, 11/23/2007 at http://www.fmprc. gov.cn/ce/ceuk/eng/sghd/t383809.htm or notes on Hu Jintao's meeting with US President Bush, also by Fu Ying in a March 2008 speech to the University of Kent: http://www.fmprc.gov.cn/ce/ceuk/eng/sghd/t416383.htm

3. Numerous such studies have been done by industry specialists, reporters, and academics. The study we used is titled *Who Captures Value in a Global Innovation System?: The case of Apple's iPod*, from the University of California, Irvine — Greg Linden, Kenneth L. Kraemer and Jason Dedrick, and can be found at: http://pcic.merage.uci.edu/papers/2007/AppleiPod.pdf

4. Accurate information about the number of migrant workers is, of course, hard to come by as many of them are unregistered and don't want to be found. Guangdong, which includes major manufacturing cities such as Guangzhou, Shenzhen, and Dongguan, is estimated to have more than 26 million migrant workers (http://news.xinhuanet.com/english/2008-01/29/content_7517049.htm) according to the Guangdong Provincial Department of Labor and Social Security. Beijing's population of migrant workers is said to top 5.1 million, about 30% of the city's official population (http://english.people.com.cn/90001/6393304.html)

5. In reference to the migrant population and migrant births in 2005, please see this article from Shanghai Daily, March 3, 2007, "Population to stay under 19m": http://www.shanghaidaily.com/sp/article/2007/200703/20070308/article_308231.htm

6. China's urbanization target is set by the government in the 11th Five Year Plan as needing to reach 47% by 2010, up from 43% in 2005, meaning approximately 50 million people must be urbanized. By 2030, the government wants the urbanization process to be complete (about 75%–80% or about one billion people to be living in cities). A March 2008 McKinsey & Company report, "Preparing for China's Urban Billion" is a good source of further information, estimating more than 350 million additional people will move to cities by 2025: http://www.mckinsey.com/mgi/publications/china_urban_summary_of_findings.asp

7. The figures of 700 to 900 million farmers/rural workers are widely reported in various places inside and outside of China, but according to China's last official agricultural census, the results of which became available in 2008, the total number of rural people actually working in farming is significantly less, about 340 million of 480 million full-time rural workers, Xinhua reported, February 22, 2008, "China saw 80 million less farmers 1996–2006": http://www.10thnpc.org.cn/english/China/243467.htm This does not include tens of millions more who are now unemployed farmers with no other work, work only part-time, or have become migrant workers who return to their hometowns during the harvest seasons, so China's total number of farmers is still the most significant part of the working population.

8. More information on the opening of the second terminal in March 2008, reported by Xinhua, March 26, 2008, "Shanghai officially opens China's 2nd largest air terminal": http://news.xinhuanet.com/english/2008-03/26/content_7861957.htm

9. More information on the Three Gorges Project can be found at the official website (http://www.ctgpc.com/) or its Wikipedia entry (http://en.wikipedia.org/wiki/Three_Gorges_Dam)

10. Information about China's rail network, the biggest in the world, is widely available. This Asia Times article provides a good overview the current state of the railway infrastructure, February 7, 2007, "China rail program takes off like a shot": http://www.atimes.com/atimes/China_Business/IB07Cb03.html

11. In the Chinese New Year 2008 travel season, 24.5 million people were using the rail system, down slightly from the previous year because of an intense snow-storm in China that closed trains, roads, and airports for several days. More information can be found here via Xinhua, February 14, 2007, "Railways carry 24 mln passengers during Spring Festival holiday": http://english.gov.cn/2008-02/14/content_889246.htm

12. For further information on the train, please see a media report (http://travel.latimes.com/articles/la-tr-tibettrain19aug19), a travel website with details of the train schedule and fares (http://www.chinatibettrain.com/), and the luxury rail service announced in a Xinhua Report, March 9, 2008, "Five-star Beijing-Tibet train service to be launched after Olympics": http://news.xinhuanet.com/english/2008-03/09/content_7751430.htm

13. A summary of recent announcements and achievements of the Chinese road network can be found here: http://www.chinahistory forum.com/lofiversion/index.php/t20721.html

14. For more information, see World Bank Development Indicators: http://devdata.worldbank.org/external/CPProfile.asp?PTYPE=CP& CCODE=CHN

15. A good summary of recent (2007–2008) regulatory actions in the mobile phone sector in China and the state of the industry was reported by Shanghai Daily, May 4, 2008, "Way to go until phone industry is fair": http://www.china.org.cn/business/2008-05/04/content_15054017.htm

16. More information on the Apple/Chine Mobile talks and their evident ending can be found at this January 15, 2008 article from Australian IT, "Apple, China Mobile end iPhone talks": http://www.australianit.news.com.au/story/0,25197,23054617-15306,00.html and a similar article from Wired: http://blog.wired.com/business/2008/01/china-mobile-an.html. Another more recent report says that formal talks are still to take place. "Our door will remain open…" said China Mobile's chairman, as reported by Xinhua, April 12, 2008, "China Mobile, Apple yet to open formal talks over iPhone launch": http:// news. xinhuanet. com/ english/2008-04/ 12/ content_7966325.htm

17. The China Network Information Center has a large amount of useful data about China's Internet. Their 21st Survey Report published in January 2008 is the most official and up-to-date at the time of writing: http://www.cnnic.net.cn/uploadfiles/pdf/2008/2/29/104126.pdf

18. A private firm, BDA China, made the estimate on the growth of Internet users reaching 220 million by February 2008, as reported by the Associated Free Press, March 13, 2008, "China outsurfs the US: research firm": http://afp.google.com/article/ALeqM5hp9rBe-PsLvpZWYjf4mxwVrz4DCKw

19. Source: CNNIC, see note 17.

20. Source: CNNIC, see note 17.

21. China's response to the Asian Financial Crisis is summarized in a report by Richard Halloran in Global Beat, January 27, 1998, "China's Decisive Role in the Asian Financial Crisis": http://www.bu.edu/globalbeat/pubs/ib24.html

22. The daughter, Yang Huiyan, controls 70% of shares in property company Country Garden. After the IPO, she became wealthier in one day than China's previous wealthiest woman, the so-called

'Queen of Wastepaper,' Zhang Yin, as detailed in this article from the Asian Pacific Post, June 12, 2007, "Richest Chinese woman married": http://www.asianpacificpost.com/portal2/ff808081131b9f8b011320-cb32cf0036_Richest_Chinese_woman_married.do.html

23. Shanghai Daily, December 18, 2007, "Government to get 10% of SOE profits": http://www.shanghaidaily.com/sp/article/2007/200712/20071218/article_342042.htm

24. As discussed in the article in Financial Times by Pei Minxin, November 7, 2005, "China Is Paying the Price of Rising Social Unrest": http://www.carnegieendowment.org/publications/index.cfm?fa=view&id=17677&prog=zch

25. More information about the 'nail house' can be found on numerous media sites, it was front-page news in many Chinese publications for its precedent-setting events. One summary from the Asia Times: http://www.atimes.com/atimes/China_Business/IC31Cb01.html

26. According the UN's Human Development Program report on *Inequality in Income or Expenditure*, China's Gini index is 46.9, while the US's is 40.8. These values are relatively close. In Japan, a country that has a much larger middle class (i.e. less of a wealth gap) the Gini index is only 24.9. More information can be found at http://hdrstats.undp.org/indicators/147.html

27. In 2007, state media reported China closed 553 coal generators, according to Xinhua, January 2, 2008, "China exceeds target in closing 43% small coal-fired plants": http://www.ccchina.gov.cn/en/NewsInfo.asp?NewsId=10367. In 2008, the country continued its campaign, shutting 83 smaller coal generators in the first quarter, according to Chinese state media, April 25, 2008, "Gov't shuts 83 small coal-fired power plants": http://www.china.org.cn/environment/policies_announcements/2008-04/25/content_15015693.htm

Chapter 4

1. Booz Allen and Shanghai American Chamber of Commerce study, March 3, 2008, "China's Shifting Competitive Advantage": http://www.boozallen.com/news/china_manufacturing_2008

2. China National Bureau of Statistics

3. China National Bureau of Statistics

4. Wages were up sharply in the first quarter of 2008, more than 18 percent year on year, reflecting the current high growth and inflation in

China, according to data from National Bureau of Statistics, April 28, 2008, "Average Wage of On-Duty Staff and Workers in Urban Units Went up in the First Quarter": http://www.stats.gov.cn/english/ newsandcomingevents/t20080428_402476836.htm. Also see "The average urban wage in China rose 15 percent to 20,856 yuan (2,875 dollars) in 2006 from a year earlier, according to government data.": http://news.xinhuanet.com/english/2008-01/21/ content_7461360.htm

5. Development of the CH-DVD has had many twists and turns, and has been in the works since 2005 at least. Toshiba was said to have courted Chinese manufacturers to pick its DVD standard over Blu-Ray but this did not satisfy the most important criterion for China's electronics industry: Avoiding paying large IP license fees to a foreign consortium as they have been doing for DVD players and other electronics. At the time of writing, there are still no commercial CH-DVD products on the market but 2008 may see their launch finally, as HD flat screen TVs have become enormously popular and inexpensive in China. For more information about CH-DVD, see the Wikipedia entry, http://en.wikipedia.org/wiki/CH-DVD, or this press release from Tsinghua University's Optical Memory National Engineering Research Center (Mandarin version) on ZDNet China: http:// stor-age.zdnet.com.cn/stor-age/2007/0907/495410.shtml and story based on a translation here: China http://www.tech2.com/india/ news/optical-drives/china-develops-new-hddvd-format/15671/0

6. The largest is the US, followed by Japan, according to Ernst & Young in a 2007 report quoted in Asia Times: http://www.atimes.com/ atimes/china_business/id14cb02.html

7. The MiniOne was profiled in a Popular Science article, August 7, 2007, "China's iClone": http://www.popsci.com/iclone

8. The story is long and somewhat convoluted, arising as it does in a virtual world, but has nevertheless attracted much real world publicity. Anshe Chung Studio's published a press release announcing Graef's millionaire status (http://www.anshechung.com/include/ press/press_release251106.html) after being reported on in Business-Week (http://www.businessweek.com/magazine/content/06_18/ b3982001.htm) and earlier at CNN (http://money.cnn.com/ magazines/business2/business2_archive/2005/12/01/8364581/ index.htm?cnn=yes)

9. The facility, which has been discussed for some time, broke ground on May 15th, 2007, according to the Tianjin Free Trade Zone website,

May 29, 2007, "Tianjin Assembly Line of Airbus A320 Series Airplane goes into operation on 15th May": http://www2.tjftz.gov.cn/system/2007/05/29/010011906.shtml

10. LNG tankers, which carry liquefied natural gas that is compressed 600 times to liquid form by cooling it to minus 163 degrees Celsius, are one of the most technically-complex ships to construct. More information can be found on China's self-developed LNG tankers in Shanghai Daily, May 1, 2008, "China secures long-term future by building its first LNG tankers": http://www.shanghaidaily.com/sp/article/2008/200805/20080501/article_357815.htm

11. Another survey puts this at 24 cars per 1000, versus 300 in Europe and 765 in the US. More information about China's car market can be found in this recent article, Detroit Free Press, April 20, 2008, "Competition for China's growing auto market is heating up": http://www.freep.com/apps/pbcs.dll/article?AID=/20080420/BUSINESS01/804200588

12. Information on the expected automotive growth rates for 2008 can be found in China Daily, April 14, 2008, "2008 auto industry mingles hope and fears": http://www.chinadaily.com. cn/bizchina/2008-04/14/content_6615667.htm. China's growing demand for SUVs and other fuel-inefficient vehicles is discussed in the New York Times, Keith Bradsher, April 21, 2008, "Beijing Pressures Automakers to Improve Efficiency": http://www.nytimes.com/2008/04/21/business/world-business/21auto.html?_r=3&adxnnl=1&oref=slogin&ref=business&adxnnlx=1210592544-+VdD5ERs9N7KufhRKvJhWw

Chapter 5

1. Turnover information from Chinese HR services firm, 51job.com, 2007, "Bosses alarmed as turnover rate tops 23 percent": http://www.recruitmentadvertising.cn/news/150.html

2. Ibid.

3. For information about China's compliance with WTO accession obligations, see the US Trade Representative's annual report to Congress, December 11, 2007, "2007 Report To Congress On China's Wto Compliance": http://www.ustr.gov/assets/Document_Library/Reports_Publications/2007/asset_upload_file625_13692.pdf

4. Li Ge and Wuxi PharmaTech profile based on author knowledge and research from China Business Weekly, March 24-30, 2008, "New

Prescription: A scientist turned entrepreneur is changing the face of China's pharmaceutical R&D industry".

5. PPG, also known as Yes!PPG, has an English version online catalog at http://ppgshirt.com and Chinese version at http://ppg.cn Another source for information about PPG and KPCB can be found at: http://venturebeat.com/2007/10/19/vcs-in-china-kleiners-shirt-factory-sequoias-farm/

6. Company promotion budget revealed by a PPG executive, quoted in Shanghai Star, February 25, 2008, "For PPG, Internet fails as magic wand for higher sales".

7. China's Internet Research Center (AKA iResearch) released findings that China's online sales were approximately 59.4 million RMB (US$8.5 billion), as reported by Xinhua via China Daily, January 22, 2008, "China's Internet shopping taking off fast: report": http://www.chinadaily.com.cn/bizchina/2008-01/22/content_6412983.htm. According to market research firm CCID consulting, China's 2008 eCommerce sales may hit 164 billion RMB (US$ 23 billion), as reported by Xinhua, January 23, 2008, "Internet market to hit 164b yuan in 2008": http://www.china.org.cn/english/business/240420.htm

8. China Internet Research Center website: http://english.iresearch.com.cn/html/e_commerce/Default.html Another indicator for fast growth of C2C commerce is China's auction giant Taobao, which more than doubled transactions in 2007, as reported by Shanghai Daily, January 23, 2008, "Taobao.com transactions surge 156%": http://www.shanghaidaily.com/sp/article/2008/200801/20080123/article_346263.htm

9. Data from March 2008 according to Nielsen Online, from Marketwire press release: http://www.marketwire.com/mw/release.do?id=843432

10. As reported in ZDNet Asia, November 26, 2007, "China's e-tail awakening": http://www.zdnetasia.com/news/internet/0,39044908,62034851,00.htm

11. This sidebox used research from a number of sources, including a Forbes Magazine article (http://www.forbes.com/2008/01/17/retail-malls-shopping-biz-commerce-cx_tvr_0118malls.html), a Wikipedia list (http://en.wikipedia.org/wiki/List_of_largest_buildings_in_the_world), the official website of the Dongguan South China Mall (http://www.southchinamall.com.cn/english/index1.jsp).

12. Whether in terms of outlets, sales volume, staff, or any other measure, KFC leads McDonald's by a wide margin as of the time of writing.

Chapter 6

1. Chinese retail spending in 2007 was at an 11 year high, at 11.6 percent in 2007, and in the month of April 2008, year on year sales we up 22 percent, showing consumption in China is accelerating. Some of the reasons are higher incomes, investment gains in property and stocks, and government policies discouraging investments and exports, as mentioned in previous chapters. For more information, see Reuters via CNBC, May 12, 2008, "Chinese Retail Sales Surge 22% in April on Year": http://www.cnbc.com/id/24587346/site/14081545

2. The launch of Starbucks bottled coffee drinks in China was assisted by the use of a 'Sub-opera' played on the videoscreens of Shanghai's subway systems called "A Sunny Day." Each mini-episode, meant to be viewed on a single subway ride, featured product placements. More information can be found on Starbucks official website, press release dated November 1, 2007, "Starbucks Bottled Frappuccino Coffee Drinks Now Available in China": http://www.starbucks.com/aboutus/pressdesc.asp?id=800

3. A publication on the Huawei website describes the 'wolf culture' from an outsider's perspective as "Huawei People = an incendiary bomb + a non-stop machine", among other terms: http://www.huawei.com/publications/view.do?id=1420&cid=2423&pid=127

4. A worker-advocacy organization, China Labor Bulletin, has a number of mentions of apparent cases of death by overwork in China. Other than the case of Hu Xinyu at Huawei Technologies, which was widely reported in both Chinese and overseas media, we did not investigate the other cases: http://www.clb.org.hk/en/node/39002

5. For more information about China's growing spa business, see International Herald Tribune, Joshua Kurlantzick, September 18, 2007, "Chinese spas: A country masters the art of relaxation": http://www.iht.com/articles/2007/09/18/arts/trchina.php

6. China is estimated to produce 60–90% of the world's vitamin C, for example, and is the largest producer of a number of other synthetic vitamins and drugs. For more information, see McClatchy Newspapers via The Seattle Times, see Tim Johnson, July 3, 2007, "China corners vitamin market": http://seattletimes.nwsource.com/html/nationworld/2003732744_vitamins03.html?syndication=rss. In terms of organic food, much of the food that would qualify for organic

growth standards in the US and other developed countries is simply just food in China, grown as it is with low-tech fertilizers, manual labor and no processing. Whether China can regulate the industry and standardize the qualification standards is another matter.

7. Ibid. Also, for information on the vitamin price-fixing cases which opened the door for Chinese expansion into the industry, the major producers were fined in a number of countries, including the US, Canada, and EU. See CBC, "7.7 million payout in vitamin price fixing lawsuit": http://www.cbc.ca/news/story/2002/02/28/ vitaminfixing_020228.html Guardian, "Vitamin cartel fined for price fixing": http://www.guardian.co.uk/money/2001/nov/21/ personalfinancenews.europeanunion

8. Only 30 percent of the dishes in the Olympic Village at the Beijing Olympics will be authentic Chinese, the rest will be western food, according to the organizers. See official Olympic website, April 29, 2008, "Menu for Olympic Village cafeteria revealed": http://en. beijing2008.cn/100days/preparations/s214328527/n214330795.shtml

9. More information on the dieting trends of Chinese women can be found in this China Daily article, March 27, 2008, "No hunger and no sweat": http://www.chinadaily.com.cn/citylife/2008-03/27/ content_6570380.htm

10. For more information about China's new sexual and social trends, including male metrosexuality, see New York Times, David Barboza, March 4, 2007, "China – The People's Republic of Sex Kittens and Metrosexuals": http://www.nytimes.com/2007/03/04/weekinreview/ 04barboza.html?_r=1&oref=slogin

11. More about organic rice farming can be found at the following website: http://english.eastday.com/eastday/englishedition/Districts/ Chongming/userobject1ai2485373.html

12. A company press release from 24 Hour Fitness details the endorsement of Yao Ming: http://www.fitcommerce.com/Blueprint/page. aspx? pageId= 276&announcementId=1157&tabId=87&tabIndex=0

13. More information about the author, Sun Wukong, the story Journey to the West (*Xiyouji*) and the Monkey King can be found at the Wikipedia entry: http://en.wikipedia.org/wiki/Journey_ to_the_West

14. This program, sometimes called the 'Through Train' was initially quite limited as it could only be performed at one bank branch in Tianjin and through one brokerage. However, this program is expected to expand in the future should the pilot be successful: http://www. atimes.com/atimes/China_Business/IH22Cb01.html

15. According to information on the UK Visa Application Centre, a three month trial will start in March 2008 to lower the cost of Chinese UK visa applications, "UK cuts visa price for Chinese tourists" via press release on its website: http://www.vfs-uk-cn.com/pressRelease.aspx

Chapter 7

1. According to official sources, China's two mobile phone carriers, China Mobile and China Unicom, transmitted 592 billion text messages in 2007, for an average daily total of 1.6 billion. This is the largest absolute number of text messages sent by a single country globally, but on a per capita basis China is behind the Philippines (where text messaging is also incredibly popular) but far above the usage in countries such as the US and UK. On the busiest days of the year, SMS can top 5 billion. For more information, see Xinhua, February 18, 2008, "Chinese Expected to Send 17bln SMS During Spring Festival": http://english.cri.cn/3130/2008/02/08/262@321436.htm

2. Via Xinhua, May 11, 2008, "China's smartphone market booms in Q1, sales up 4.8%" http://english.people.com.cn/90001/90776/6408262.html

3. China's Internet Network Information Center (http://www.cnnic.net.cn/uploadfiles/pdf/2008/2/29/104126.pdf) and China Internet Research Center (http://english.iresearch.com.cn/html/instant_messenger/Default.html)

4. CAGR, the year to year growth rate may be more or less depending on the year, but generally growth has been plus 18 percent in the last several years with exceptional growth following the opening of the advertising markets. For more information, see this article from CRI, February 2, 2008, "Olympics Fuel Ad-Spending Surge in China": http://english.cri.cn/4026/2008/02/02/164@319910.htm

5. China's WTO entry commitments required it to allow joint ventures by the end of 2003, and wholly-owned advertising agencies by the end of 2006. Virtually every large global advertising firm now has one or the other in China.

6. China's Internet Network Information Center, press release, December 26, 2007, "CNNIC Releases 2007 Survey Report on China Weblog Market Number of Blog Writers Reaches 47 million Equaling One Fourth of Total Netizens": http://www.cnnic.cn/html/Dir/2007/12/27/4954.htm

7. At the time of writing, Xu Jinglei's blog was number one by a large margin, with more than 153 million hits to date. Blog ranking provided by Sina.com (Mandarin): http://blog.sina.com.cn/lm/top/rank/

8. See note 6.

9. A direct link to the Google.cn page can be found here (Mandarin): http://www.google.cn/intl/zh-CN/renrou/. Paraphrase English translation and commentary on the phenomenon: http://www.zonaeuropa.com/200804a.brief.htm#004

10. More information on these stories can be found as follows. Shanghai Daily via China Daily, March 16, 2006, "High-heeled kitten killer apologizes": http://www.chinadaily.com.cn/english/doc/2006-03/16/content_540375.htm The Independent, Clifford Coonan, September 4, 2006, "China's internet vigilantes target British ex-pat cad": http://www.independent.co.uk/news/world/asia/chinas-internet-vigilantes-target-british-expat-cad-414557.html Xinhua via China Daily, March 18, 2007, "Photo of 'extinct tiger sparks controversy": http://www.chinadaily.com.cn/china/2007-10/18/content_6188481.htm. Shanghai Daily, April 17, 2008, "Patriotic fervor swells in MSN campaign": http://www.china.org.cn/china/national/2008-04/17/content_14971209.htm

11. Data from survey by Internet Society of China, as reported in Xinhua, January 21, 2008, "China's online game players to reach 59 million in 2008, survey finds": http://news.xinhuanet.com/english/2008-01/21/content_7467275.htm

12. iReaseach, a Shanghai-based Internet research firm, pegged market share by trade volume at 83.6 percent for TaoBao,8.7 percent for TenCent's PaiPai auction service, and 7.7 percent for eBay/Eachnet: http://english.iresearch.com.cn/html/Default.html

13. eBay paid a total of US$ 180 million in two investments, first to acquire a 33% share for US$30 million and then acquired the remaining 67% share for US$150 million. For more information, see Marketwatch, June 11, 2003 "EBay buys remaining stake in EachNet": http:// www.marketwatch.com / news / story / ebay-pays-150-mln-remaining/story.aspx?guid=%7BA1A483FE-1AC6-4826-A7F9-3A864-2E47814%7D

14. Yahoo! bought a 40 percent pre-IPO stake in Alibaba, parent company of TaoBao, for US$1 billion. See China Daily, August 11, 2005, "Yahoo buys US$1 billion stake in Alibaba": http://www.chinadaily.com.cn/english/doc/2005-08/11/content_468252.htm

15. Information on the formation of the joint venture between Li's Tom.com and eBay via Tom.com Investor Relations, December 20, 2006, "eBay Inc. and TOM Online Announce Joint Venture Agreement To Enable Next Phase Of E-Commerce Growth in China": http://pr.tom.com/pdf/20061220_en.pdf

16. As reported in Shanghai Daily via China Economic Net, May 6, 2008, "eBay China's Users Need Not Pay Fees": http://en.ce.cn/Business/Enterprise/200805/06/t20080506_15372716.shtml

17. Data for this section comes from official 2007 company corporate earnings announcement dated March 19, 2008 (http://www.tencent.com/ir/pdf/news20080319a_e.pdf) and information about the Q-bi can be found via Wall Street Journal, March 30, 2007, "QQ: China's New Coin of the Realm?": http://online.wsj.com/public/article/SB117519670114653518-FR_svDHxRtxkvNmGwwpouq_hl2g_20080329.html. In the first quarter of 2008, TenCent's profits grew over 85 percent year on year.

Chapter 8

1. Though the Shanghai Composite Index closed off its highs reached in October 2007, it still closed out the year up 97 percent, according to Reuters, December 28, 2007, "China stocks end year up 97 pct, uptrend to slow": http://www.reuters.com/article/rbssFinancialServices-AndRealEstateNews/idUSSHA20340620071228

2. Tony Tan, a former broker turned *feng shui* master, correctly predicted the 2007 bull run, and predicts poor performance in the China stock markets in 2008 at least until April. Coincidentally, China's markets made a recovery in late April off their lows, whether due to the government intervention or the *feng shui* forces in this year of the Rat, nobody can really say. This Bloomberg article has more details: http://www.bloomberg.com/apps/news?pid=20601213&sid=aXLferGUnAlA&refer=home

3. A comprehensive summary of all of the recent real estate regulatory actions in China in 2007 and early 2008 can be found at the following website from law firm Morrison & Foerster LLP, February 13, 2008, "China: Further Changes In China's Real Estate Regulations": http://www.mondaq.com/article.asp?articleid=56920

4. Figures in the book differ due to various exchange rates used in conversions being reported in separate media. However, the point that

China is near or greater than the US in terms of public financing remains. For example, Asia Times reports "According to data provided by PricewaterhouseCoopers, the value of IPOs in Shanghai and Shenzhen topped HK\$496 billion (US\$63.5 billion) in 2007 while the US market raised a total of HK\$492 billion. The London Stock Exchange was third, raising HK\$387 billion; Hong Kong was fourth with HK\$295 billion last year." (http://www.atimes.com/atimes/China_Business/JA10Cb01.html) This means China's IPOs raised more than did US IPOs, but according to PricewaterhouseCoopers, directly Greater China IPOs raised 62 billion dollars in 2007, March 2007, "IPOs in Greater China raise record high of US\$62 billion": http:// www.pwc.com/extweb/ncpressrelease.nsf/docid/5E94F15-FBACE557C852572CA00557AE9

5. Based on share prices at the time interval indicated.
6. As reported in Asia Times, June 26, 2007, "The bubble bursts for Pu'er Tea": http://www.atimes.com/atimes/China_Business/IF26Cb01.html
7. 345,000 millionaires at the end of 2006, according to survey by Merrill Lynch as reported in AFP, October 17, 2007, "China has 345,000 millionaires: study": http://afp.google.com/article/ALeqM5ixQlU1Gegh-Wewhn1PFb2nZwzEPPg
8. Based on data from Zero2IPO Group, a private research firm, January 23, 2008, "US\$3.25B VC Investment Touches New High, Fundraising & Exit Active": http://www.zero2ipo.com.hk/china_this_week/detail.asp?id=5753
9. Venture Beat, October 19, 2007, "VCs in China: Kleiner's shirt factory, Sequoia's farm": http://venturebeat.com/2007/10/19/vcs-in-china-kleiners-shirt-factory-sequoias-farm/
10. The 3Com sale to Huawei was called off after a review by the US Committee For Foreign Investment in the United States, according to International Herald Tribune, February 21, 2008, "Sale of 3Com to Huawei is derailed by U.S. security concerns": http://www.iht.com/articles/2008/02/21/business/3com.php. Also see Associated Press via USAToday, February 20, 2008, "3Com withdraws buyout application": http://www.usatoday.com/money/industries/technology/2008-02-20-3com_N.htm
11. For example, nearby Asian countries such as South Korea, Japan, Malaysia and the Philippines all run trade surpluses with China. Europe overall has a large trade deficit, though trade between China

and Germany is well-balanced, France, UK Italy and Spain all run large deficits, according to China's Ministry of Commerce, 2007 yearly trade statistics: http://english.mofcom.gov.cn/aarticle/statistic/ie/200802/20080205371690.html

12. For more information on the reasons why China should and should not revalue the RMB at a faster pace, see The Economist, May 17, 2007, "Lost in Translation": http://www.economist.com/finance/displaystory.cfm?story_id=9184053

13. JP Morgan's head of China research, Frank Gong, predicted a 10 to 15 percent rise in mid-to late-2008, as reported in Shanghai Daily, April 30, 2008, "Yuan may advance 10-15%, says expert.": http://www.shanghaidaily.com/sp/article/2008/200804/20080430/article_357698.htm

14. More information about the global activities and sizes of Sovereign Wealth Funds, see the Sovereign Wealth Fund Institute: http://swfinstitute.org/. Also, more information about China Investment Corporation can be found from a *60 Minutes* report, April 6, 2008, "China Investment An Open Book?": http://www.cbsnews.com/stories/2008/04/04/60minutes/main3993933.shtml

15. In May 2008, the People's Bank of China, China's central bank, again raised the reserve ratio, to 16.5 percent. The PBOC has used the reserve ratio as its main policy tool to reign in liquidity, and will continue to do so, as reported by Thomson Financial News via CNBC, May 14, 2008, "China to continue using reserve ratio hikes to control liquidity — central bank": http://www.cnbc.com/id/24611511/for/cnbc

Chapter 9

1. A NASA study released in March 2008 shows clear evidence by satellite imaging of how particulate pollution spreads from China to other parts of the world via air currents in as little as ten days, according to Geology.com, March 2008, "Satellite Measures Pollution From East Asia to North America": http://geology.com/nasa/monitoring-pollution-by-satellite.shtml

2. China has in fact accelerated its use of coal generation in 2006 and 2007, introducing dozens of new coal power plants a year even while shuttering some of the older, less-efficient ones: "'In 2006, China put into operation 105 gigawatts, which is [equivalent to] the entire electricity

generation system of France,' [An analyst from Suez International, Mark Josz] said. He said 90 per cent of that generation was from coal plants, and China followed by adding 91 gigawatts of coal generation in 2007." Vancouver Sun, March 13, 2008, "China spurs comeback for coal as energy source, panelists say": http://www.canada. com/vancouversun/news/story.html?id=167a9c83-5b31-44cd-bbba-4146fd8ae9f4 China's energy generation by source and other statistics can be found at the US Department of Energy's China page: http:// www.eia.doe.gov/emeu/cabs/China/Electricity.html

3. More information on the Yangtze white dolphin, the *Baiji*, can be found at its Wikipedia page: http://en.wikipedia.org/wiki/Baiji

4. China has the world's 3rd largest reserves of coal after the US and Russia. It is the world's largest producer and consumer due to its coal-intensive power generation policy. For more information see, the Wikipedia pages on Major Coal Producing Regions (http://en. wikipedia.org/wiki/Major_coal_producing_regions#China) and the Coal Reserves page (http://en.wikipedia.org/wiki/Coal#World_coal_reserves)

5. According to Xinhua, January 16, 2008, "South China province reports worsening air quality": http://english.peopledaily.com.cn/90001/90782/90872/6339255.html

6. As reported in China Daily, January 16, 2008, "Group wants more polluters in court": http://www.chinadaily.com.cn/china/2008-01/16/content_6396814.htm

7. There are several surveys of this kind and methodologies used. On one list, by the Blacksmith Institute, and NGO, China has only two of the top ten worst-polluted cities (http://www.blacksmithinstitute.org/ten.php), while the World Bank's top 20 list in 2007 can be found here: http://siteresources.worldbank.org/INTDATASTA/64199955-1178226923002/21322619/LGDB2007.pdf. It is also reported on via the CBS website: http://www.cbsnews.com/stories/2007/06/06/eveningnews/main2895653.shtml

8. China, for example, mandates a common mobile phone recharger for all phones sold in China to reduce electronic waste, Shanghai keeps excess cars off the road by selling a limited number of license plates every month and uses the money raised for public transportation, and China's new Energy Conservation Law promulgated in 2008 mandates more energy-efficient buildings, to name three regulatory or legal examples. While China does have stricter environmental laws in many areas, enforcement of those laws remains another matter.

9. According to data from the Beijing Municipal Bureau of Environmental Protection, as quoted in Shanghai Daily, May 3–4, 2008, "Beijing's air quality is improving by the day": www.shanghaidaily. com/sp/article/2008/200805/20080503/article_358141.htm

10. In fact, China's National Development and Reform Commission says the national target is 150 million square meters by 2010, and by 2020 should hit 300 million square meters, providing hot water to hundreds of millions of people, according to official Chinese media, March 13, 2008, "New Energy in China": http://www1.cei.gov.cn/ce/doc/cenm/200803130536.htm

11. Information about Suntech Power via its official website: http://www. suntech-power.com/about/history.php. Also, from CNN, May 7, 2007, "Shi Zhengrong: China's sunshine boy": http://edition.cnn.com/2007/BUSINESS/05/06/ft.suntech/index.html

12. In the past, Shenhua has licensed clean coal technology from Shell (http://www.shell.com/home/content/china-en/news_and_library/press_releases/2004/coal_casification_30032004e.html), and had announced it was working towards a partnership with Dow to build a clean coal plant in China: http://www.chinadaily.com.cn/bizchina/2007-05/16/content_873402.htm

13. Some of the companies on the list included cement firms, mining companies, and chemical producers. The list was made public in China's 21st Century Herald newspaper, via Sina.com.cn (Mandarin), February 26, 2008: http://news.sina.com.cn/c/2008-02-26/092015020772.shtml English translation of the above article can be found at China Digital Times: http://chinadigitaltimes.net/2008/02/green-securities-act-blocks-10-polluting-public-companies/

14. The case of Wuxi and Tai Lake is the exception rather than the rule when it comes to the government getting tough, but it is a very concrete example things can change. For years Wuxi had hosted polluting factories and drew its economic livelihood from them, but the pollution was just too much. More details can be found from China's state-run media: http://english.zhb.gov.cn/zwxx/hjyw/200710/t20071008_109896.htm and http://www.china.org.cn/english/environment/227180.htm Details of the pollution blacklist can be found at http://www.china.org.cn/archive/2007-07/31/content_1219199.htm

15. Information from various government sources, as quoted in Shanghai Daily, November 22, 2007, "Pollution fuels China drinking-water crisis": http://www.shanghaidaily.com/sp/article/2007/200711/20071122/article_339013.htm. And, Wikipedia, "Water resources of the

People's Republic of China": http://en.wikipedia.org/wiki/Water_
resources_of_China

16. For more about China's north/south water imbalance, see People's
Daily, March 10, 2001, "Northern China is One of World's Most Water
Deficient Areas": http://english.people.com.cn/english/200103/
10/eng20010310_64651.html. Information about China's drying rivers
can be found at Newsweek, 2007, "Where China's Rivers Run Dry":
http://www.newsweek.com/ id/35593

17. The current plight of the Yellow River is dire, two recent reports
have noted: National Geographic, May 2008, "Bitter Waters: Can
China save the Yellow—its Mother River?". Also, see New York
Times, November 19, 2006, "A Troubled River Mirrors China's Path
to Modernity": http://www.nytimes.com/2006/11/19/world/asia/
19yellowriver.html?_r=1&oref=slogin

18. Since 1998, China has spent billions, and increased the pace once it
was awarded the Olympics in 2001. Beijing alone spent 120 billion
yuan, about US$17 billion, to clean up pollution before the Olympics,
as reported in Xinhua, March 11, 2008, "Chinese FM spokesman: China
confident of hosting clean, safe Olympics": http://news.xinhuanet.
com/english/2008-03/11/content_7767813.htm

19. According to the Beijing Olympics official website, January 27,
2007, "Beijing strives for reducing energy consumption": http://en.
beijing2008.cn/35/33/article214013335.shtml

20. Regarding increase in blue sky days, see Xinhua, May 2, 2008, "Beijing
reports more 'blue sky' days in first four months": http://news.
xinhuanet.com/english/2008-05/02/content_8090524.htm

21. For more information about the planned pollution controls to be used
during the Olympics, see New York Times, January 24, 2008, "Smoggy
Beijing Plans to Cut Traffic by Half for Olympics, Paper Says": http://
www.nytimes.com/2008/01/24/world/asia/24beijing.html. And via
Xinhua, March 6, 2008, "Beijing still Mulling Timing of Vehicle-cut
Measure": http://english.cri.cn/3100/2008/03/06/189@ 330744.htm

22. Though China signed the Kyoto Protocol agreement, technically
it is not subject to its limits as China is classified as a developing country along with India and other developing nations.
This was the main point of contention that kept the US from
signing. There is some worry that China's emissions are accelerating more quickly than expected, leading China to become the
world's largest carbon emitter sooner than expected. See National

Geographic, March 18, 2008, "China CO_2 Emissions Growing Faster Than Anticipated": http://news.nationalgeographic.com/news/2008/03/080318-china-warming.html

23. On increasing the national target for wind power generation to 100,000 MW by 2020, see Shanghai Daily via Xinhuanet.com, April 28, 2008, "Fanning wind power capacity": http://news.xinhuanet.com/english/2008-04/28/content_8065702.htm

24. The plastic bag manufacturer confirmed the closing via telephone with a Bloomberg reporter. See Bloomberg, February 26, 2008, "China's Biggest Plastic-Bag Maker Closes Down, Xinhua Reports": http://www.bloomberg.com/apps/news?pid=20601080&sid=ayzGeRNUdBcc

25. The Shanghai Plastic Bag Company put up the notice, as reported in Shanghai Star, April 7, 2008 "Plastic bag law may have silver lining".

26. More information about the Biolux biodiesel refinery planned for China at Reuters, January 14, 2008, "Biolux sees huge biodiesel potential in China": http://www.reuters.com/article/summitNews/idUSHKG32396420080114

27. This goal is provided by China's National Development and Reform Commission (NDRC), as reported in China Daily, September 15, 2007, "Renewable Energy to Be a Priority for Nation": http://en.chinagate.com.cn/news/2007-09/15/content_8888744.htm

Index